CAL

A GUIDE TO THE WORLD'S LARGEST
UNIVERSITY AND THE BAY AREA

Steven Warshaw
David A. Warshaw
General Editor

An Endymion Book
A Product of Diablo Press, Inc.
Berkeley, CA 94707

© 1983 Diablo Press, Inc.
P.O. Box 7042
Berkeley, California 94707

LIBRARY OF CONGRESS CATALOGING
IN PUBLICATION DATA

Warshaw, Steven.
  Cal, a guide.
  1. University of California (System)—Description—Guide-books.
2. University of California, Berkeley—Description—Guide-books.
3. Berkeley (Calif.)—Description—Guide-books.   I. Warshaw, David   A.   II. Title.
LD761.W37   1982   378.794'67   82-12788 ISBN 0-87297-055-8 (pbk.)

ISBN: 0-87297-055-8

Made in the United States of America

ACKNOWLEDGEMENTS

This book is based upon the widely acclaimed volume, *Diablo's Complete Guidebook to the East Bay* which was first published in 1962 and remained in print for many years. The present book is a completely updated version of the original material, the accuracy of which is authenticated with the generous help of the persons and institutions cited below. The author and editor, however, are completely responsible for any flaws which may appear in the work. They are grateful to the legion of specialists who helped to review data, and who in almost all cases patiently read and reread the manuscript for accuracy and comprehensiveness. In sections relating to the University of California, this included Ray Colvig of the Public Information Office of the Berkeley campus, Carolyn Terman of the Systemwide Administration Public Information Office, Guy C. Joy, Director of U.C. Extension, John Pheack of the Public Information Office of the Lawrence Berkeley Laboratories, Barbara Ando of the Public Information Office of the Lawrence Hall of Science, and J.R.K Kantor, University Archivist, The Bancroft Library. Other readers included Albert K. Norman, the noted regional specialist, and Fred C. Hutchinson, the Berkeley historian and former city attorney, and Bob Yamada, of the Berkeley Historical Society. Selected walking tours in the Architectural Guide to Berkeley section were taken, with permission, from *24 Walking Tours of Berkeley, California* Copyright 1980, The Berkeley Architectural Heritage Asssociation, P.O. Box 1137, Berkeley, California 94701.

Thanks are also due to the Public Information Offices of each of the nine campuses of the University of California, for the use of photographs of all the campuses.

No guidebook can remain complete without the assistance of its readers. The publisher welcomes suggestions for improving this book and will revise future printings with respect to them.

CONTENTS

INTRODUCTION

This book was not written by an academic or a similarly subjective insider, but by gifted professional writers who have a love affair with the University of California. So do I; and it's for that reason that I am grateful to be able to introduce a great book about a great university.

On the personal, purely individual level, I am drawn to the book because I graduated from Cal and later was privileged to serve it as a Regent for sixteen years, and at times as Chairman of the Board of Regents. But there is another, far more important level which would have made the text compelling even if the University of California were nothing more than a rumor in my life, as it is in the lives of millions of other Americans. "It is in the University that the soul of the people mirrors itself," a British statesman once wrote, referring to all such institutions. I agree.

Civilization itself, in the broadest sense, is somehow bound up in the nature of universities. They reflect a society's most serious effort to realize its principles. Cal, because it represents an immensely productive region which was only a recently a frontier, reflects a strident, optimistic, competitive, yet shyly poetic land. It mirrors what is unique and essential in California: the energy, joy, and idealism which are inescapable in a place so vast, abundant, and so lately discovered as California.

The authors of this book have conscientiously stressed this point in their design of the book. First, they devoted almost half of the text not only to the University at Berkeley, but to other campuses as well. Theirs is the only work which contains a concise historical guidebook to the University and its environment. Nor have they neglected the civilization about the school, dealing as they do with regional histories, tours, transportation, and such cultural aspects as restaurants and recreational facilities. The book is, as claimed, "Ten guidebooks in One!"

Reading about the University in this way, I was struck by the context in which the school finds itself. The book's historical outline tells how the precursor of the University was written off as a failure because "anything that does not succeed in California in three months will never succeed." That's how people thought, and still often think, of what the University is and what it should produce. Some expect it to show instant profits, and others expect it to offer life daily in behalf of instant principles. But these are not the functions of this or of any other University. Cal's function is to make the deepest, most enduring contribution to society that is possible, and to survive so that it can go on doing so.

The book shows plainly how Cal has succeeded in these respects. Though a miraculous choice of leaders, it has become one of the world's most influential schools though, as a public institution, it is vulnerable both politically and economically. It has succeeded, not for three months, but for more than a hundred years because it has won the affection and respect of its community.

If asked what they know about the University of California, people in many parts the world are likely to respond that the school had something to do with the development of the atomic bomb and that during the 1960's its students began what seemed then to be a revolution. These are important parts of the school's story, but, as the book shows, they are not the whole of it. Cal has made immense contributions to literature, art, music, the life sciences, to mining and agriculture, as well as to our understanding of physics and of political thought. There is no aspect of the humanities or of the sciences in which it has not at some time or another excelled. Thus it has made itself not only a meaningful, but a necessary part of our lives.

The same forces which enabled the University to progress in these intellectual ways have, in the recent past, caused many of its members to act politically. It would take an exceptionally sullen, passive student body to learn principles and then fail to act upon them during a crisis. Cal students, always free and intense, acted in the most dramatic possible way during the 1960's and 70's. Rightly or wrongly, they made the political contributions they thought best; and even today, while we are still paying the price for the events of those decades, we must credit them for acting out of conscience. The book sharply focuses student reactions to the Civil Rights and Free Speech crises, to the Vietnam War, and to what has come to be called the "People's Park Incident," as well as to such more recent political movements involving nuclear disarmament and investments in South Africa. Its historical view enabled me, while reading it, to appraise essentially emotional events more rationally.

I, and many other policymakers at the University, at first felt great sympathy for the students who called for social change during those decades. Like the student dissidents, we, too, wanted social justice and a country at peace with itself and with the world. But we soon parted with many of the dissidents over questions of method. They had begun to alienate the only groups capable of sustaining the long movement towards their goals. We longed to make them understand that progress is never gained by contemptuous gestures.

Students today take a longer view—and they will do so more and more if they read the history in this book. Knowing the history of their school, they are more likely to avoid the false issues that divert attention from the country's unfinished business. America's future does not belong to those who are timid, fearful, or rash. Rather, it belongs to those who can blend passion with reason and courage.

For all of these reasons I'm pleased to have the insights that the book offers. It may be, as Camus wrote, that "We are all condemned to live together." Yet with the kind of calm, rational material that this book offers, we may hope to make our lives as just and pleasant as possible.

William Coblentz

ORIGIN

On May 1, 1853, a gaunt, thin-lipped Congregational minister named Henry Durant arrived in San Francisco in the flow of prospectors, traders, and speculators. He was 50, a New England aristocrat, a former Yale divinity student who had taught in Eastern schools and was moving west to begin a college in a region that was still violent with gold fever. The Home Missionary Society of New York had agreed to sponsor him after he had answered its want ad.

When Durant arrived, San Francisco's population was 100 times more than when California became a U.S. possession in 1848. In that year, President Polk issued a statement that broke all restraints on the movement westward. "The accounts of the abundance of gold in that territory are of such an extraordinary character as would scarcely command belief. . . ." The migrations were still increasing five years later, although the first mining boom was almost over, and San Francisco's 42,000 people were beginning to sense their first depression. The miners were coming back. Most of them were looking for any kind of work. Some of them collapsed, drunk, into the thick mud of the unpaved streets. They were not removed, normally, until some passing city employee decided to put their corpses elsewhere, or was compelled to by the odors.

On the shore, Durant met the Reverend Samuel H. Willey, an agent of the Home Missionary Society of New York. Willey had been one of the first Yankees to arrive in California. He was on a ship in New Orleans when Polk announced the discovery of gold in the West. He watched the celebration, and then he went into his cabin to write in his diary, "Men seem to forget their souls in their interest for gold." His mission was to start a church, but after land-

ing in Monterey, he decided that Californians needed a school
more.

Willey had done all that he could to prepare the way for the
college. At Monterey he worked with Thomas Oliver Larkin, who
was one of the most influential men in the new state. Larkin put
him in correspondence with a relative who was a Harvard Overseer,
the Reverend William H. Rogers. Any new college in California,
the Overeseer wrote, "must be the growth of time;" its founders
would have to accept "what will equal a New England high school at
first." Willey had also become chaplain to California's first Constitutional Convention when it met in Monterey, and he persuaded the
convention to agree to a college "with such branches as the public
convenience may demand, for the promotion of literature, the arts,
and sciences."

Willey, 32, was unwilling to be as patient as Rogers advised. The
Jesuits had begun Santa Clara College (now the University of Santa
Clara), and the Methodists were beginning Wesleyan College (now
the University of the Pacific in Stockton). Willey himself had nar-
rowly missed starting a college. He failed because the courts were
too slow to adjudicate his land claim. He took Durant to Nevada
City before a joint meeting of the Congregational Association of San
Francisco, his own organization, and the Presbytery of San Francisco. The group immediately accepted Durant. In 1853, he and
Willey set out to organize the college on a budget of $30,000. They
decided to start the new institution in Oakland in order to avoid San
Francisco's distractions, and so they named it Contra Costa ("opposite shore" in Spanish) Academy.

"A wheezy little steamer," Willey wrote, "had got into the habit
of crossing the Bay two or three times a day to carry passengers. It
was pretty regular except that it was liable to get stuck on the bar
now and then. In this case (their first trip) it took us safely over.
Oakland we found to be indeed a land of oaks, having one street,
Broadway, extending from the landing toward the hills, with a few
buildings here and there on either side, and a few houses scattered
among the trees."

Their first building was the Washington Pavilion, a former
fandango house at Broadway and Fifth Street. They considered it
temporary. They kept looking for another site and soon found four
square blocks at 12th and Franklin Streets that they thought suitable. Soon afterward, Durant saw a mass meeting at the foot of
Broadway, where he often walked. He discovered that it was get-

ting ready to seize all of Oakland's vacant land. That would have included the new campus.

Durant walked into the crowd. He waved his hat and began to speak. He gave a short lecture on education and told about the school and its site. The crowd fell silent. Then someone yelled, "Three cheers for the school!" The crowd voted for a committee to save the campus from itself and other squatters.

While a contractor was being hired, Durant announced courses in French, German, Spanish, Latin, and Greek. He offered to teach them all himself for $10 a week. His housekeepers, a Mr. and Mrs. Quinn, offered board, washing, and domestic care for another $2.50 a week. But the Quinns became concerned about a missing paycheck one month while the school still had only three students. "Whatever did not succeed in 2 1/2 months in California," they predicted, "never would succeed." To get their money they started a tavern in the Academy, and Quinn fought back when Durant started to throw him out. Then, Durant wrote, "He got into a rage, laid his hands on me with considerable force, and was pushing me away, when suddenly he became pale as a cloth, lifted his hands over his head and began to pray. He begged that I would pray for him that God have mercy on his soul. His religion came to my relief."

The force of Durant's personality saved the school from squatters and housekeepers, and later from the contractor of the new building. The contractor submitted a fraudulent bill and tried to take possession of the property. Durant moved into it. He slept with an axe under his bed, waiting; and finally the contractor and a friend came to declare themselves the owners.

In his memoirs, Durant wrote, "I rose, then about two feet taller than usual; I felt as if I was monarch of all I surveyed. Said I, 'You will not only commit a trespass upon my property, but you will do violence upon my body. I don't intend to leave this room in a sound condition. If you undertake to do that, you will commit a crime as

The College of California, U.C.'s precursor, in 1861

well as a trespass.' That seemed to stagger them, and finally they left me in possession."

The school enrolled 50 pupils in the spring of 1855, and it gained a state charter as the College of California. Durant developed a faculty of eight. He was able to reduce his own teaching. This growth encouraged the trustees to look for a campus away from the rapidly developing town of Oakland. In 1858, after widespread searching, they settled on a place three miles north of Oakland (see *University: Plan*). Durant persuaded state agents to look for a campus site in the same place in 1867, and they chose one near the college. While admiring the college's site, Governor Frederick F. Low, a leading sponsor of the college, suggested a merger. "You," said Low to Willey, "have . . . scholarship, organization, enthusiasm, and reputation, but not money. We, in undertaking the state institution, have none of these things, but we have money. What a pity they could not be joined together."

Low's proposal revived a controversy of the 1850's: could California be associated with a private religious school? The Legislature had agreed to provide public funds for that purpose in 1851, but under pressure from separatists, it repealed its action in 1852. During the next decade it sold the "seminary lands" given it by the federal government for joining the Union. It gained another 150,000 acres when in 1862 President Lincoln signed the Morrill Act to grant 17.4 million acres ro the states for "people's colleges." It had the means to begin its own school, and by 1867 seemed determined to use public funds and land only for the "agricultural college" that the federal act obliged it to build soon.

But the governor's proposal suddenly reversed state policy; the trustees of the College, evidently surprised by him, let it be known that they, too, had reservations about any merger. They were more concerned with teaching the humanities than the sciences, and were worried by the public's determination to train students in the "mechanical arts." The positions were compromised. The trustees were willing to accept the state's help if they could join the government of the new university and include liberal arts in its curriculum. By this move they gained relief from their financial problems. The state found that the College was willing to be non-sectarian and that there would be no great public outcry at its incorporation as a public insititution. Moreover, California gained the well-chosen new campus, 160 acres that Durant had found, as well as a framework for its university.

There were religious overtones in the University at first, but even the most vigorous separatists knew that most of the country's educated men had been to religious schools. They were unconcerned. There were no objections to the historical ceremony on Founder's Rock in which men dedicating the site of a new public university "offered prayer to God for his blessing on what we had done, imploring His favor upon the College which we proposed to build there, asking that it might be accepted of Him, and remain a seat of Christian learning, a blessing to the youth of this State, and a center of usefulness in all this art of the world." For soon afterward no other American university could claim more academic freedom to dissent than the University of California. The most inflexibly interpreted portion of the Charter was a statement regarding secularism:

"It is expressly provided that no sectarian, political, or partisan test shall ever be allowed or exercised in the appointment of Regents, or in the election of professors, teachers, or other officers of the University, or in the admisssion of students thereto, or for any purpose whatsoever. Nor at any time shall the majority of the Board of Regents may be of any one religious sect, and persons of religious denomination, shall be equally eligible to all offices, appointments, and scholarships."

DEVELOPMENT

People came to California for every kind of gain but education. Having few students migrate to it in its early days, the new University depended upon an education system that was barely more than an accident. The first non-Indian settlers, the Franciscan fathers, had come to start that system in 1769, but their mission was among Indians rather than settlers, whose work left no time for books. The Franciscans, in fact, considered education a way toward faith rather than learning. They prevented some settlers from exploring it too far; they excommunicated Juan Bautista Alvarado, who became a revolutionary civil governor, and Mariano G. Vallejo, a distinguished general who was Alvarado's uncle, for reading Jean-Jacques Rousseau.

The Spanish founded secular schools under Governor Diego de Borica in 1794. He sent tough retired soldiers armed with *disciplinas*, cat o' nine tails, into one-room classes at San Jose, Santa Barbara, San Francisco, San Diego, and Monterey. But when he left in 1800, the system disappeared. There was almost no formal schooling until Governor José Figueroa, upon arriving in 1833, learned that there were only three schools in California, none of them very efficient. He set up six more that lasted through the regime of Juan Bautista Alvarado.

Alvarado became governor by firing a single cannonball at the Mexican capital in Monterey. The administration fled, and Alvarado, a brilliant renegade in all ways, took over. One of his first acts was to order that more teachers be brought from Mexico. He made education compulsory for children six to eleven. When he left government in 1842, Americans had begun to trickle into California.

Their educational inheritance was the system that he began.

Mrs. Olive Mann Isbell, an overland immigrant, began the first American school in 1846. She seated 24 students on boxes around a fire in an earth-floor stable on the grounds of the Mission Santa Clara. But California's merchants refused to allow taxation for schools. In San Francisco in 1851, one hundred children marched up Montgomery Street to show the reluctant businessmen that there were enough of them in the city to warrant public education. They were led by the Reverend Samuel H. Willey, the resourceful organizer of the new university. That was only three years before the organization of Contra Costa Academy, predecessor of the University of California. It was after the first state Constitutional Convention declared that a school must "be kept in every school district at least three months in every year."

The splendid intentions of the Constitution's authors were unrealizable until the 1860's. Throughout the first decade of statehood, taxation for schools was local, and there were county and city school superintendents, and city boards of education. There were local boards to grant teaching certificates. Challenged by this confusion and the plainly inadequate financing, the Legislature kept extending its powers over education. In 1866, it passed a Revised School Law prepared by State School Superintendent John Swett. This fixed the state and county school taxes at adequate levels and established school libraries, county teachers' institutes, and city boards of examination.

San Francisco opened the first public high school in 1856. Communities were expected to pay for their own high schools. Many could not afford to, some did so but poorly, and some provided bad schools. For 50 more years the Legislature refused to support secondary education. The new University needed 30 more years to begin coping with the state's irresponsibility in the matter of financ-

The first women students, arriving in Berkeley in 1870

ing good secondary schools. In 1884, it began an accrediting system so that it could admit without examination students having excellent records. By this means it drew high schools under its academic influence. Directed by advisers from the University of Michigan, whose success many California educators frankly admired, the University sent appropriate faculty members into every department of every high school, scouting the best students for its growing campus.

During its first full year, 1869–70, the University enrolled 40 academic students. By 1874, largely because 19 high schools had been started or were under way, it was able to enroll 191. There were 910 academic students in 1900, and the total number in all departments, both academic and professional, was 2,660.

The admission of women in 1870 further increased the potential. The first 17 coeds could not have been happy inside the gates. They were regarded as outlanders and were neither respected intellectually nor glorified physically. The *Blue and Gold Yearbook* of 1906 contained an article condemning coeducation on grounds that it cost women charm. That was a daring piece of research for its day: there were as many women as men on the campus in that year. For all of their problems of gaining social acceptance, women did accelerate the progress of higher education in California. Of a total of 2,229 students in Berkeley in 1900, 1,027 were women, and in 1910 there were 1,403 women in a total of 3,746. Still, until 1910 there were no contests for "queens" of the campus or of associations, and the lore became filled with clumsy jokes concerning the "pelicans," as the coeds were called, probably because they wore starched white dickies—shirtfronts tied to their waists. Women who studied were known as "queer birds."

The University came under severe political attack during its early years. One important source of the hostility was the Granger Movement, which wanted education to be limited largely to agriculture. Another appeared after its first two buildings were occupied in 1873: San Franciscans tried to have it moved to their city, and to encourage the move they had to fight with every political maneuver possible. For one or another of these reasons, legislators later accused builders of the University's two major colleges of accepting graft.

More philosophical charges were made by Henry George, the brilliant writer and economist who was editor of a newspaper in Oakland. George aimed invective in Berkeley's direction. The University, he said, was using the public's hard-won taxes "to educate rich men's sons." But the central cause of his complaint was a mere one cent for every $100 of assessed property in California. For the first time in its history the University succeeded in that measure to win freedom from abrupt changes on policy by successive Legislatures. Although still responsible ultimately to state officials, its life was not to be staked, from that point on, in every discussion with every powerful legislator. The Vrooman Act, the tax enabling law, was a landmark in the University's development. To welcome the news of the 1889 appropriation under it, the school band and two battalions of cadets went to Berkeley Station to meet University officials returning from Sacramento. On campus a student rose to offer a few richly worded hopes:

"If, in the past, her influence has been such that numbers, who have gone out from her gates into the life of this State and other states, have become powers among their fellows, what cannot we claim for her when the hopes, which we may now reasonably hold, are made realities; when we shall have a group of noble buildings facing the Golden Gate; when the size of our teaching corps shall be adequate to the demands made upon it; when our student body shall grow so as to rival the enrollment of Harvard or Yale?"

Development took place in episodes. There have been three principal ones:

1. The Administration of Benjamin Ide Wheeler

When the University's potential became evident during the 1890's, its Regents began to search for a strong president. They found one in Benjamin Ide Wheeler (see also *University: Plan— Wheeler Hall*).

Wheeler was lean and intense. He was a clergyman's son who was born in New England and educated there and in Germany, for whose schools the faculty at Berkeley had a traditional respect. Wheeler had studied in Greece and was Professor of Greek at Cor-

Benjamin Wheeler and Phoebe Hearst,
leading a graduation procession

nell when the University's Regents, in search of a firm hand, began to negotiate with him. He examined the history of the University's presidents. Few, he found, had survived many years in office. Most either were sacrificed to committees of the Legislature, faculty, or special interest groups, or they became administratively paralyzed and so resigned. He offered to take the job if the balance of power on campus were changed. He wanted complete control over faculty appointments, removals, salary determinations, and organization. The Regents approved through a voting majority of 11, with four dissenters. They made Wheeler responsible only to themselves.

He arrived in 1899. Five thousand people came to see him inaugurated. He leaned forward into the crowd and said earnestly, in a low, commanding voice, "We all are students; all are learners; all are teachers. . . . Education is the transmission of life." He contrasted life and death of the educational spirit: Berkeley, he suggested, was in need of fresh vitality.

The University responded to Wheeler. During his 20-year tenure its student body was increased from 2,229 to 11,692. It had completed one of the world's great architectural competitions the year before his arrival, and he directed its execution. He helped to finance 11 new buildings and drew a new wave of brilliant scholars to the West. Wheeler viewed all of this with the immense satisfaction of a man who has seen his planning work. Impeccable in a European-tailored suit and wide-brimmed hat, he came to symbolize the University, an almost legendary figure who, after working hours, occasionally would ride his white mare over the undeveloped hills of the campus.

Wheeler planned for the University's growth in the remote future. He developed campuses across the state, and during the decade after he retired in 1919, as a direct result, the University grew from 11,692 students to 25,794. There were three principal sources of the new students: veterans of World War I, the growing number of high school graduates who during part of the decade were admitted without tests or qualifying grades, and migrants to the Los Angeles Area who went to the new southern campus.

The faculty accepted Wheeler at first; but later it worried about his nearly absolute power over its members. In 1919 it organized what has been known since as the "faculty revolution," in which it regained the power of nominating its new members. It did not institute this change until 1920, when Wheeler had retired; and then, having restored the balance of power (see also *University: Govern-*

ment) it became one of the world's most independent faculties, able to express itself in ways as predictable as committees and as spontaneous as mass meetings, without fear of recrimination. Wheeler created a strong faculty by causing it to react to his strength. That, it developed, was one of the most important results of his administration.

2. *The Administration of Robert Gordon Sproul*

Although Robert Gordon Sproul was not a professional scholar, he was elected to *Phi Beta Kappa* and *Tau Beta Pi* while studying engineering at Berkeley. His great strength was his capacity to understand people and his willingness to be understood. A San Franciscan, he stayed in the Bay Area after he was graduated. He joined the efficiency department of the City of Oakland. He went to the University as cashier, rose to become assistant secretary to the Regents, comptroller, vice-president, and president. He had the support of the alumni. An anecdotal speaker who was plain and direct, he was likeable, and he combined that skill with political insights that enabled him to build the University into a position of academic and numerical superiority. Faced by an investigation of the University's budget, for example, he succeeded in getting the Legislature to appoint him to the investigating committee. But his most important presidential work, in his own view, was his support of a young assistant professor named Ernest Orlando Lawrence, inventor of the cyclotron (see *University: Plan*). Sproul used his charm, which was candor, to get Lawrence money for research. The young physicist became a principal guide to the Atomic Age: he won the Nobel Prize by the time he was 40. Other Nobel Laureates, perceptive scientists, and brilliant students came increasingly to the laboratory that he established, and the University under Sproul rose to new eminence. It and the region around it became one of the world's great scientific centers, for Sproul proved increasingly able to develop the profound sense of a university community.

As movement toward California began to exceed any internal migrations known in history, the administration found itself needing rigid admission tests. Sproul began these in 1931, when junior colleges were established to supplement the University system, and later, too, when the state college system evolved. He thereby raised the quality of University education, and endowments, honors, and construction reached record levels. But so did enrollment. The struggle to maintain quality deepened as more students came.

3. *The Administration of Clark Kerr*

After World War II, Governor Earl Warren met Robert Gordon Sproul to discuss his concern for the future of labor-management harmony in California. He and Sproul agreed that an Institute of Industrial Relations at Berkeley might reconcile some labor-management groups that had been saving their differences for the postwar period. Kerr, by then a Professor of Economics, was put in charge of the Institute in 1945; he kept that job through 1952.

During this period the Board of Regents considered itself to be under pressure to attack the political left. It insisted that all faculty members sign a loyalty oath, the strategy of which was to trap the left into signing or quitting. This would have exposed a few to economic boycotts, or perhaps prosecution, for some remote association. At the time, 1950–56, the oath had an effect greater than any of these alternatives. Some faculty members would not sign the oath;

Robert Gordon Sproul and Clark Kerr, with Nobel Laureate Glenn T. Seaborg at left, as Kerr became U.C.'s president in 1958

they were fired. The oath caused many faculty members of con-
science to resign, whatever their political conviction or history.
These faculty members found a spokesman in Kerr. He himself
signed the oath, but he argued, in the full view of the Regents and
Legislature, that refusal to sign should not be a reason for dismissal.
He chose freedom over declaration of patriotism.

He won the attention and respect of the faculty, and its support
when the Berkeley chancellorship became available in 1952. As
chancellor, he defended the campus against centralization into the
University's growing statewide administration. He became president when Robert Gordon Sproul retired in 1958. He was only 47,
and lithe and active, a small-boned man with infinitely blue eyes,
who almost always had a tan acquired in his garden or playing with
his three children.

Kerr sought to maintain the University's high academic standards
in the face of its exploding student population. Accordingly, certain
industrial and creative arts courses were eliminated during his tenure. To Kerr, the president's assignment was to decentralize, plan,
and modify growth in all campuses.

Kerr stirred a great controversy within the university community
when he tried, unsuccessfully, to resist Governor Ronald Reagan's
pressures to dramatically cut the university's budget. Reagan forced
Kerr's dismissal in 1967.

THE FREE SPEECH MOVEMENT

(From The Trouble in Berkeley, Copyright 1965, Diablo Press, Inc.)

In the fall of 1964, the University of California in Berkeley experienced a kind of trouble that hinted at problems infecting all American education. A group of its students rebelled against an administrative order limiting the content of their speech and advocacy, and they demanded that the University rid itself both of the order and of the personnel capable of issuing it.

In one respect, at least, the rebels, whose group was called the Free Speech Movement, were not disputed by the Administration: the University's simplicity was gone. One hundred years before the conflict two Congregational ministers, Sam Willey and Henry Durant, had started the school with fifty students. They paid a husband and wife $2.50 a week to run their campus, which contained a single building, and meanwhile they spelled each other teaching French, German, Latin, and Greek, and politicking for a state charter.

By the time of the rebellion the University was spread over nine campuses: regions each the size of a modern town, linked by a name, a ledger sheet in the state budget, and some administrators who used a small fleet of cars and airplanes to communicate with each other. In place of its first four administrators and scholars the University employed 40,000. Instead of the 100,000 Californians and the dying gold rush there were more than 18 million people and an economy in which it was necessary to waste materials in order to keep up with production.

The University no longer had to beg for the right to be involved with the state. The reverse was true. Its enrollment was over 72,000. It had to turn down thousands of applicants every semester. Its annual operating budget was more than one-half billion dollars; and its research grants, pouring out of government, foundations, business, and industry, ran to more than $175 million. In the beginning, the University got its Charter because one of its chief sponsors, Frederick F. Low, also became governor. Low remarked to Sam Willey, when the site of the Berkeley campus was being explored, "You have . . . scholarship, organization, enthusiasm, and reputation, but not money. We, in undertaking the state institution, have none of these things, but we have money. What a pity they could not be joined together." By the time of the rebellion they were inseparable. "The University," Clark Kerr, its president, said in defense of his Administration during the struggle "is intertwined with all society."

Kerr thought that the changes at the University of California suggested a "new university" in the United States. He called it the "Multiversity."

This word, it turned out, had been used before Kerr by university presidents in Iowa and Minnesota. Kerr stressed it when delivering the Godkin Lectures at Harvard University in 1963, in the original draft of which, when prepared by his staff, it appeared as "multi-campus university." Thus a description of an intrinsically widespread university became one of a basically involved and complex one. In the whole drama that followed no other word, nor any act of Kerr's, so threatened individuality and therefore so provoked the rebels as "Multiversity." Kerr's book, *The Uses of the University* (Harvard University Press, 1963), which included the Godkin Lectures, amplified his thinking:

The current transformation will cover roughly the quarter century after World War II. The University is being called upon to educate previously unimagined numbers of students; to respond to the expanding claims of national service; to merge its activities with industry as never before; to adapt to and rechannel new intellectual currents. . . .

The university has become a prime instrument of national purpose. This is new. This is the essence of the transformation now engulfing our universities.

The sense of the Multiversity appeared to identify the University with the expanding web of power being developed in the name of automation, national defense, and research and development. This identification was what the University's rebellious students refused to accept. The students feared the establishment which the University was voluntarily supporting. Often when the national purpose seemed well defined by official policy, as in the American military involvement in Asia, they dissented from it. And they resented the increasing distance between their teachers and themselves. (In Berkeley, lectures are often given in auditoriums over microphones; tests are graded by teaching assistants, and there are so many final papers to be graded that the teaching assistants often subcontract them among fellow students.)

At the time of the conflict student idealism in Berkeley and elsewhere was being expressed within the larger struggle for minority rights in the United States. The spring and summer before, hundreds of Berkeley students affected major employers in Northern California, demanding, while chanting in marches and sit-ins, that Blacks be allowed equal job opportunities with Whites. Hotels, restaurants, department stores, and automobile dealerships felt their anger, sensed their power, and surrendered at least some small part of prejudice. Many students went to the southern United States to affect racial attitudes there through nonviolent action. They returned, after three students were tortured and murdered and others were whipped and beaten, with the psychology of soldiers home from an unfinished war.

Before the beginning of the new semester that fall, the 1964 Republican National Convention was held in the Cow Palace in neighboring San Francisco. The far right dominated Republican politics. Barry Goldwater, who became the inevitable Republican candidate after winning the California primary election during the previous summer, had taken positions which, if enforced from the Presidency, would have changed the basic direction of the civil rights struggle: the movement for Black equality either would have been deflated or exploded into violence—probably the latter.

Students in Berkeley organized protests. They picketed the Cow Palace knowing, probably, that they were speaking more to the world than to the Republicans inside; for the Republican political commitments had been made and were irreversible.

Recruitment for the picketing of the Cow Palace took place in front of the Student Union building on the University campus. There, students favoring causes traditionally set up folding tables on which they placed petitions, leaflets, and receptacles for contributions. The university permitted free speech on campus, but had not always done so. The past University president, Robert Gordon Sproul, had forbidden all political meetings in 1934, during the conflicts of the Depression, but the political climate had changed. The Administration's insistence that the staff sign a loyalty oath in 1950 had racked the faculty and, when liberal influence was restored, the oath had been modified. The ban on Communist speakers, imposed in 1951, was eliminated in 1963 under the pressure of litigation by students and the American Civil Liberties Union.

Soon after he became president in 1958, and again in 1961 and 1963, Clark Kerr issued a series of directives which codified the verbal understandings that the University had made with students on questions of free speech on the campus. Through the Kerr Directives he also interpreted this essential element of the University Charter: "The University shall be entirely independent of all political or sectarian influence and kept free therefrom in the appointment of its Regents and in the administration of its affairs." In Kerr's understanding, this meant that the "University and the name of the University must not be used to involve the University as an institution in the political religious, and other controversial issues of the day."

University administrators expected that aloofness would gain them freedom from the senseless persecutions of demagogues. No public university could spend all of its time defending itself from the few elected officials who would not distinguish words from acts and who, in the fashion of the day, were threatening to punish people and institutions that allowed the full use of the First Amendment. And yet while it was necessary to disassociate the University from any hint of stigma, the administration had an obligation to the scholarly pursuit of truth; it could not abandon open forums without resigning its function.

The recruitment tables were banned, however. The one major exception was at Bancroft Way and Telegraph Avenue. There, the University allowed political action. Many administrators at the University thought that recruitment was possible on that strip of land because it belonged to the City of Berkeley rather than to the University. Kerr knew otherwise; he had instructed the treasurer of the University to transfer the land to the city of possible. Other business interfered with the transfer, though. His instructions weren't carried out.

A committee of the University had been discussing whether or not the bicycles, tables, and crowds at Bancroft and Telegraph constituted a hazard. At that time, a combination of events gave the University more to think about in its concern for the student safety on Bancroft. First, it was strenuously seeking the passage of a state bond issue for education in the coming election. Second, William F. Knowland, the editor and publisher of the *Oakland Tribune*, was the California manager of Barry Goldwater's campaign for the Presidential nomination. The University Administration denied that its attempts to ban assemblages on the campus were the result of pressure from Knowland.

At this point Mario Savio, Jack Weinberg, and others organized the Free Speech Movement (FSM), one of the first politically effective student groups in the United States, to protest the University's ban on political activity on campus. The University attempted to suspend them for defying the ban of assemblies. As the Administration and the FSM negotiated, thousands of students rallied to protest the disciplining of Savio and Weinberg. Governor Edmund G. Brown called out the California Highway Patrol, and local law enforcement authorities sought to break up a sit-in which students organized in the Sproul Hall Administration building. Eventually professors, teaching assistants, and students from other University campuses struck in support of the FSM, and the University was

shut down. Owen Chamberlain, the Nobel Prize-winning physicist
at Berkeley, said: "I am trying to listen, and I ask you to listen. See
if they are not saying: Respect our civil disobedience—it is sometimes better than foregoing the rights you believe to be yours." Jack
Weinberg, held captive in a police car surrounded by thousands of
supporting students, summed up the reasons for the popularity of
the Movement:

*These themes have been so well received because of the general
feeling among the students that the Unversity has made them anon-
ymous; that they have very little control over their environment,
over their future; that the University society is almost completely
unresponsive to their individual needs. The students decry the lack
of human contact, the lack of communication, the lack of dialogue
that exists at the University. Many believe that much of their
coursework is irrelevant, that many of their most difficult assignments are merely tedious busy work with little or no educational
value. All too often in his educational career, the student, in a pique
of frustration, asks himself, 'What's it all about?' In a flash of in-
sight he sees the educational process as a gauntlet: undergraduate
education appears to be a rite of endurance, a series of trials, which
if successfully completed allows one to enter graduate school; and
upon those who succeeded in completing the entire right of passage
is bestowed the ceremonious title, Ph.D.*

The newspapers said that the trouble in Berkeley had generated the
greatest mass arrest in the history of California. Six hundred and
thirty-five policemen took more than 800 students into custody over
a period of 12 hours. In the chilly darkness of a largely uninhabited,
barren and rolling countryside, lines of cars miles long were parked
on the normally busy highway in front of the Santa Rita Rehabilitation Center, 35 miles south of Berkeley. Most of the cars contained
students, faculty members, or University personnel who, whether
or not they were in sympathy with the arrested students, came to
offer bail.

　　Throughout the country, educators acted as though a sensitive
nerve had been touched. A famous professor of philosophy, writing
from his vantage point in New York City, set to work on a polemic
against student irresponsibility. University presidents braced them-
.selves for the responses on their own campuses.

　　After the University and FSM had finally worked out an

agreement allowing free speech on campus, it had appeared as though the drama had ended. It hadn't. There were charges pending against 773 students, who were represented by lawyers distinguished both for ability and for championing libertarian causes; the trial of the students became a matter of principle. The arrested students filed claims totalling $4.5 million, charging brutality by police and deprivation of rights. Moreover, students on other campuses had begun to take actions resembling those in Berkeley: 110 students at the University of Kansas had sat down in the president's office to gain a nondiscrimination clause in the regulations governing fraternities and sororities. At St. John's University there was a rally to reduce administrative censorship of the school newspaper.

State legislators threatened to investigate the entire University and to reduce its budget unless the offending students were punished. In Washington, D.C., the UnAmerican Activities Committee of the House of Representatives joined in the effort to rebuke the rebellious students. Edward Carter, the Chairman of the Regents, demanded punishment for the offenders, too, but Kerr refused this on grounds that in doing so he would reopen the free speech controversy and would fail in his obligations to due process of law. Instead, Kerr and Acting Chancellor Martin Meyerson broke a new storm over Berkeley. They offered resignations, not to the Regents, but to the press. Reactions were obtained by the press, too, before the Regents could hear Kerr officially present his point of view. On every campus chancellors, faculties, and students voted overwhelmingly to ask Kerr to remain president of the University. Kerr's supporters among the Regents were thus well armed by the time of the meeting. The Governor led them. He insisted that due process of law be followed and that Kerr—who had still not officially submitted his resignation, be asked to remain. The Governor prevailed; both Kerr and Meyerson agreed to stay in office, and both were assured of new and greater strength.

This vote of confidence in Kerr was to be temporary, however. Governor Brown was defeated in the 1966 election by Ronald Reagan, who promised the voters harsher punishment for Kerr for not dealing with the students with more severity. Reagan forced Kerr's dismissal in 1967.

If there were victories during the trouble in Berkeley, they were shared by all sides. Students gained a new consciousness of their own maturity and commitment to the cause of human dignity. Faculty gained a new awareness of how far circumstances had drawn it from the common defense of academic freedom. The Administration had been shown how impersonal it had become. The people, perhaps, were aroused sufficiently to think about the sea of ambiguities into which modern society is drifting.

The Free Speech Movement of 1964 established Berkeley as the most political university in America, if not the world. By 1968, universities everywhere were reproducing its demonstrations. Berkeley, and American education, were never to be the same.

1967–

Governor Reagan's dismissal of Clark Kerr as University president reflected public anger over the riots in Berkeley. For many years, the public had accepted the University of California, and the state's higher education in general, without question. But during the 1960's, it perceived that its central values were being attacked through the violent confrontations and acts of civil disobedience at Berkeley. Clark Kerr, who had taken a middle ground during tense periods, thus was forced out. The end of his tenure represented a turning point in the University's history, for it marked the beginning of a period in which the school was more politically sensitive to both students and public.

For the next six years the school was headed by Charles Hitch. During this period, in 1969, a new crisis arose in the form of the People's Park incident. Governor Reagan, adamant as ever, summoned the National Guard at Hitch's request to suppress the students and street people who occupied the unofficial Park. (See *Berkeley, 1967–* .)

In 1973, the Regents chose David S. Saxon, a physicist, as president. During his tenure, the school sought to respond to criticism that it was neglecting teaching in favor of research and that it was ignoring the consequences of its discoveries. To focus more completely on teaching it restored the semester system, for students had complained that the division of the academic year into quarters had put them on an assembly line. The University's greater emphasis on teaching was accelerated, too, by the withering of financial sources: state and federal governments, facing harder economic times, were reducing their subsidies to research.

During the 1970's most American students, sensing the downturn in the economy, began to think less about social issues and more about themselves. At Berkeley, the result was a less political student body. A survey of Berkeley students conducted in 1977 disclosed that 43 percent considered themselves to be "middle-of-the-road" politically, while 14 percent were "conservative," 39 percent "liberal," fewer than 1 percent "far right," and only 3 percent "far left." Only 29 percent urged disobedience when laws violate personal values, a decline from 37 percent just the year before and from 70 percent in 1976. Even more startling, 17 percent believed that the administration had the right to ban some speakers from the campus. One student leader, expressing himself in bad English but in accurate thought, summarized the mood at Berkeley:

People are a little more sophisticated now than they were ten years ago. We read utility rather than philosophy. We play with mathematics rather than feel. You've got to be sensitive and logical to convince people you're right.

This is not to say that political confrontations have disappeared from Berkeley. One major issue, for the far left, has been the University's investment in companies which participate in the economy of South Africa. (In 1977, on the Santa Cruz campus, this issue resulted in the largest mass arrest—of over 400 students—since the Free Speech Movement.) But the engagement between the University and protesting groups has taken a more subtle turn. The chief of the University Police, when arresting students who were protesting the South African investments, half-apologized for his action, a remarked contrast to the police brutality of the 1960's: "We want to give people options at every step of the way," he told his future prisoners. "We want to do this in a dignified way that meets your needs." Where but in Berkeley, some people remarked, would an arresting officer be so accommodating?

In recent years another political movement has engaged many Berkeley students. A well-organized group has sought to end the University's weapons research at Livermore and Los Alamos. Why, the students demanded, should the University aid in the design and construction of weapons which threaten to destroy humanity itself? In answer the Regents have pointed out that the Livermore and Los Alamos labs bring federal contracts of $625 million a year to the

University—more than half of the total University budget. President Saxon defended the labs, saying, "It is self-illusory to think that the University will control U.S.foreign policy."

The University community has divided sharply over this issue. In 1970, 43% of the Berkeley faculty voted to detach the weapons labs from the University. This group formed an alliance with Governor Brown, who in 1980 said, "The weapons program is getting more and more out of the hands of democratic control and more in the hands of the computer. The University is blocking democratic controls by providing a cover for the weapons labs." However, the Regents denied Brown's efforts to reject government contracts, which, therefore, were renewed in 1980 for five years.

Another major issue facing the University concerned the school's role in the promotion of racial equality in America. It was formidably raised in 1977 when a white engineer named Allan Bakke applied for admission in the Medical School at Davis, but was twice rejected. Bakke sued the University, contending he was denied admission to because the school gave preferential admission to less-qualified minority students. The "reverse discrmination" case, as it became popularly known, was appealed to the courts. It represented a major policy question not only for U.C., but for universities nationally. The California Supreme Court ruled against the University's special admissions program, saying it violated the Equal Protection Clause of the U.S. Constitution. The U.S. Supreme Court overturned that ruling, holding that racial quotas are permissible when schools choose which students shall be admitted. These quotas, the court said, serve a legitimate state purpose by encouraging equality. Yet the court also ordered that Bakke be admitted to the Davis Medical School, stating that he had been denied his Constitutional rights.

The Bakke case was significant in that it was the first time the issue of affirmative action, which had been instituted in response to the demands of miniorities, had reached the U.S. Supreme Court for final adjudication. But the court's decision was ambiguous. Since Bakke was admitted and the special admissions program left intact, it is still uncertain as to whether the University may legally change its academic standards in order to increase minority enrollment.

Over the years, other issues have dogged U.C. Should the faculty should be allowed to engage in outside consulting jobs? Should the school cooperate with the Central Intelligence Agency (CIA) and the Defense Department on military projects? To what extent

should U.C. apply itself to research, granting that research con-
sumed energies which might have been devoted to teaching?

All of these have been subjects for continuing, intense debates,
all of which could not have taken place before the Free Speech
Movement of 1964. The FSM established Berkeley, both on campus and on, as a leading political forum. Ever since those tumultu-
ous days, the University has included social and political concerns
in its guiding motto, *"Fiat Lux!"*—"Let There Be Light!"

GOVERNMENT

The governmental units of the University of California are the Board of Regents, the Academic Senate, and the Administration.

1. The Board of Regents.

Driven into the cement before each entrance of the University's campuses are bronze plaques reminding visitors that they pass by permission of the Regents. All official business is conducted in their corporate name. State law gives them "full powers of organization and government, subject only to such Legislative control as may be necessary to insure compliance with the terms of the endowments of the University and the security of its funds." This includes selecting the president and reviewing his appointments, budgeting, and other decision making, which are powers defined by the State Constitution.

Governors appoint Regents. No single governor is likely to appoint many of the 16 who are selected by that means, however: the Regent's term of office is 12 years by contrast to the governor's four. But the governor is an *ex officio* Regent himself, and so are eight others: the Lieutenant Governor, the Superintendent of Public Instruction, the Speaker of the Assembly, the President and Vice-President of the Alumni Association, the President of the University, and a student who serves a one-year term.

The concept of regency was written into the University's charter at the suggestion of a state superintendent of schools in the 1860's. Its literal author was John W. Dwinelle, an official of the Congregational-Presbyterian union that sponsored the College of California, the University's predecessor. He and other supporters of the idea may have been thinking of religious boards of elders when they created regencies. In any case, they accomplished their purpose: Regents have often saved the University from outside parsimony or hostility; they are ordinarily wealthy and/or influential and so serve, too, to bring the University endowments, as well as to bring it businesslike government.

2. Academic Senate.

It is comprised of the permanent faculties of the University colleges, and of the principal administrative officers of the university. Its committees govern scholarship and protect professional self-determination. To serve the first function it determined in conference with the administration what students shall be admitted and given certficates and degrees, and authorizes courses of instruction, teaches them, and supervises students. For the second, it counsels chief campus officers in the election of departmental chairpersons who represent the administration within departments and propose permanent faculty members to deans and committees of professors. New appointments are made when the appropriate faculty has chosen three persons and submitted their names, through the chairpersons, to the chancellor of the campus on which they will serve. The chancellor makes the appointment after consulting with members of a committee of the Academic Senate. Technically, the president and Regents may veto appointments. Neither has used this power since the "faculty revolution" of 1920, when, after Benjamin Ide Wheeler retired as president, the faculties regained the control over appointments that he had taken from them (see *University: Development.*).

The independence of the Academic Senate tends to assure free expression among both students and faculty, a quality that first baffles and then pleases whoever comes from more restricted environments and is exposed to some of the more vigorous debates at the University. The faculties of few other public universities have similar status: Oklahoma State, Michigan State, University of Colorado, University of Idaho, and the University of Michigan are among them.

3. The President and His/Her Administration (see University: Development.)

ASSOCIATED STUDENTS OF THE UNIVERSITY OF CALIFORNIA (ASUC)

When students considered havoc their birthright the Associated Students of the University of California was organized to govern them. In 1887, ASUC supplied rules for mass meetings and for social and cultural events. It began to promote these events, and to sponsor campus athletics as well. But this later appeared to be insufficient self-government. In September, 1902, packs of students overran the horsedrawn railway system by which many of them commuted to rooms in Oakland. Newspapers suggested that all of Berkeley's students were undisciplined. Some reform became urgent to placate the community.

Sponsors of the changes were strongly affected by Germanic traditions of education. In the *Blue and Gold Yearbook* of 1889, of the 56 faculty members listed, 21 had been to German or Austrian universities: Heidelberg, Berlin, Gottingen, Vienna. Benjamin Ide Wheeler was president, and he had also been to Heidelberg. He, too, was angry about the attacks on the railways. He encouraged a settlement out of court. Then he set about helping to alter the ASUC according to his and the faculty's lights. His Germanic tradition differed from the English and French upon which most American universities were founded. It urged complete and early independence upon students. His determination to help the students gain self-government grew out of the half-forgotten but once widely famous Jim Whipple Case.

Jim Whipple was captain of the football team in 1899. He had failed a course but decided to ignore a faculty order not to play in a "Big Game." (See *University: Traditions.*) The team won because of him, and he became a hero. Students would have rebelled at official disciplining of Whipple, and the administration cannily assisted in the formation of a committee of leading seniors to hear the case. According to one report, Whipple, on the recommendation of the committee, was suspended for the period of the winter vacation. In fact, he got his degree 18 months late, but with his academic luck that might have happened anyway. Whatever the truth, student government matured because of him: the principle of student juries became embedded in what was called "senior control." Soon afterward, undergraduates formed the Students' Affairs Committee. The idea of self-government has not been challenged since. In 1919 it was so strongly held that freshmen were expected to take an oath of self-government and independence, a method that nineteenth century Heidelberg would have cheerfully approved.

Today, ASUC is a $12 million operation, run by 35 elected student representatives, 90 professional staff, and over 400 student employees. ASUC's philosophy is that non-academic activities are an important supplement to the normal educational experience. Accordingly, ASUC offers a wide range of services, both to the students and to the general public. These include restaurants, cafeterias; a recreation center; a bus service; child care services; a travel agency; an arts and crafts center; and a book store. ASUC owns the *Pelican*, the campus humor magazine, and the *Blue and Gold Yearbook*.

ASUC uses an assessment system of student fees, much in the same way labor unions use a check-off system of their wages to finance union activities. These funds are supplemented by profits generated from the many services operated by ASUC. The profits support over 200 student social, political, and cultural organizations. ASUC also founded the U.C. Student Lobby, the first organized student advocacy organization outside the parameters of university government. Headquartered in Sacramento, the U.C. Student Lobby has served as a model for similar organizations across the country.

A GUIDE TO STUDENT SERVICES

Many of the student services available are operated by the ASUC. Others are university services. Since business hours may vary, the telephone numbers for each office is listed so that the reader may call for exact information.

Campus Safety Program
Telephone: 642-1431
The Campus Safety Program provides lighted safe walk routes, emergency phones and a rape prevention and education program. For more information, call the Campus Safety Coordinator.

Career Planning and Placement Center
This office offers workshops and seminars on resume writing, job search strategies, identifying job skills, and summer jobs. Advisers are available by appointment to help students and alumni with any aspect of career planning. A Career Library (T-6, second floor) provides directories of employers and past job listings. A computerized career information sytsem is also available. Students considering careers in business, industry, government, social services, and non-profit organizations should go to the upper floor of Building T-6, 111 Wheeler Hall, or to 26 Barrows Hall. Students considering careers in education should go to the ground floor of building T-6. Students and their spouses seeking part-time, temporary, odd-job, internship, or summer employment should go to 111 Wheeler Hall. Students interested in work-study should go to the Office of Financial Aid, 207 Sproul Hall.

Committee for Arts and Lectures (C.A.L.)

C.A.L. is a special University department (not associated with ASUC) which sponsors lectures, films, plays, and a wide variety of cultural events on campus for students and the public. Most C.A.L. events are held in Zellerbach Auditorium or in Zellerbach Playhouse. C.A.L.'s offices are on the basement floor of Zellerbach Auditorium. Tickets to C.A.L. events are available through the University Box Office.

Counseling and Psychological Services
Building T-5
Telephone: 642-2366

The Counseling Center offers educational, career, and personal counseling. The Center has an extensive library collection of occupational and educational materials, as well as college and professional school catalogs. Lists of scholarships, fellowships, and loans are available. The staff consists of professionally trained counselors. All information gathered in the course of counseling is confidential and is released only with the student's consent.

The Gay Counseling Program
Telephone: 642-5012

This program is staffed by professionals and volunteers. Both individual and group counseling are offered without charge to students. Information about appointments should be directed to the Cowell Hospital Information Desk.

Humphrey Go-BART

This is a free shuttle bus, offered between 7 a.m. and 7 p.m. from the Downtown Berkeley BART Station to the campus and to Strawberry Canyon, the Botanical Gardens, and the Lawrence Hall of Science. The night shuttle runs from 7 p.m. to 1:50 a.m. Sunday to Thursday, and until 12:30 a.m. on Fridays during the Fall and Spring semesters. Humphrey Go-Bart offers door-to-door service after 10 p.m. on its night schedule.

Information Desk
Lobby, Student Union building
Telephone: 642-3361

Speakers Bureau: 642-7202
Call to obtain information and to register for programs on: Stress Management, Nutrition, Meditation, Back self-care, stop smoking, weight control, health assessment, fertility awareness.

Student Information Center
102 Sproul Hall
Telephone: 642-6412

The student information center offers referrals, information, or advice for nearly every conceivable student question. Student counselors are available for personal or administrative problems. Other functions include legal advising through the Ombudsperson, a Notary Public for matters relating to the University, student orientation programs, and the Help Center to assist in class enrollment each semester. Students may make official business telephone calls to other U.C. campuses from the Center free of charge.

Student Learning Center
Building T-8
Telephone: 642-7332

Individual and group tutoring is offered in specific courses, especially lower division science and math courses, reading speed and comprehension, writing, (with emphasis on introductory composition courses), notetaking and other study skills. Computer-assisted instruction is available in several subjects, and counselors can also assist in preparation for graduate or professional school examinations (e.g., LSAT, MCAT, GRE, and the GMAT.) The Center is open to all students, with priority given for individual help to EOP/ Affirmative Action students and athletes.

Student Pre-Professional/Pre-Graduate Advising
400 Eshleman Hall
Telephone: 642-5207

This office offers advice for students entering one of the health professions, including dentistry, medical technology, medicine, nursing, osteopathy, podiatry, physical therapy, and veterinary medicine; the legal profession; or other graduate programs. The office maintains a letter of evaluation service and collects and sends letters of reference required for application to graduate and professional schools.

Studio
Lower Level, Student Union building
Telephone: 642-3065
The Studio is a workspace where students not enrolled in art classes can learn and practice ceramics, photography, painting, calligraphy, stained glass, and various types of printing. The Studio offers classes for persons at all levels of skill.

Travel Center
Lobby, Student Union building
Telephone: 642-3000
Open to the general public, the Travel Center specializes in student budgets for travel anywhere in the world. Ticket arrangements may be made Monday through Friday, 9:30 a.m. to 5 p.m.

University Box Office
Lobby, Student Union building
Telephone: (tickets) 642-9988
Information: 642-3125
Athletics Tickets: 642-5150

For any conceivable question about the university. Campus maps, brochures, bus schedules, and movie schedules for the Pacific Film Archive are distributed from this desk. Newspapers and chess boards can be checked out from the desk for use in the Heller Lounge.

KALX (90.7 FM)
311 Eshleman Hall
Telephone: 642-1111
Request line: 642-KALX
KALX is the campus radio station. Student-operated, KALX offers a wide variety of programming 24 hours a day. Students interested in volunteering should go to 311 Eshleman Hall.

Psychiatric Services
83 Cowell Hospital
Telephone: 642-9494

Services are available to all Berkeley students who need counseling on problems of a university or personal nature. The emphasis is on the individual, and not on "mental illness." All information is held in professional confidence. Individual and group services are available.

Student Advocate
318 Eshleman Hall
Telephone: 6422-5291
Elected by his or her fellow students, the Student Advocate serves as "defense counsel" on behalf of students who face disciplinary action by the University.

Student Health Service
Cowell Hospital
Medical Emergencies: 642-3188 (24 hours)
Future appointments: 642-5012
(8 a.m.to 7 p.m., Monday through Friday) Same-day visits, Advice Nurse: 642-6890, room 102.
Contraception and Gynecology Clinic: 642-7687
Educational programs: 642-7202

Greek Theatre Tickets: 642-8024
Hertz Hall Tickets: 642-2698
Wheeler Auditorium Tickets: 642-4290
The University Box Office sells tickets for campus entertainment, as well as for tickets to Bay Area events. Students may sign up to usher at major theaters, including the Curran, the Geary, and the Orpheum in San Francisco. Credit card orders are taken on the phone. State Park permits are also obtainable, as well as tickets to Lincoln Center in New York City. The University Box Office is the largest ticket seller in Northern California.

CAMPUS PLAN

There seems no alternative to the campus, now that it is built. Henry Durant and other University founders saw an infinite number of alternatives. Horace Bushnell, an itinerant New England minister, was chief scout for the trustees of the College of California, the University's predecessor, when they were looking for land. Everything he nominated seemed to them to be too arid, remote, or expensive. They eliminated Clinton, Napa Valley, San Pablo, and San Jose. Then Durant called attention to land owned by his friend Captain Orrin Simmons, a retired sea captain who had sold a San Francisco hardware business. It was on Strawberry Creek north of Oakland. He liked the outlook and climate of the place.

The trustees accepted Durant's choice after local owners offfered the College free land. It bought most of the north half of the campus for $1,200. Then William Hillegass, an adjacent owner, got news of the decision. He held out 17 acres for two years. The College could not have paid him and would have withdrawn if Samuel H. Willey, one of its founders, had not discovered a way to profit from the arrangement by homesteading the acreage.

The nine trustees came to the site together on April 16, 1860. Willey later described what happened: "We looked about for some permanent landmark around which we could gather for some simple ceremonies of dedication. This rock appeared to be the only thing that met the requirement of the occasion, and we made our way higher (see Founder's Rock, below). From this elevated spot the grounds were all before us, covered with a crop of growing grain, and bordered with such noble trees as were nowhere else to be seen. The whole plain, indeed, was grainfield from the Bay back to the hills, and not a house that could properly be called a dwelling was in sight."

The trustees had to pay Orrin Simmons $35,000 for his ranch. They paid George M. Blake and George Leonard $8,000 each for another 40 acres, and they finally gave Hillegass $9,000 Hillegass, Blake, and Leonard had each paid $5,000 for 160 acres in 1856. Another original resident, Frank K. Shattuck, had paid $4,200 for 130 acres. When the college took title, Willey did the subdividing; he reserved 160 acres for the new campus and sold 160 acres for $500 an acre, payable in 20 monthly installments.

The campus was planned by Frederick Law Olmsted, the first

Sather Tower was intended to "raise the vision."

American landscape architect. He had been manager of General Fremont's mining estate in Mariposa County for two years. He was ready to return to planning Central Park in New York but was persuaded instead, in 1865, to work on a park in San Francisco and later, as a sideline, on the campus. His plan was complete but only a small part of it, the broad central axis centering on the Golden Gate, was used by the men who finally did the building.

Yet the plan seemed settled in 1873, and 1,000 people paraded from Oakland to Berkeley, moving on a warm fall day up Telegraph Avenue in carriages whose trotting horses drew them for ceremonies before the first two buildings of the campus, North and South Halls. David Farquharson was the designer of the buildings. They were heavy and dark but elegant and comfortable: one of red brick garnished with rich woods and lavish millwork inside, and one of wood, painted white. They were sited along along the central axis that Olmsted had drawn. It became Campanile Way.

No planner affected the campus during the next 15 years. There was no school of architecture and no one to press for the rational allocation of land. Then Bernard Maybeck arrived. (See *Architecture*.) He was the son of a German-born carpenter who apprenticed him to woodcarving in New York when he was 17. He had studied at the *Beaux Arts* in Paris, worked aimlessly in Florida and Missouri, and designed cottages with an English architect in San Francisco. Maybeck understood the region, its materials, and its architecture.

In 1896, after Maybeck came to the University to teach, Mrs. Phoebe Apperson Hearst visited President Martin Kellogg to offer a school of mining in memory of her husband, the silver millionaire and senator. One account of the visit suggested that "There she was with the money in her hand, and like a good executive President Kellogg assured her that if she would return in a day or two he would be able to show her what they could do with the money. A hurried call to the engineering department found no talent to produce in 24 hours a drawing of an imaginary building. But someone did recall that 'There was that architect fellow, Maybeck, around, and if an architect was good for anything maybe this was it.'"

Maybeck produced the design. Mrs. Hearst approved, committed the money, and was drawn closely into the work of the University, whose future she profoundly affected. But Maybeck was discontented with the random placing of a single building on the campus. He told this to a new Regent named J. B. Reinstein, who agreed with him and went off to tell his friend Mrs. Hearst how he

Mrs. Phoebe Apperson Hearst,
Regent and patron of
the University

was persuaded that the University urgently needed a plan.

Mrs. Hearst had millions of dollars and a central interest: education. She founded and subsidized girls' schools, children's schools, Episcopal schools; she gave scholarships and fellowships in wholesale lots; she helped to finance the University of Pennsylvania and tried to start a national university.

She had never been to college; she had only accidentally left her native Missouri. In 1862 George Hearst, the son of a Missouri farmer, briefly left his California mining interests to visit his sick mother in Franklin County, Missouri. There he saw Phoebe Apperson. She was 20, the daughter of a physician and a Southern belle.

They married and moved to San Francisco. But she found herself alone as ever. He was in the Legislature by 1865, and he kept a hand in his copper mines in Montana and lead mines in South Dakota. Governor George Stoneman appointed him U.S. Senator, but when he tried to become governor himself in 1882, evidently while preparing to run for the Presidency, Stoneman, once a popular general, beat him. The Hearsts had one son, William Randolph, who by the time his father died was immersed in building a newspaper empire. Mrs. Hearst was left to her millions and her compelling social interests.

*Henri Jean Emile
Bénard, first architect
of the Berkeley Campus*

She liked the idea of a plan for the University. At the Palace Hotel in San Francisco, she sat down to write to the Board of Regents, of which she was to become a member: ". . . and I desire to say that the success of this enterprise shall not be hampered in any way by a money consideration." The Board accepted her offer.

Mrs. Hearst began the project by sending Maybeck and Reinstein to Europe in 1897. They toured the major cities interviewing architects and distributing a multilingual circular containing the floridly worded terms of a contest that opened the planning to all of the world's designers. "It is believed to be possible," the circular said, "to secure a comprehensive plan so in harmony with the universal principles of architectural art that there will be no necessity of remodeling its broad outlines a thousand years hence, than there would be of remodeling the Parthenon, had it come down to us complete and uninjured. . . . "To this the London *Times* responded that "Never, perhaps, since Aladdin built his famous palace, certainly never since Wren sought and was deprived of the opportunity of rebuilding London according to his own splendid conception, have architects been offered so unique and so transcendent a chance of deserving and achieving immortality."

The prize was $10,000 and worldwide fame. One hundred and five architects submitted entries before the deadline of the preliminary competition. Their plans were accepted by the American counsel at Antwerp, Belgium, and on July 10, 1898, were moved with appropriate showmanship to the Belgium Royal Museum of Fine Arts, where they were put under guard and examined by four jurymen. The jury picked four of the entries, adjourned, and reassembled at Berkeley Station on August 30, 1899, when it went in carriages with professors to address the students beneath the oaks of the campus. That evening the jurymen went to San Francisco's City Hall to meet Mayor James D. Phelan and to undergo a storm of social planning: there were fancy-dress parties for them across the northern half of the state.

The winner, Emile Henri Bénard of Paris proved a classicist for whom the Parthenon remained the highest achievement of human construction. His plan reflected the desire of western classicists for symmetry. It proposed three major axes, two crossing Campanile Way, and two plazas from west to east, ending with buildings on the terraced slopes of the Berkeley Hills. The humanities buildings were at the core, the stadium at the south, and science buildings at other extremities. Bénard suggested winding extensions of city streets among the fruit trees and grain fields at the west gate, among the oaks, bays, and Monterey pines at the two branches of Strawberry Creek, at the southwest corner of the campus.

When the celebrating was ended it became possible to inspect Bénard's plan more closely under Berkeley's own vivid light; and people who had accepted without complaint the bad prose that began the contest to see the relationship between it and the winning entry that it had inspired. In Berkeley the plan proved pompous and expensive; Bénard's own estimate of its cost was $80 million. Bénard worked to change the plan. He did all that he could and left for Paris. The only building left, ultimately, was the President's Mansion.

Maybeck had a suggestion. He outlined it in an article in the *Blue and Gold Yearbook* of 1900. It seemed to him that local architects who tried to advance the plan would be subject to local pressures, and that the University should hire one from another city. He kept pleading fundamentals: "In building a new university, it is certain that some of the faults of older institutions will be avoided if thought be given to the general arrangement of the plan."

Maybeck's argument eliminated himself as the one to be hired, and he and Mrs. Hearst, for whom he was building a lavish student-faculty gathering place behind the mansion she had rented at Piedmont Avenue and Channing Way, joined to support John Galen Howard, wealthy New York architect who was fourth in the competition. As a result, Howard designed the Hearst Memorial Mining Building that Maybeck had started, and in 1902 became supervising architect for the campus, which he replanned in 1908.

He proposed detached buildings. He put them on the broad, formal, east-west axis that Olmsted drew in 1866. During his first 12
years on campus he planned 11 major buildings. After a successful
bond issue in 1914 work began on three other designs by him:
Wheeler, Gilman, and Hilgard halls. These, added to his other
prominent work—including the mining building, Charles Franklin
Doe Library, and Agriculture Hall—made up most of the University.

   Howard, like Bénard, had the notion that antiquity is the most
pertinent symbol of higher education. Most of his plans were borrowed from classical Greece and Rome; he favored the Roman and
Renaissance. He had none of Maybeck's enthusiasm for wood and
local materials. He imported white stone that effusively radiates
Berkeley's bright sunlight. He was campus architect until 1927.
There have been plans since, but his was preponderant.

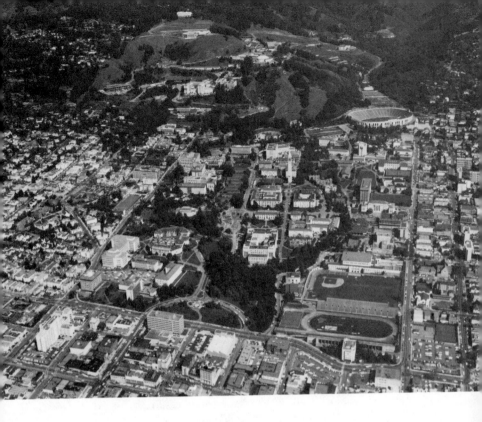

CAMPUS BUILDINGS

There are five academic colleges at Berkeley: Agriculture, Chemistry, Engineering, Environmental Design, and Letters and Science. There are eight professional schools: Business Administration, Education, Forestry, Law, Librarianship, Optometry, Public Health, and Social Welfare. The campus offers preliminary work leading to professional study in dentistry, medicine, nursing, or pharmacy.

The Berkeley campus includes 1,232 acres. These are its buildings, organized in groups and related by the number code to the map on pages 110–11. *(Dates indicate the year of completion):*

1. University Hall. University and Oxford Streets. C-1.
Contains all statewide offices, inluding those of the president, Regents, Agricultural Extension Service and Agricultural Information, and Systemwide Information in Room 349.

2. *Extension and Press Building*. 2223 Fulton Street. (1962)

Extension

During the winter of 1890–91, the faculty began to lecture in the Unitarian Church of Oakland. It did so at the suggestion of Professor Charles Mills Gayley, who had organized a group of professors that set out to determine whether the kind of adult education that was commonplace in England, and that had been started on the East Coast, could be adapted to California. There was reason to be encouraged: traveling lecturers were being well received in Northern California.

First, Gayley himself offered a course in Shakespeare. The class was assigned to the auditorium of the California Academy of Sciences in San Francisco. The average attendance quickly reached 400. This success led other faculty members to offer classes. Professor Thomas Bacon offered a course in history. It attracted 200 adult students, and the enrollment soon was doubled. Professor Irving Stringham's course in mathematics attracted 25 students at first, and after four weeks its enrollment was trebled. Dozens of extension courses followed, and clearly reflected the educational hungers of the times: they included "Transition from Medieval to Modern History," "Propaedeutic to Higher Analysis," and Ethics. "History of Modern Europe" was one of the most popular courses. Others were the "Logic of Mathematics" and "The Epistles of Horace."

Extension became a self-governing part of the University in 1902. For 11 years afterward, its teachers were volunteers. Then the Legislature offered funds to establish five Extension bureaus: correspondence, class instruction, public lectures, public discussion, and municipal reference.

Today, 1,600 instructors conduct classes for 50,000 students each year. The Extension Department, which is completely self-supporting from student fees, is known for offering courses in fields which cut across traditional departmental lines. Examples include: international studies, natural environmental studies, graphic design, counseling, publishing, bookselling, alcohol studies, gerontology, arts administration, and the use of computers for data processing.

Special continuing education credit (denoted as "ceu") is offered for students who need evidence of study for licensing requirements, for employers, or professional organizations which require evidence of study.

The vast majority of Extension students have a bachelor's degree. Sixty percent of Extension students are between 25 and 28 years old, and another 30 percent are aged 39 to 66. A large percentage of Extension students, 48 percent, take courses for job-related reasons, 37 percent are enrolled for personal growth, and 15 percent are working toward credentials or a degree.

Extension courses are held in numerous field stations away from the Berkeley campus. Courses for teachers, managers, or engineers, are held in appropriate settings. Students in natural environmental studies work in Mendocino, Monterey, or in the Sierra Nevadas. U.C. Extension also operates a successful international program at Oxford University, Canterbury, and Leningrad.

Press

Established in 1887, one of the oldest university presses in the United States, it publishes about 150 clothbound books a year, 60 paperbacks, and 10 reprints in the California Reprint Library Series. The University Printing Department now is maintained separately. Its founders were master craftsmen whose appreciation of graphics became a tradition, yet students made up the staff and were the source of the modern Press.

3. *Agricultural, Biological Group.*

Improving agriculture has been one of the University's central aims since the Organic Act of 1868. The College of Agriculture was not significant academically, however, until 1875, when Eugene Woldemar Hilgard became professor in it. Daniel Coit Gilman, second president of the University, who was so harried by political attacks that he left after two years to become president of Johns Hopkins University, brought Hilgard to Berkeley to satisfy hostile Grangers. He had to suggest that "volunteers" enroll in agriculture to keep the distinguished professor busy. Hilgard made the course popular; he stayed to build the college.

The modern college is chiefly used for theoretical research, and applications are developed on the campuses at Davis and Riverside.

Vitamin K, the anti-hemorrhaging agent, was determined, isolated, and synthesized in Berkeley. The college also produced a simple compound with four times the vitamin's clotting powers. Among the college's other major accomplishments is the ability to predict the size of deciduous fruit on the evidence of the previous winter's temperatures, permitting farmers more economic stability than they had previously known.

One of the college's more dramatic accomplishments took place when citrus trees of Southern California were being destroyed by mealy bugs. Berkeley scientists sent ladybugs out against the pests; but the friendly insects were attacked by the Argentine ant. A Berkeley scientist explored the world's temperate zone to find the source of the mealy bug and its nemesis. He wired from a place near Australia, "I have found the mealy bug's home and with it the arch-enemy, a diminutive wasp which bores a hole in the mealy bug's back, lays its eggs within the insect, and when hatched out the baby wasps devour the vital portions of the pest." The wasp is microscopic. He sent some of them to Berkeley, where they were nursed to adulthood and turned loose among the stricken trees. Within weeks, California's citrus industry was declared saved.

Agricultural Extension, which is associated with the college, is situated in University Hall. Supported by the University and the U.S. Department of Agriculture, its work is to extend the University's agricultural discoveries to farmers. Not a part of Extension (see *No. 2, this section*) it began in the University's second year, 1870, and became far more active in 1913, when it established its farm adviser program. Through this means it sent agents into any county where 20 percent of resident farmers petitioned for one. Today, its advisers are in 52 of the 58 counties (The others have no substantial farming.). Their salaries are paid by the University, and their expenses are paid by the county in which they work.

Agricultural Extension also sponsors home demonstration agents and organizations of boys and girls (4-H) who aid agricultural progress. It is preparing to serve all farm producers, and presently does most through thousands of bulletins that may be obtained in Berkeley through Public Service, University Hall. Stored at the University Mailing Division, 2000 Carleton Street, Berkeley, these publications constitute the largest source of farming information west of the U.S. Department of Agriculture in Washington, D.C.

In Alameda County, the University Agricultural Extension and the Department of Agriculture have headquarters at 224 W.

Winton Avenue, Hayward. There, advisers counsel in agriculture and home economics, and help, too, to solve domestic problems ranging from food preserving to raising children or vegetable gardens.

a. Warren Hall. 1955. B-2.

Named in honor of Earl Warren, former governor of California who later became Chief Justice of the United States Supreme Court, this building houses the School of Public Health. It is also the site of the Cancer Research Genetics Laboratory. Warren Hall maintains a lively exchange of personnel and data with the State Department of Public Health, whose headquarters are in the beige building opposite the campus on Berkeley Way.

b. Mulford Hall. 1948. C-2.

School of Forestry. Named for the late Walter Mulford, Professor of Forestry and Dean of the School of Forestry, this School was begun in 1915. It is operated throughout the year: in summer it teaches required courses in woodlands. The first and second floor corridors of its building include a public exhibit of woods called Woods of the World, which is open Monday through Friday, 8 a.m to 5 p.m., and 1 p.m. to 5 p.m. on Saturdays.

c. Agnes Fay Morgan Hall. 1954. B-2.

Here are laboratories for the study of nutrition, food science, and dietetics, in a building named for a great Professor of Nutrition whose career on the faculty covers most of this century. The building has an extensive library, exhibits, and a cafeteria in which food is prepared by student dieticians.

d. Hilgard Hall. 1918. B-3.

The building was named for Professor Eugene Woldemar Hilgard, founder of the College of Agriculture who was a member of the University's faculty for more than 40 years. The corridors have an exhibit called Soils of the World, open Monday through Friday, 8 a.m. to noon, and 1 p.m. to 5 p.m. on Saturdays.

e. Agriculture Hall. 1912.

Like Hilgard (above) and Giannini (below) halls, this building is in a modified Renaissance Italian design; it has corner quoins and tile roof.

f. Giannini Hall. 1930. B-3.
The building was named for Amadeo P. Giannini, founder of the Bank of Italy (in California), which became the Bank of America. He helped finance it and many of the University's agricultural projects and scholarships.

g. Stanley Hall. B-6.
Molecular Biology and Virus Laboratory.

4. University House. 1902-06. B-3.
This is the official guest house used by the president and chancellor for receptions, but it was the presidential mansion from 1911 to 1958. Clark Kerr, when inaugurated president, chose to remain in his own house in El Cerrito. The official building is grayish tan sandstone; its design is Italian Renaissance. There are two marble lions before its arcaded loggia entrance. Inside are rare tapestries including a Beauvais dating from the sixteenth century, and Renaissance paintings and furniture.

5. Education-Psychology. B-3.

a. Haviland Hall. 1924. B-3.
School of Social Welfare. Funds for this building were provided by Mrs. Hannah N. Haviland as well as the state.

b. Tolman Hall. 1962. B-3.
Education is among the largest departments on campus, and is widely noted. In addition to complete coursework, it is famed for its summer program for professional teachers, its supervised teaching program in local schools, its continuous demonstration secondary school and its research, which is assisted by extensive audio-visual equipment and a large library.

The Department of Psychology is ranked among the best in the country. Its fame springs in large part from the discovery in it that learning causes chemical changes in the brain. It is also noted for its long and fruitful work in child psychology. Moreover, on Grizzly

Peak Boulevard in Berkeley, it operates a laboratory in which comparisons are made among the behaviors of animals.

6. *Architecture-Engineering Group. D-5.* (See *University: Plan,* for origins of the School of Architecture.)

In 1868, the Legislature provided for the College of Engineering. For a time John LeConte, Professor of Physics and Industrial Mechanics (and University president, 1876–81), was the sole member of the College of Mechanical Engineering. (See *LeConte Hall, No. 14, this section.*) After his retirement, W. T. Welcker, Professor of Mathematics, reorganized the school into the College of Civil Engineering. Today, the faculties and classes of engineering are in five main buildings. In them course work emphasizes design, development, and research. The college includes the Institute of Engineering Research, which has grants in the millions to investigate such subjects as electronics, surface wave mechanics, metallurgy, ceramics, heat transfer, stress analysis, and fluid flow, particularly at low temperatures. The college's Department of Civil Engineering includes the Institute of Transporation Studies. Its research relates to the planning, design, and operation of airports, highways, and other transportation facilities.

a. *Earth Sciences Building. 1961. B-4.*

This building is relatively new to the architecture-engineering neighborhood of the campus and has only a tenuous intellectual association with it. It houses Geology, Paleontology, and Geography, including the Museum of Paleontology, one of the most detailed exhibits of its kind in California. The Museum of Paleontology is open weekdays 8 a.m. to 5 p.m. and weekends 1 p.m. to 5 p.m., except when the University is in session. Maps are available on the 5th floor, as are public telephones and restrooms. The University Seismographic Station is also in this building. The Geology Department also operates seismographs in a 100-foot tunnel in a quarry above the Botanical Gardens in Strawberry Canyon.

b. *Hesse Hall. 1924. B-4.*

Named for Professor Frederick G. Hesse, pioneer in industrial mechanics, this structure contains equipment used in instruction and research in fluid mechanics. Here and in other buildings of the group are some of the world's largest machines for testing structural

Senator George Hearst, whose mining fortune assisted in the development of the University

members. There is also a Hydraulic Engineering laboratory and displays.

c. McLaughlin Hall. 1931. B-4.
It houses the main administrative office of the Colleges of Engineering, with its classrooms and laboratories.

d. Wurster Hall. 1964. D-5.
A large cast concrete structure, Wurster Hall houses the College of Environmental Design, and exhibits of student and faculty projects. Also in this building are landscape architecture, and city and regional planning. The building was named for William Wurster, late Dean of the College of Environmental Design, and for his wife Catherine, Professor of City Planning.

e. Cory Hall. 1950. B-5.
Department of Electrical Engineering and Computer Science. Named for Clarence L. Cory, late Professor and Dean of the College, this building is used for the study of cosmic rays. Weather balloons often are seen rising from its roof, where there is also a 10-foot radio telescope installed by the Office of Naval Research. The telescope tunes in on four to eight millimeter waves from space.

f. Hearst Memorial Mining Building. 1907. B-5.
John Galen Howard, who planned most of the campus, designed this building for Phoebe Apperson Hearst, who gave it to the Uni-

versity as a memorial to her husband, Senator George Hearst. Its style is Italian Renaissance. The building contains pictures of mining operations in early California, and displays of ore specimens and other exhibits in mineral technology. Mining students take full courses here, to the extent of physically mining (see *Lawson Adit*, *below*), and also must spend six weeks in surveying camps each summer as well as at least one summer during their training in a mine, mill, smelter, or oilfield. The Departments of Materials Sciences and Engineering are housed in this building.

g. *Lawson Adit. 1916.*
This shaft under Charter Hill was dug by mining students for mining engineering, fire research, rescue work, and direct mining experience. (Open to the public by appointment.)

h. *O'Brien Hall. 1947. B-4.*
College of Engineering. Fluid Mechanics displays.

i. *Etcheverry Hall. 1964. A-4.*
Department of Engineering.

j. *Bechtel Engineering Center. 1980.*
Named for Stephen Bechtel, a 1923 graduate of the University, and founder of Bechtel Engineering Corporation.

7. *Medical Science Group.* (See also *University: San Francisco Campus.*)

a. *Donner Laboratory. 1942. B-5.*
Here beside Founders' Rock, scientists apply physics, chemistry, and the natural sciences to biology and medicine. Built when the cycoltron began to open new fields for medical research, since 1942 it has employed physicists, chemists, mathematicians, physiologists, and medical doctors for dozens of biological experiments. Its staff has extensive equipment of its own, and it also has access to the facilities of the Lawrence Berkeley Laboratory. Donner Laboratory is headquarters for the academic Division of Medical Physics, where many students are trained in biophysics and medical physics.

b. Stanley Hall. 1952. B-6.

This building was named for Professor Wendell Stanley, the Nobel Laureate of 1946. It contains a Molecular Biology and Virus Laboratory. Basic research is conducted on all types of viruses—animal, bacterial, plant, and human—with the objective of learning more about virus diseases and their control, about genes and heredity, cancer, and the nature of life. The laboratory's significant achievements include the discovery of an infectious viral nucleic acid, the first isolating of an animal virus (human polio) in crystalline form, and striking advances in techniques for studying viruses with the electron microscope. Its scientists reconstituted virus, the tobacco mosaic, one quiet day when they might have expected thunder. These achievements have made the Laboratory one of the most advanced in the world, a fact indicated by the number of its foreign visitors.

8. Residence Halls. Units 1 and 2. E-6. Unit 3, E-4.

a. Stern Hall. 1942.

This woman's residence hall was designed by William Wurster, who later became head of the School of Environmental Design, and Harvey Corbett, both alumni of the University. It houses 137 women students. The hall was a gift of Mrs. Sigmund Stern. An addition to house 110 more students was completed in 1981.

b. Bowles Hall. 1929.

This residence hall for men was given to the school by Mrs. Mary A. Bowles in memory of her husband, Philip E. Bowles, a Regent. It houses 204 students. Kleeberger Field, nearby, is used for intramural sports.

9. Lawrence Berkeley Laboratory. B-6.

Professor Ernest O. Lawrence's invention of the cyclotron in 1929 made Berkeley a center of nuclear physics research; since Lawrence won the first Nobel Prize at Berkeley, the Lawrence Berkeley Laboratory (denoted as "LBL") has earned an international reputation and eight Nobel Prizes.

When Lawrence presented the findings of his research before a meeting of the National Academy of Sciences in 1930, Robert Gordon Sproul, the University's president, became convinced of Law-

Ernest O. Lawrence's first cyclotron included coat hangers and used wires.

rence's talent and worked to finance it. As a result, some of Lawrence's most important early work was endowed by William H. Crocker, the banking millionaire of San Francisco for whom a University Laboratory was named. Many other Alumni responded to Sproul's enthusiasm with endowments of the University's scientific activities.

The University's pace was suddenly quickened by the expectation of discovery. Lawrence won the Nobel Prize before he was 40. He accelerated particles, nuclear science, and life at Berkeley. Nuclear physics at Berkeley began to attract brilliant teachers and students from across the world. Many stayed and some of those who did were of the highest scientific intellect: Emilio Segré, Edwin McMillan, Luis Alvarez, Owen Chamberlain, Glenn Seaborg, and Edward Teller. Their presence attracted more great teachers, researchers, and students. Berkeley gained what appears to be permanent leadership in nuclear physics, and the stimulation strongly encouraged the development of other disciplines on the campus.

The Lawrence Laboratory has two divisions: Berkeley and Livermore. (Livermore is known as the Lawrence Livermore National Laboratory.) The Livermore division, 40 miles southeast of Berkeley, is a highly-guarded center whose central purposes are to develop weapons and to achieve the fusion of light nuclei with the resulting release of energy. It has many other chiefly peaceful goals, including nuclear propulsion and nuclear mining. Its scientists have confined a heavy hydrogen plasma at a temperature of 60 million degrees F. for one thousandth of a second, a fact suggesting that man is capable of turning the world's most destructive force into its most useful one.

On the campus, LBL is often called "The Hill." Computers, cyclotrons and accelerators: these are the chief tools of this modern Mount Olympus with some of the character of a U.S. boom town. Trucks and heavy building equipment buzz along the narrow roads of The Hill, continuously expanding what is assuredly one of the most active corners of the campus.

Its major buildings are visible from much of the East Bay. The Engineering services Building is a four-story structure housing mechanical, electrical, and plant engineering staffs, and service groups including accounting, purchasing, and business administrators. Clinging to the side of The Hill overlooking the campus and Bay, and instantly recognizable by its form, is a round building housing a 184-inch cyclotron, which can accelerate particles to 750 million electron volts.

The Hill also has an 88-inch cyclotron (60 mev deutrons), a Bevetron (6.2 billion electron volt protons), a heavy ion linear accelerator (HILAC, 120 Mev carbon nuclei), and a 72-inch hydrogen bubble chamber to detect nuclear interactions. It has its own Chemistry Building, and a four- story annex for it that is designed

The view from Lawrence Berkeley Laboratory

Seven of the eleven Nobel Laureates of the Berkeley campus. (1980) (Top row, left to right,) Donald Glaser, Edwin McMillan, Melvin Calvin, and Emilio Segré. (Bottom row, left to right,) Luis Alvarez, Glenn Seaborg, and Owen Chamberlain.

for radio-chemistry laboratories, special laboratories for heavy-element chemistry, and a series of conference rooms, offices, and shops. There is also a Physics Research Building with a six-story annex, smaller laboratories, and decontamination buildings.

The Lawrence Berkeley Laboratory is internationally known for many accomplishments, including the discovery of fifteen of the

107 known chemical elements of the periodic table. These include
Lawrencium, (Element 103, named to memorialize Professor Ernest O. Lawrence, who died in 1958.) Californium, Berkelium, Nep-
tunium, and Plutonium; the discovery of antimatter; the determination of the chemical pathways of photosynthesis, and the application
of this work to problems in energy production and in agriculture;
the founding of the field of nuclear medicine, including the radioac-
tive isotopes used in radiation therapy; in collaboration with the
Stanford Linear Accelerator Center, the discovery of new nuclear
particles and the construction of PEP, the most powerful electron
accelerator in the United States, and the invention and development of the Time Projection Chamber, the world's most sophisticated nuclear-particle detector.

No classified work is done at the Lawrence Berkeley Laboratory.
Defense and classified research is conducted, however, at the Lawrence Livermore National Laboratory.

Operated by the University under contract with the U.S. Department of Energy, the Lawrence Berkeley Laboratory consists of
3,000 scientists and technicians conducting research in nuclear science, biology and medicine, high-energy physics, and molecular
and materials science. Research is also conducted in the analysis of
environmental problems, new energy technologies, particularly in
geoscience and geothermal energy, fossil fuels, and solar and fusion
energy.

Tours of the Lawrence Berkeley Laboratory can be arranged for
high school and college classes. A tour for the general public is also
offered every Tuesday at 2 p.m. To make reservations, call the LBL
Visitor Center at 486-6727. The tour lasts two hours and includes a
look at the large accelerator, a current research project, and a
multi-media show which gives the history of the Laboratory and a
description of current research projects. Specialized tours may also
be arranged for groups with specific interests. Humphrey Go-BART
connects the University with LBL, beginning from Shattuck Avenue at Center Street in downtown Berkeley. Parking is limited, so
visitors are urged to use the shuttle whenever possible.

10. The Lawrence Hall of Science. 1968. C-7

For visitors, the Lawrence Hall of Science, a museum not to be
confused with the Lawrence Berkeley Laboratory, is one of the
major attractions of the Berkeley campus. Located on a hill overlooking the central campus and the Bay Area, the Hall offers unique

exhibits which enable visitors to learn about science by participating in teaching experiments, in computers, astronomy, mathematics, biology, and the physical sciences. The Hall of Science also offers supplementary educational programs designed to enrich school curricula. Teachers may arrange for workshops on a short-term or on a series basis at the Hall, which is equipped with classrooms, a library, lecture hall, cafeteria, bookstore, live animal exhibits, and a planetarium. Science films, lectures, and workshops are offered to the public on a regular basis. Over 250,000 people visit the Lawrence Hall of Science each year.

For further information on tours, classes, membership, programs for schools, lectures, the Summer Science Camp, and visiting hours, call the Hall of Science at 642-5132.

Transportation to the Lawrence Hall of Science is available on A.C. Transit line #7. Call A.C. Transit at 653-3535 for schedule information. Humphrey Go-BART stops at the Hall of Science, originating at Shattuck Avenue and Center Street in downtown Berkeley, across from the Berkeley BART station. Each shuttle accommodates up to 20 people at a time. There is no charge for the ride. Call 642-5149 for schedules. Because of its steep incline, Centennial Drive is unsafe for large, heavily-loaded vehicles. The Hall of Science provides limited, free parking for cars.

11. Recreational Area. C-7.

a. Botanical Gardens. 1926. C-7.

Thirty sheltered acres at the head of Strawberry Canyon contain more than 8,000 species of plants from around the world, containing more than 50,000 plants. The Gardens include 5,000 rare rhododendrons and 2,000 cacti and succulents growing in natural settings of sand and stone. Many of these plants were gathered in China and Tibet, and in South America, by T. Harper Goodspeed, Director Emeritus of the Gardens. There is also a vast rose collection, a palmetum, and an herb garden. They comprise one of the most individualized arboretums of the world.

Twelve acres of the Gardens are intensively cultivated. They serve as a laboratory as well as a public exhibit. Within five other acres chiefly covered by pines and redwoods, there is an open air theater that is a memorial to Stephen Mather, first director of the

U.S. National Park Service. The Garden also has picnic tables that are less well known than most in the East Bay. They, and the Garden itself, are open to the public and are reachable by auto and by Humphrey Go-BART. The Gardens are open during regular business hours every day of the year except Christmas. Guided tours are offered on the weekends, and may be arranged at other times by appointment.

For tour information, call 642-3343.

b. Strawberry Canyon Recreational Area. 1958. C-7.

Above Memorial Stadium there is a section famous for a natural beauty more rugged than the sloping land beneath it. Here are tennis courts, playing fields, a clubhouse and swimming pools, and a picnic ground. The central features, the Elise and Walter Haas Clubhouse with its Lucie Stern Pool, were the gift of Mr. and Mrs. Haas of San Francisco, with a bequest from Mrs. Haas' aunt, the late Lucie Stern, to the students, faculty, and employees of the University. (Open weekdays noon to 6 p.m.; Tuesdays and Fridays; the lower pool is open until 7 p.m. On weekends, the Area is open 11 a.m. to 6 p.m.) The upper pool is set up for lap swimming and high diving. The Strawberry Canyon Recreational Area is open to registered students of U.C. Berkeley and their families, members of summer institutes, staff (academic and non-academic), staff families, and alumni and their families. Guests of persons associated with the University are admitted. Proof of University status is required for admission. Strawberry operates a popular recreational camp for children during the summer.

For further information, call 642-5575. For tennis court reservations and equipment checkout, call 642-8342. For information concerning BORP, the Disabled Program, call 849-4662.

c. California Memorial Stadium. 1923. D-7.

The University's interest in sports developed fitfully. In 1872, a student publication announced, "Baseball has revived and football has died." More accurately, the popularity of baseball continued while football's became submerged. For years each class sent four members to a local baseball league that played young businessmen or students of rival schools. In 1883, the class historian apologized that "We are not much in athletics. We cannot put a baseball nine on the diamond, and we win no field-day medals. However, though we are not athletes we can console ourselves that we did not come to College to learn pedestrianism nor to acquire the art of swinging the dumb-bells. No, we had in view a higher aim—the cultivation of the intellect."

Within 40 years, this position became reversed. Track teams were formed in 1878, and in 1892, after going nowhere in particular they were encouraged by the success of Walter H. Henry, Class of 1893, who set a world's record by running the 120-yard hurdles in 15 3/4 seconds. California won two-thirds of its intercollegiate games in 1895. It developed a formidible name among eastern athletes. On March 19, 1892, just 11 years after organizing its first football team, it began its "Big Game" tradition with Stanford (see *University: Traditions*). All school pride was staked on either team each year. On November 13, 1904, California lost the 14th game, but to a huge house that helped finance California Field, for whose funding the Associated Students added a $15,000 bank loan.

By then football had become rough: the captain from Berkeley, according to one report, "battered until his mind was gone, stuck at his post until he was led from the field weeping." In a game among engineering students of that period, a student named Jesse Hicks died of a broken neck. The University and Stanford agreed to forbid football. President Wheeler described the game as "a body of evolutions rather than a sport and had come to be a game for special experts rather than a free athletic sport suited for amateurs."

Both the University and Stanford decided to encourage some alternate game. They chose rugby. The two schools resumed their football rivalry through a rugby match in 1906 at Berkeley. Clinton R. Morse, recorder of California's football history, saw the game and wrote, "The old 'grads' were disgusted, but curious enough to give the game one more chance . . . the large majority of spectators, those who come because it is the game of the year, to see the pretty dresses and hear the rooters squeal, didn't care whether the teams were playing rugby or backgammon." After the third annual rugby game with Stanford, even Morse was "quite converted to that style of play."

But football, by then governed by new intercollegiate rules, was on the way back. Some sportsmen, including Morse, mourned the loss of rugby. Their enthusiasm for the milder game was overcome by followers of Andrew Latham Smith, the accomplished Pennsylvania coach. He appealed to American manhood: "Amongst all intercollegiate athletics American football stands as the leader—the focus to which the lens of virile interest ultimately directs us." The ASUC, which at that time controlled athletics at Berkeley, hired Smith, and he developed the "wonder teams" of 1920 through 1924. His first star was Harold T. "Brick" Muller, the first West Coast All-American. Muller later bacame a physician in Berkeley, a fact that encouraged many football fans to point out that the game did not exclude all scholarship.

They began to raise money for a stadium that would memorialize students who died in World War I. In contributions ranging from coins to big bills, they gave $1,017,000 to build the California Memorial Stadium. Neither the state nor the University gave any funds for it. Solicitors had a slogan that came full circle from the ". . . we had in view a higher aim—the cultivation of the intellect" of 1883. "The pigskin is mightier than the sheepskin," they shouted.

The Stadium was completed in time for the biggest of the "Big Games" and has been used for the ones held in Berkeley ever since. As the University grew the seating capacity was increased from 76,000 to 82,000, (but the temporary seats have been removed), and the structure was used for large-scale events including com-

California Memorial Stadium can seat up to 76,000. International House is in the foreground.

mencement exercises. Remodeling begun in 1981 created new office space for the Department of Intercollegiate Athletics as well as an Athletic Hall of Fame Museum.

Student interest in rugby and soccer has never diminished over the years, and teams playing those sports often meet in the Stadium. The University has continued interest, too, in tennis and in rowing, in which its crews were unbeatable in the beginning of the century and in 1928, 1932, and 1948, years when it won Olympic laurels.

12. *Hearst Greek Theatre. 1903. B-6.*

At the opening day of the Theatre John Galen Howard, its designer, solemnly confessed that he had transposed it from Greece and had changed nothing. "No line," he said, "no surface, no slight-

A Greek Theatre performance, ca. 1925

est detail has been fixed in its design without the careful consideration of all the documents to which we have access in a spirit of
deepest reverence for the past . . . "

The Theatre enabled the University to move rapidly into the
highest level of cultural presentations at a time when it lacked them
almost entirely. The first performance was Aristophanes' "The
Birds." It was given in Greek. Critics noted that the audience, although unable to understand the words, seemed transfixed by the
sight of the classical play in classical surroundings. Such performances are still given by touring companies from Greece.

In 1906, the actress Sarah Bernhardt came to the Greek Theatre
for an unscheduled performance. She turned up one month after
the earthquake and fire of 1906 that had destroyed the theater in
which she was scheduled to play in San Francisco. With national
fanfare, she and her company moved their play, Racine's "Phaedre,"
to Berkeley. Among palms, Oregon pine chairs, and the symphony
concert dais, a setting to which meticulous critics afterward objec-
ted, the great lady moved many to tears, and she later offered her
own brilliantly improvised comment: "It has always been a dream
of mine to play Phaedre sometime in the open air, but I never
dreamed of doing it in Greece."

The Theatre has been used for the annual Charter Day ceremonies, and for dramatic and operatic productions, meetings, rallies,
concerts, special events, political speeches, and the annual "Big
Game" bonfire. Accordingly, it has been visited by many of the
greatest persons of this century. Therefore in this structure, unique
for the United States, students on May 16, 1903, were treated to
the blustering of Theodore Roosevelt in surroundings almost identi-
cal to those in which the ancient Greeks of Epidaurus once saw
Sophocles played; and they had a glimpse of the Bay like the Mediterranean behind them. Students have also been addressed by
Chief Justice Earl Warren, U Thant, Secretary General of the
United Nations, and Secretary of State George Marshall for Charter
Day ceremonies in the Greek Theatre.

The reception building includes a fifteenth-century Flemish
Gothic tapestry, Italian marble bas reliefs of the fourteenth century,
and French stone bas reliefs. They and the Theatre itself were given
to the University by William Randolph Hearst at his mother's suggestion. In 1946, the Hearst Corporation gave $400,000 to remodel
the Theatre; this was done in 1957, and the Theatre was rededi-
cated.

The Theatre can accommodate more than 10,000 people and is frequently used for concerts which are not sponsored by the University. Schedules of concerts held in the Greek Theatre and tickets to those events are available at the University Box Office in the Student Union Building.

13. Chemistry-Physics-Mathematics Group.

a. LeConte Hall. 1924 and annex 1950. C-5.

John LeConte and his brother Joseph were descendants of persecuted French Huguenots who came to America about 1698 and who, by 1810, were slave owners in Georgia. They came from three generations of scientists; the attic of their plantation was a chemical laboratory where they worked each day or met the famous scientists, usually botanists, who came to see their father Louis. Both went to the University of Georgia near their home, and they became M.D.'s at the College of Physicians and Surgeons in New York.

John became professor of natural philosophy and chemistry at the University of Georgia. Joseph studied at Cambridge, taught at Oglethorpe University, and joined his brother on the University of Georgia's faculty. He was a "natural scientist," a term which in those days included chemistry, geology, and natural history. Both went to teach at South Carolina College until the school was abandoned during the Civil War, and then they both joined the Confederate Army. John, a major, supervised all of the Confederacy's Nitre and Mining Bureau at Columbia; Joseph, a pharmacist early in the war, later went to his brother's agency. They tried to resume life in Georgia after the war. They found it in ruins, and so both accepted offers to join the faculty at Berkeley in 1868. Both brothers led in the University's development. John became its president in 1876. He retired in 1881 from the presidency but continued to teach until he died in 1891. In addition to this building, the University has a small monument to the LeConte brothers. It is on the path at the eucalyptus grove off of Oxford Street.

In this hall orginated one of the greatest collections of physical scientists the world has known (see *University: Development*). Ernest O. Lawrence developed the cyclotron in it. Since then, founders of the Atomic Age—the likes of J. Robert Oppenheimer, Edward Teller, Edwin McMillan, Luis Alvarez, Owen Chamberlain, Emilio

*John LeConte, Professor of Physics,
University president*

Segré—have made this department academically famous. It has
been generally famous to laymen, too, at least since one of its professors, Harvey White, taught physics over a national television
network.

b. Birge Hall. 1962. C-5.
(See *Bacon Hall.*)

c. Campbell Hall. 1959. C-5.
Named for William Wallace Campbell, Professor of Astronomy,
who became president of the University after distinguished sevice
as director of Lick Observatory. The building contains the departments of Astronomy and Letters and Science.

d. Latimer Hall. 1962. C-5.
College of Chemistry Complex. Named for Professor Wendell Latimer, a famous chemist.

e. Hildebrand Hall. 1966. C-6.
Named for Professor Joel H. Hildebrand, one of America's most

Joseph LeConte,
Professor of
"Natural Sciences,"
John's twin

honored chemists, the building contains an extensive chemistry library. The building also houses graduate and undergraduate chemistry teaching laboratories. Hildebrand was a co-leader with Professor Gilbert N. Lewis, who was dean of the College of Chemistry for 30 years, in the "Faculty Revolt" of 1919–20 which regained faculty control over the Academic Senate and University policies. Well-known for his vigorous life-style, Hildebrand was an early president of the Sierra Club. He was an avid skier well into his seventies until his family forced him to quit. He continued his research on a semi-retired basis through his nineties, and the University celebrated Professor Hildebrand's 100th birthday in 1981.

f. Gilman Hall. 1917. C-5.
Named for Daniel Coit Gilman, the University's second president (see *University: Development*), who came from Yale's Scientific School, this building houses part of the Deparment of Chemistry.

g. Biochemistry Building. 1964. B-2.

h. Lewis Hall. 1947. C-6.

The first major building completed under the University's building program after World War II, it is named for the late Gilbert Newton Lewis, Professor of Chemistry and Dean of the College for 30 years. Lewis and many who followed him in this department won international fame: Wendell Latimer, Joel Hildebrand, and William Giauque among them.

i. Physical Sciences Lecture Hall. 1964. B-5.

j. Evans Hall. 1967. B-5.

Mathematics, Statistics, and Computer Sciences, as well as the University's Computer Center, an increasingly active region.

14. Sather Tower. ("Campanile"). 1914. C-4.

The University's best-known landmark is more commonly called the "Campanile," Italian for "bell-tower," a word chosen because the structure was modeled after St. Mark's Campanile in Venice. The Renaissance atmosphere that it casts over the central part of the campus is reinforced by the formal esplanade that surrounds it, and by its appearance: its white granite glimmers in the sunlight, and its slightly cracked exterior gives it a look of antiquity. The inside has an elevator, a dark stairway, and storage space in which there are 50 tons of fossils, mostly from the La Brea tarpits of Los Angeles: no Medici could have planned it better.

Mrs. Jane K. Sather intended the tower as a memorial to herself, and Sather Gate (see *Student Union, No. 29 this section*) as a memorial to her husband Peder, a banker who had been trustee of the College of California, the University's predecessor. She wanted people to look upward. She died three years before the tower was finished.

Mrs. Sather spent $200,000 for the tower and another $25,000 for its original 12 bells. They were made in Loughborough, England, in 1917. During World War I they were hauled past enemy submarines in the North Atlantic and eventually into San Francisco Bay. They range in weight from 349 to more than 8,000 pounds. One of the largest bears an etching of a poem written by Isaac Flagg, a Professor of Greek: "We ring, we chime, we toll; lend ye the silent part—some answer in the heart, some echo in the soul."

In 1979, the Class of 1928 provided funds for 36 additional bells to create a carillon.

The bell that chimes the hours, together with the clock mechanism that works it, once was in a tower of Bacon Hall, an original University building opposite the tower's east side. The others were made for the tower. They intone Bach and Beethoven, school songs on Fridays, and ironies before finals week: *The Hanging of Danny Deever*, or *One More River to Cross*.

The four clock faces, 250 feet from the ground in the 307–foot

Sather Tower ("The Campanile") under construction, 1915.

high tower, are 63 feet in circumference. The base of the tower is 35 feet square and extends 50 feet below the ground into a grillwork of heavy I-beams. Below these beams are large reinforced shafts, so that the tower itself, formed of steel and sheathed in stone, may sway but is unlikely to fall in an earthquake.

The carillon is played each weekday at 7:50 a.m., noon, and 6 p.m.; each Saturday at noon and 6 p.m., and each Sunday at 4 p.m. Twenty-five cents pays the fare for an elevator ride to the top narrated by a chatty and knowledgable operator along the way. The view is one of the best in the Bay Area. There is a small window display in the lobby of the tower containing University memorabilia outlining the University's history. A schedule of the tower's hours of operation is posted at the front entrance.

Big C: From Sather Tower or its vicinity it is possible to see this letter of concrete imbedded in Charter Hill above Strawberry Canyon. Normally, it is covered with gold paint. It was built in a single day, March 18, 1905, by enthusiastic students. (See *University: Traditions.*) Stanford has periodically painted its most prominent color, red, over the Big C, as one of the traditional pranks emanating from the Stanford-Cal rivalry.

15. Bacon Hall. 1881. (Birge Hall.) 1962. C-5.

Birge Hall, which houses the Department of Physics, replaces the former campus showplace, Bacon Hall, which once was the University's elegant library and art gallery, and whose story is more than a footnote to campus history. All of the original art in the gallery was a gift of H. D. Bacon. The hall was an original building that characterized the early stages as well as Birge Hall, which characterizes the present ones. Part of its library belonged to the expatriated German liberal Francis Leiber and was purchased for the University by the San Francisco merchant prince, Michael Reese, who also came from Germany; many books were Bacon's, and the rest came from the College of California, the University's precursor, and from the University itself. The art gallery included a Rembrandt among its 65 paintings; there was some immensely heavy statuary by Heinrich Dannecker and Johann Halbig; the work was comissioned by Henry Douglas Bacon of Oakland, a wealthy, idealistic businessman who knew President Lincoln and was inspired to dedicate works of art called "Genius of America" and "The Abolition of Slavery."

All of this stone obviously impressed early University authorities, but it worried them too. Wondering whether the floor would hold it, someone from the Engineering Department suggested that a platoon of students march through the building. They did; the floor did not budge; the Department established a success at testing materials.

Bacon Hall's early days were as distinguished as those of any building on any campus. In the year that it was completed, Darius Ogden Mills gave $75,000 for a Chair of Intellectual and Moral Philosophy and Civil Polity. Three years later, George Holmes Howison became the first Mills Professor of Philosophy. Having become famous at the University of Berlin and Harvard University, he was reluctant to teach at Berkeley, but when he did the University's Philosophical Union, as he later called his lecture forum, became one of the most influential in the country. William James introduced the Pragmatism School at the Union in 1898.

16. School of Business Administration. Barrows Hall. 1964. D-5.

"The business between California and Asia is already very great," said State Senator Edward Tompkins when he was financing the University's Agassiz Professorship in 1872. "Its future is beyond any estimate that the most sanguine would dare to make. The child is now born that will see the commerce of the Pacific greater than that of the Atlantic. It is carried on with people of whose languages we are wholly ignorant. It is therefore of the utmost consequence to California that the means shall be provided to instruct our young men, preparing for lives of business activity, in the languages and literature of Eastern Asia."

Tompkins' analysis proved prophetic; trade with Japan, the Republic of China, and South Korea grew to record levels during the 1970's. In 1979 diplomatic relations with the People's Republic of China began to improve, and the first Chinese ships and planes since World War II began to arrive in San Francisco.

The promise of Asian trade periodically encouraged more business instruction at Berkeley. There seemed no other reason for a school of commerce. Arthur Rodgers was in the graduating class that heard Tompkins in 1872. In 1896, by then a Regent, he proposed that a College of Commerce be organized. Three years later President Wheeler told San Francisco businessmen how much the college would mean to them: "We are going to have there a school

which shall prepare men to aid you in finding out what the world
wants. Germany has sent her consuls into the outer world as trade
agents. You never found a German consul in city of Asia Minor who
was appointed because he was somebody's man. You find men put
into places by the German government because they have been
trained to the work. American merchants are going to find out, if
they have not already done so, that we have suddenly become an
exporting rather than an importing nation."

Business Administration, founded with three students, has a
present enrollment larger than any other University college except-
ing the College of Letters and Science, and has developed a range
of courses including accounting, banking, foreign trade, government foreign service, transportation, and marketing.

Barrows Hall was named for David Prescott Barrows, a Professor
of Political Science who became a University president. The Hall
also houses the Departments of Political Science, Economics, and
Sociology, in adddition to the School of Business Administration.

17. South Hall. 1873. C-4.

This is the oldest building on the campus. It and North Hall,
which stood on the present site of the Library Annex, were the first
opened when the University moved from Oakland to Berkeley.
They stood alone on a treeless plain, visible for miles, the frontier of
American learning. South Hall now houses the School of Library
and Information Studies.

18. Main Library. 1911. C-4.

After Charles Franklin Doe gave $720,000 of the $1,4 million cost
of this building's construction, the University was able to move its
books from Bacon Hall (see No. 15, this section) to one of the largest
buildings of its kind. Despite the sentiment associated with Bacon
Hall, members of the University quickly recognized that the intellectual and physical center of the campus had been moved with the
books. Indeed, the authors of eight campus master plans have af-
firmed that the University revolves about its library.

The Library, sixth largest in the country, has more than 5.75
million volumes in 20 branches and sections.

Library Services. These include typing rooms, the lost and found
office, periodicals, rare books, documents, including official publications of foreign countries and of the United Nations, maps, and a
photographic service.

The *Loan Desk* is on the second floor. Call and registration cards are necessary. A number is given for each call card. When the book is available or a report has been made, the number appears on a call-board. The General Catalog is adjacent to the Loan Desk; a subject index is in a nearby room.

Two smaller libraries are parts of the Library Building:

The Bancroft Library.

Hubert Howe Bancroft, born in Ohio, moved to California in 1852 and soon became a stationer. He traveled widely, visited book dealers everywhere, and by 1882 he had collected 40,000 books, manuscripts, and newspapers, chiefly on the history of the western United States. He kept this library in a San Francisco building and twice saved it from fires. He moved it in 1884. In 1905, the Board of Regents bought the Library from him. The collection named for him has been expanded to 40 million manuscripts; these include papers on California and Mexico and Latin America, as well as pa-

North and South Halls, 1874

Doe Library

pers by distinguished authors on politics, journalism, law, and science. The Rare Books Collection of the Bancroft Library includes about 400 incunabulums for research in the humanities; fine printing materials with an emphasis on modern English, American, and European authors; modern poetry archives; medieval manuscript books and documents; and papyruses.

The University Archives contain the official documentation of the history of the University of California and all its campuses, and its precursor, the College of California. The collection includes student publications, faculty writings, handbills and memorabilia, and an indexed collection of photographs of university scenes.

The Regional Oral History Office includes a collection of tape-recordings and typed memoirs of persons who have shaped the history of the Western United States. Emphasis is on California politics, agriculture, the California wine industry, state and national parks and forests, and University of California history.

The Mark Twain Papers is a non-circulating collection of the author's manuscripts, correspondence, and other documents. The papers are available to any qualified researcher in the library.

A magazine editor once insisted that the Bancroft's librarians estimate the value of its books. "Three to ten million," they offered. Even this flexible price tag is inadequate; the items have no price: they are irreplaceable. An example is the diary of Patrick Breen. He kept it in his cabin at Donner Lake in 1846–47, while the Donner Party slowly froze, tried to break over snowbound mountain passes into California, and died in cannibalism. They might have been saved if their guide had met them on time on the eastern side of the Sierra, or if they had not believed a stranger's tale that the mountains were passable. "It is distressing," Breen wrote. He got through.

The Morrison Reading Room of the University Library

Moffitt Undergraduate Library. 1970. C-4.
Named for James K. Moffitt, a paper manufacturer who became a Regent, the library expanded the collection in the Doe Library.

Morrison Library.
West of the north entrance, this is a bibliophile's vision of solid comfort realized in the form of open shelves with popular books and records; lithographs, prints, etchings, and woodcuts that are periodically rented to members of the University, and easy chairs informally placed. Books of this library are not circulated, with the exception of newly published volumes in the "X-8" collection.

Inter-Campus Library Buses.
The University operates a connecting bus service to the Davis, Santa Cruz, and San Francisco campus libraries, as well as the library at Stanford University. All buses stop at the west campus entrance of the Berkeley campus. The buses are open to students, faculty, and staff only. For information on schedules and reservations, inquire at the University Library.

Branch Libraries and Their Buildings.
Architecture (Wurster Hall); *Anthropology* (Kroeber Hall); *Astronomy-Mathematics-Statistics* (Campbell Hall); *Audiovisual Media Center* (Moffitt Undergraduate Library, 1st floor); *Biochemistry* (Biochemistry); *Biology, including anatomy, bacteriology, biochemistry, botany, nursing, physiology, zoology* (Life Sciences Building); *Chemistry* (Hildebrand Hall); *Chinese Studies* (Barrrows Hall); *East Asiatic, including Chinese, Japanese, and other Asian languages* (Durant Hall); *Earth Sciences* (Earth Sciences Building); *Education and Psychology* (Tolman Hall); *Energy Information* (Building T-4); *Engineering* (Bechtel Engineering Center); *Environmental Design* (Wurster Hall); *Forestry* (Mulford Hall); *Forest Products* (Richmond Field Station); *Industrial Relations* (2521 Channing Way); *Health Sciences Information Service* (Building T-7); *Library School, including library science, printing, publishing* (South Hall); *Music* (Morrison Hall); *Native American Studies* (Dwinelle Hall); *Optometry* (Minor Hall); *Physical Education* (Hearst Gym); *Physics* (LeConte Hall); *Public Health* (Warren Hall) *Rhetoric* (Dwinelle); *Social Welfare* (Haviland Hall); *Survey Research Center* (2538 Channing Way); *Water Resources Center*

(North Gate); *Women's Center* (Building T-9). These others are mostly limited to faculty and graduate students: *Agricultural Economics* (Giannini Hall); *Entomology* (Wellman Hall); *Graduate Social Science Library* (Stephens Hall); *Institute of Governmental Studies* (Moses Hall); *International Studies* (Stephens Hall); *Transportation Studies* (McLaughlin Hall); *Law* (Boalt Hall).

19. Wheeler Hall. 1918. D-4.

This building, which contains Wheeler Auditorium, the Department of English, and the Office of Summer Sessions, was named for

Wheeler Hall

Benjamin Ide Wheeler, president of the University from 1899 to 1919 (see *University: Development*). He was a New Englander trained in German universities, and the combination tended to make him an educational Spartan. By insisting that the University's government grant more power to the presidency before he would take the office, he succeeded in becoming the first president for an extended period. His inaugural address contrasted life and death and urged the University to choose educational life. At the dedication of Wheeler Hall 20 years later he said: " . . . here, by the contagion of sympathy, each generation will inspire its sons and daughters to nobler living; here by the mystery of inspiration, vi-

*Henry Durant, a
founder of
the University*

sion shall awaken and personality shall give its spiritual lifeblood to
the handing on of life, like as fire by the handing on of the racer's
torch. Go now to thy place, old stone! Take up thy long burden of
the years!"

Wheeler Hall is immense by contrast to the buildings contructed
before it. Its 59,199 square feet include 62 classrooms, almost twice
the number in North Hall, which it was designed to replace. The
auditorium is used for films, concerts, lectures, and plays.
"Wheeler Oak," and "Wheeler Steps" are traditional meeting
places for students. The original oak at the east end of the steps
died. Its site was marked with a plaque, and another oak was
planted nearby.

20. Durant Hall. 1912. C-3.

This building was constructed for $150,000, more than $100,000 of which came from the widow of Judge John H. Boalt, whose name honored it and later was moved with its contents, the School of Law, to a new Boalt Hall (see *University: Boalt Hall*). The present name is derived from the Reverend Henry Durant of the College of California, who became the University's first president. The building contains the Oriental Center, the Department of Oriental Languages, and the East Asiatic Library.

21. California Hall. 1906. C-3.
Originally housing the president's office and the Bancroft Library, this houses the chancellor's office and the Graduate Division.

22. Life Sciences Building. 1930. C-3.
This is one of the largest academic buildings in the United States. Covering three acres; its five stories house scientists who once were scattered in wooden buildings across the campus. They include workers in anatomy, physiology, pathology, hygiene, bacteriology, biochemistry, botany, and zoology. The building also houses the Hormone Research Laboratory. Among the collections in the building are the Museum of Vertebrate Zoology (including mammals, birds, reptiles, and amphibians), and the Botany Herbarium, where the public may bring any plant for free identification.

Important scientific developments have taken place in this building; they include basic research in botulism, and the biological control of insects.

The eucalyptus grove behind this building is a prominent landscape design feature of the campus. Its blue gums, some of which are over 200 feet tall, tend to reduce the monumental scale of some campus buildings that need reducing. The swaying trees are acridly pungent and are remembered by many thousands of alumni as a pleasantly scented meeting place.

23. Dwinelle Hall. 1952. D-3.
This building was named for John W. Dwinelle, who introduced the bill in the 1868 Legislature which created the University. Classrooms and offices are in this building. There are auditoriums for large lecture classes, public lectures, and symposia. In the basement are studios for limited radio and closed-circuit television productions, and a laboratory for teaching languages by tape-recorders. So is the University Theater in which student dramatic productions

John W. Dwinelle,
whose legislative bill
created the University

are given. (Information about plays is available at the Office of Dramatic Art in Dwinelle Hall Annex.)

Behind the building's rear parking lot is a triangular glade on which many students picnic on warm days, and on which some classes are held. At the apex of the triangle is a statue of two sensitive-looking young men shown getting ready for football. It was the work of a deaf sculptor, Douglas Tilden, a graduate of the California School for the Deaf.

The Football Players was the gift of James D. Phelan, a San Francisco politician. He was an important regional landowner, and he was deeply competitive. To encourage rivalry between Stanford and the University, in 1897 he offered the statue to either of the two teams that would win two successive annual football games against each other. In 1898, the University overwhelmed Stanford 22-0; in 1899, it won 3-0. Thus, the statue helped to establish the tradition of the Big Game. (See *University: Traditions.*)

24. Callaghan Hall. 1947. C-2.

This building is used by the University Naval Reserve Officer Training Corps for cadets. It is named for Admiral Daniel Judson Callaghan, who was killed in action on the bridge of the USS San Francisco off Guadalcanal in 1942. He was once in charge of the Naval ROTC in Berkeley, and he taught Naval Science at the University in the 1930's.

25. *Edwards Field and Track Stadium. 1932. D-2.*

The track team succeeded in making the University nationally famous for athletics in a number of victorious years, particularly in 1895, when it won the Western Intercollegiate with all of the fanfare of a dark horse. The 12 members of the team trained rigorously. They had a "light breakfast about eight" when they were on the road, someone reported, "meat and baked potatoes, milk for the light men, and oatmeal for the heavyweights . . . no coffee or tea, no smoking or drinking nor profane language in playing allowed."

The Field and Track Stadium was completed in a year that the team won Olympic laurels, having been financed jointly by the Associated Students and the University. It was named to honor the late Colonel George E. Edwards, who taught mathematics on campus for more than 40 years, but who is more widely known, perhaps, for his interest in sports.

The 22,000-seat Stadium is used for intercollegiate competitions, training, and drills. High school track teams meet there too, and more rarely, student rallies and commencement exercises have been held on the field grounds. The field has two eight-lane straightaways of 220 yards each, however, and so is uniquely equipped for track. Olympic trials are frequently held in Edwards Field, which draws large crowds of spectators.

27. *Harmon Gymnasium for Men. 1933. D-2.*

Here are two pools, special gymnasiums for wrestling, boxing, fencing, gymnastics, squash, and handball, and training quarters and locker facilities. The main gymnasium seats 7,000 and is often filled for basketball games, University meetings, dances, or concerts. The building replaced one financed by A.K.P. Harmon of Oakland and was itself financed by the Associated Students, Alumnus Ernest V. Cowell, and the State of California. Recently, the students voted to tax themselves in order to finance the expansion of Harmon Gymnasium, which will include an enclosed Olympic-sized swimming pool along Bancroft Way. The expansion is scheduled for completion in 1984.

28. *Alumni House. 1954. D-3.*

The 12 graduates of the first four-year class of the University became: a Congressman, a governor, two University professors, three lawyers (including a Regent), two financiers, one minister, and two state and federal special appointees. That kind of talent begged to be organized. The roots of a formal group were in the Associated Alumni of the Pacific Coast, which included western graduates of all universities. It met in 1864. Within six years the association was made formal. By 1875, the University permitted the student publication *The Berkeleyan* to write alumni in order to ask for articles. Then letters from alumni appeared regularly, and in 1895 *The University of California Magazine*, an official alumni publication, was encouraged to appear.

The Association that sponsored the magazine represented Berkeley alumni but not those of the Affiliated Colleges of San Francisco, as the University's San Francisco schools were called. A rival group, the Council of the Associated Alumni, was formed. Slowly the alumni welded a statewide organization.

Proof of the Association's permanence came in 1918 when it began to send representatives to meetings of the Board of Regents. By 1921, it had a Board of Visitors that inspected the campus with

The University's first graduates, known as the "Twelve Apostles."

the aim of discovering how alumni might help to finance new projects. By then it represented a powerful reservoir of support for education: it had 600 branches and 20,000 members in California. It made the University the most uncommonly equipped land grant college in the United States.

Today, the California Alumni Association is a highly organized association consisting of nearly 90,000 University graduates worldwide. Its purpose is to organize the social, political, and financial activities of University of California alumni. Membership in the Association is extended not only to students of graduating classes, but also to any person who has attended a U.C. campus for one quarter or one who has accumulated 12 units of credit either on a University campus or through University Extension programs.

Many benefits accrue to members of the Alumni Association, including discounts to University recreational facilities, free library cards on any University campus, access to the Lair of the Bear, (the family camp in the Sierra Nevadas), access to group insurance plans, discounts on University of California Press books, travel benefits, internship programs in Sacramento, Washington, D.C., and the United Nations, and an active scholarship program which helps more than 600 students annually. The Association also publishes *California Monthly*, an informative feature magazine which is sent to all members. Visitors to Berkeley may want to pick up a copy; it is a good orientation to current events on the campus.

Student Union Center. 1960–61. D-4.

When an architectural competition was held for the design of these buildings, one thin and graceful line stood out from among the hundreds within the models. It is a hyperbolic paraboloid whose counterpoised angles seem to skitter here in a movement toward the massive Student Union Building. The architect took this shell-like line, revolved it, and repeated it in many places throughout the Center: there are hints of it in the concrete wall in front of the Dining Commons, in the low wall in front of the building itself, and in the patio fence.

Inside, the thin-shelled concrete roof, which is many roofs joined together, forms a series of clerestories. The Commons portion of the Center, situated on two widely separated levels, has the look of determined lightness that is underscored by the inverted Bauhaus lights, placed as if they were symbolic torches in the acre of concrete around the building, and in the Parisian kiosks nearby. The

Commons includes two cafeterias, one on each level. Both lunch and dinner are available in the building. Breakfast, lunch, and coffee are available on the terrace. The Golden Bear, the building's restaurant, offers a more complete menu and service at the tables.

The Commons also incudes game rooms for students, and an Art Activities Room for painters, sculptors, ceramicists, and photographers. It is near the entrance to the main cafeteria.

Ludwig's Fountain is between the Dining Commons and the Student Union. It is so named because a German short-haired pointer answering to the name of Ludwig began swimming in it on the day that it was filled with water. The fountain had no statue from which to gain a name; students who got some relief from finals by tossing bones to waterlogged Ludwig decided to name the place for him. Then President Kerr heard about the informal decision. He recommended the name to the Board of Regents, which promptly gave its imprimatur.

The Student Union has been a more controversial design than the Dining Commons. It appeals to many visitors because its architect was willing to break with the tradition of institutionalisms that are usually reserved for university buildings. It has no trace of Greece or Rome: it is simply a Berkeley building at the University of California.

Critics of the Union talk about it as though it were a hefty ballerina trying to dance Billy the Kid to the music of Wagner; far from being light, they say, it is top-heavy and awkward. The defense points out that the building, for its great size, is remarkably free of ponderousness.

Upper story is elongated because it contains a massive ballroom (from which there is a magnificent view of San Francisco and the Bay).

The building is the height of a seven-story apartment house. It includes bowling alleys, a barbershop, meeting rooms, and cafeteria and beer cellar, the Bear's Lair, on the lower level. Near them is the ASUC Bookshop, (open to the public) an enterprise begun in 1882 over a rootbeer barrel in North Hall; it presently grosses more than one million dollars a year. There is also a store which sells textbooks exclusively. There are numerous sundry shops which serve the needs of students. Public restrooms are on all floors of the Student Union. An information center, exhibit area, and lounges are on the main floor. The Visitor's Information Center is at the southern end of the Main Lobby. Group and individual tours of the campus may be arranged through its offices. The Travel Center, an agency which specializes in student rates for travel anywhere in the world, is also in the Main Lobby area. The Pauley Ballroom, financed by an oilman who was a Regent of the University, occupies most of the top floor, where there is also the Tilden Meditation Room, a serene but splendid memorial to a student by his parents.

In addition to operating student government and its cooperative businesses here, ASUC is publisher of the *Blue and Gold Yearbook*; the *California Engineer*, a technical magazine; and *The Occident*, a literary magazine. Another ASUC publication, *The Pelican*, a humor magazine, has its own building.

Zellerbach Hall, operated by the Committee for Arts and Lectures, is directly west of the Student Union building in Lower Sproul Plaza. It was financed with the help of alumni, friends, students, and staff, who contributed $3.5 million. ASUC borrowed the rest through a federal agency.

31. Sather Gate. 1910. D-4.
With the Campanile (see *Sather Tower, No. 14, this section*),

Sather Gate and Sather Tower ("The Campanile")

Sather Gate has been a traditional symbol of the University, and before the construction of the Student Union Center was its most distinguished outpost. Despite construction beyond it, the baroque grillwork remains the campus' most popular meeting place, as it has been since Mrs. Jane K. Sather presented it to the University in memory of her husband Peder Sather.

32. Sproul Hall. 1941. D-4.

This is the administrative and business center of the Berkeley campus, with the exception of the Office of the Chancellor, which is in California Hall. It includes the Undergraduate Admissions Office (the Graduate Division is also in California Hall); Academic Information; Campus Events Calendar (visitors may subscribe to *The Friday Paper*, a weekly, in this office.) (Room 101); Financial Aids (2nd floor); General Information (Room 101); Records (Room 120); the Campus Police Department (Room 2, basement); and the Student Resources and Information Center (Room 102). In the lobby near the main entrance is a card file showing the names and addresses of all students presently enrolled at Berkeley.

The building is named for Robert Gordon Sproul, a president of the University.

33. Pelican Building. 1957. D-4.

This is the home of *The Pelican*, the campus humor magazine whose editor, because he is required to be rash, bold, or excessively truthful, is often is in jeopardy of suspension. If he has none of these qualities, he loses his audiences to off-campus humor.

The building was the gift of Earle C. Anthony, the late founder and first editor of the magazine in 1903. He also gave the bronze pelican in front. The magazine's name was once slang for studious coeds, perhaps because they wore starched shirtfronts.

34. Eshleman Hall. 1965. E-3.

Named for John Morton Eshleman, Class of 1902, a campus editor who became lieutenant governor, this building houses offices of the ASUC, the Student Senate, most university student clubs, and the Offices of Counseling and Advising Relations with Schools.

35. Stephens Memorial Hall. 1923. D-5.

This Tudor-Gothic building is a memorial to Henry Morse Stephens, for 20 years Professor of History. Stephens Union was the headquarters of the ASUC, in conjunction with Eshleman Hall, (Now Moses Hall. See *No. 34, above, for the newer Eshleman Hall.*) until the completion of the Student Union buildings. It now houses the Hans Kelsen Graduate Social Science Library, and Offices for the Academic Senate and for the Ombudsman.

36. Hearst Gymnasium for Women. 1927. D-4.

One day in the 1920's Bernard Maybeck, Berkeley's greatest architect, was seen wearing a "tube of a black overcoat, with two tubes of black pant legs flapping against his ankles." He watched the removal of sections of Hearst Hall, (which had burned in 1922) the meeting place for University people he had designed for Mrs. Phoebe Apperson Hearst, to the site of a new campus gymnasium for women; its few remaining arches could be nowhere more appropriate than the gym, according to some architectural critics. Workmen dropped a section, and it rolled into a ditch. Maybeck ran to it lovingly. It was intact. It was placed in the gym as William Randolph Hearst's tribute to his mother, who was dead.

Later this building became the gym—without arches. Maybeck and Julia Morgan, his associate who designed William Randolph Hearst's San Simeon Castle south of Monterey, made it the campus' most distinctive structure, however. Like San Simeon, it has Grecian overtones. There are three large gymnasiums, three smaller ones, three outdoor swimming pools of Italian marble, several recreation rooms, and an indoor rifle range used by the campus ROTC. In addition to the usual sports, its playing fields are used for archery, soccer, folk and interpretive dancing, and as a practice area for the famous California Marching Band. A large area in the basement is a warehouse for collections in anthropology.

Women's intercollegiate athletic competition has existed at Berkeley since 1896, when U.C. and Stanford played basketball. Cal won that game by a score of 2–1. In 1973, the Women's program was still operating under the auspices of the Department of Physical Education. This meant that women's athletics had no official University recognition. The program's budget was just $5,000.

In 1976, Women's Intercollegiate Athletics (WIA) gained formal departmental recognition. Under the direction of Dr. Luella Lilly, the Women's Intercollegiate Athletics Association budget grew to $450,000. Women's athletics had finally come into its own at Berkeley. WIA presently fields teams in 12 sports in which more than 350 women compete.

37. May T. Morrison Hall. 1958. D-5.

This building contains facilities of the Department of Music: classrooms, practice rooms, offices, storage for instruments, including a collection of fine violins, violas, and bows presented to the University by Ansley K. Salz, and the 45,000-volume Music Library, with its records and listening room. The Hall is the gift of May T. Morrison, Class of 1878. Her contributions to the University total more than $2,470,000. In 1921, after her husband died, she gave the University his books and his library's furnishings for the Alexander F. Morrison Library. (See Library, No. 18, this section.)

38. Alfred Hertz Memorial Hall of Music. 1958. D-2.

Every Wednesday at noon, there is a concert in this hall's acoustically brilliant, 715-seat auditorium. The building was given to the University by Dr. and Mrs. Alfred Hertz. He conducted the San Francisco Symphony, 1915–30. The stage of this small auditorium might be likened to the symphony's: there is room for an orchestra of 110 pieces and a chorus of 200 voices. There is also an organ that can be screened from the audience. Built by Walter Holtkamp, it has 2,997 pipes and 46 stops. It was a bequest of Mrs. Edmond O'Neill and her husband, a chemistry teacher on campus for 54 years.

39. Faculty Club. 1903–14. C-5.

Bernard Maybeck made the basic design for this building. It has been remodeled at least twice, but it still reflects his plan and the nature of "Early Berkeley" architecture: unmistakable textures in materials; fenestration placed so that the inhabitants of the structure can look out onto vegetation and experience rapidly changing light, as here where the banquet table overlooks a semi-enclosed patio planted with ajuga; unfinished wood permitted to become naturally weathered.

The outside sheathing has woods placed in several dimensions, so that sunlight casts mobile shadows of varying intensity across it. The low-pitched roofline seems to blend with the site. There is a thick growth of landscaping whose parts are widely contrasted in size, shape, and color.

Faculty members supplied funds for this building.

42. *Cowell Memorial Hospital. 1929. D-6.*

This is a complete health service for students, accredited by the American College of Surgeons. The first of its kind, it was developed from an idea of 1902 that the University might save its students health, time, and money by supplying medical treatment. Funds for it were given by Ernest V. Cowell and the State of California. Cowell's estate gave additional funds for the annex, which doubled the hospital's size in 1960.

The round building nearby was designed by architect Michael Goodman as a laboratory for Professor Melvin Calvin, Nobel Laureate in 1961 for his discoveries in photosynthesis.

In 1977, Cowell Hospital became the first public university hospital to offer abortions to students on campus.

43. *Kroeber Hall. 1959. D-6.*

Alfred L. Kroeber, one of the world's most honored anthropologists and a Professor Emeritus at the University, died at a scientific meeting in Paris one year after this building was completed.

The hall named for Professor Kroeber contains the departments of Art and Anthropology. Intended for teaching and for public instruction as well, the art galleries and the Lowie Museum of Anthropology are open to students and public alike. (The museum is closed during the summer. For hours and fees, call 642-3681.)

44. *School of Law. 1951. D-4.*

This building's facilities for 1,000 students were financed by Garret W. Enerey, a San Francisco attorney who was a Regent, and the State of California. Luke Kavanaugh, a San Francisco court reporter for 41 years, bequeathed funds for its courtroom.

The building incorporates Boalt Hall, the School of Law, which is a replacement for a hall that was built in 1911 by the California Bar Association; and Mrs. John H. Boalt, widow of a San Francisco judge.

The University's School of Jurisprudence was formed with the construction of the original hall. The Dean, Professor William Carey Jones, previously taught in the Latin Department and in 1904 organized the School of Law, in which he taught both Roman law and jurisprudence. He was instrumental in organizing the government of Berkeley.

At the end of each spring semester, the building's courtroom is the scene of mock trials. A group resembling a youthful supreme court convenes. The participants in the drama are all second-year law students, and the only ones excused from the activity are those who win both honors and the publication of an article in the law review. On the basis of the trials, which take at least 50 hours of research and writing, and at least 20 hours of rewriting, six students are named the best lawyers of their class. The 12 authors of the best briefs also are given law books and membership in the Board of the court. The court's name, "Moot," is defined as an undecided legal question. During trial periods, cases are presented Monday through Thursday at 7:30 p.m. The public is welcomed.

The Earl Warren Legal Center is used for research, demonstrations, exhibits, and training.

(See also *Affiliated Units of San Francisco: Hastings College of the Law.*)

45. A group of university research scholars work in institutes both on and off-campus:

Jones Child Care Study Center
2425 Atherton Street (between Channing Way and Haste Streets.)
The Center was formerly known as the Institute of Human Development.

For more than 30 years the Center has kept records of the physical, motor, and mental development of a widely separated group of people, tracing them from infancy to maturity, considering their personalities, interests, attitudes, and patterns of emotional expression. The Center is concerned mainly with pre-school children and involves a number of University departments: psychology, education, home economics, and scholars in child development.

Survey Research Center. 2538 Channing Way.
It uses statistical tools, including sophisticated computers, to examine social problems including juvenile delinquency, political behavior, public health, education, and public administration.

Adolph C. Miller and Mary Sprague Miller Institute for Basic Research in Science. 2334 Bowditch Street.

The area to the west is Faculty Glade. It is used for picnicking and occasionally for classes.

40. Women's Faculty Club. 1923. C-6.

41. School of Optometry. (Minor Hall) 1946. D-6.

Founded with support of the California Optometric Associaton in 1923, this school's research is still partly financed by a share of annual license fees paid by registered optometrists. The laboratory is fully equipped to produce eyeglasses, contact lenses, orthoptics, and corrective aids for subnormal vision. Supervised by the faculty, students are trained for all forms of optometric practice, and offer them, to the general public, in the course of their work. An addition to the building was completed in 1979.

The Faculty Club, ca. 1943

Established in 1956, this Institute finances pure research by professors and research fellows.

Institute of Personality Assessment and Research.
3657 Tolman Hall
Scientists in this institute study the development of creativity in individuals. The Institute was organized in 1949 with a grant from the Rockefeller Foundation.

Institute of International Studies.
215 Moses Hall
This clearinghouse is for scholarship related to its Asia Studies, Slavic Studies, Latin American Studies, and International Population and Urban Research. It is also the campus center for scholars from abroad.

OFF-CAMPUS BUILDINGS

46. International House. 1930. E-7.

International House's function is to provide a setting where foreign and American students and professors may live together, and in doing so to promote intercultural understanding. International House also provides programs, tours, and seminars designed to integrate foreign students into American life and into the Berkeley campus. Students from over 70 countries have lived in "I-House," as it is known. I-House accommodates about 500 students.

Non-resident memberships are available to students who wish to use some of the facilities at I-House. Complete dining facilities are offered, including lounges and a recreation center. International folk dances are held every Sunday evening in the Great Hall.

A Mexican-style architectural landmark of the Bay Area, I-House boasts a spectacular view of the Golden Gate Bridge, which can be seen from its cafe at the top of Bancroft Way.

Housing Information for Students (The Housing Office.) 2401 Bowditch Street.

Supported by student registration fees, the Housing Office is available only to currently registered students of the Berkeley campus. Students are asked to show their registration cards before admitted to the Office. Services offered by the Housing Office include:

Rental counselors; information about university-operated housing including co-ops, fraternities and sororities and International House; rental listings of rooms, apartments, houses, and places to share; jobs in exchange for rooms in the community; files of available roommates; disabled students assistance; liaison with the Faculty Wives Committee for new foreign students; mediation of housing complaints; lease analysis and tenants' rights information; maps, model leases, inventory forms, a tenant brochure, and information bulletins.

The Faculty Wives Foreign Student Hospitality Committee.

This committee helps foreign students integrate into the community. The programs begin three weeks before the start of the Fall Quarter. In personal interviews, the committee members provide information to foreign students about the community, help to obtain household items, and assist in locating rentals. For information on how to participate in the program, check with the Housing Office.

University Child Care Service.

The University operates a Child Care Program for registered students with children between the ages of three months and five and one-half years. A small after-school program for children in grades 1 through 3 is also operated at the Smyth-Fernwald Apartments.

Families with the lowest incomes are given the highest priority, and fees are charged on a sliding scale based on family income. Parental participation is required.

For specific dates and application deadlines, write to: Child Care Services. 2401 Bowditch Street, Berkeley, California 94720, or telephone (415) 642-1827.

Social Memberships

Associate Social Memberships are available to students who are non-residents of the University-operated housing system. Students may buy meal contracts and can participate in organized social activities in University housing.

The Physically Disabled Students Office. 2515 Channing Way Berkeley, California 94720. (415) 642-0518.

Housing Services maintains a special file of accessible housing in the community for disabled students. University residence halls and the Co-ops reserve space in their facilities for disabled students, and attendants are available in the dormitories. The office also offers help with admission procedures, pre-enrollment, transportation, parking permits, and in finding student aides.

Summer Housing

Students planning to attend the Summer Session may purchase room-and-board contracts in the residence halls. Applications are available in March. Accommodation without meals is not offered with a Summer Session contract. Students are urged to apply before June to ensure a room assignment. For more information, contact the Summer Housing Department, 2401 Bowditch Street, Berkeley, California 94720. (415) 642-5796. Students not living in the residence halls during the summer do not have priority for residence hall assignments in the Fall Semester.

The Cooperative Housing System
2422 Ridge Road Berkeley

In 1933, a group of impoverished students founded a housing cooperative, based on the "Rochdale Principles" borrowed from 19th Century England. Under these principles, all members are owners of the housing cooperative, and each member is required to perform the household chores necessary for the maintenance of the house. In exchange for this work, each member receives reduced rent and lowered food costs. The Co-op System in Berkeley is a member of the United States Co-op Association, part-owner of Associated Cooperatives, which operate a supermarket chain the the Bay Area. The Co-op is democratically controlled by its members, and is a non-profit organization. In Berkeley, the Co-op owns and operates 15 houses with a capacity for nearly 1,000 residents. The Co-op also owns several apartment buildings near the University. Each facility is fully equipped with common dining facilities which are managed by the students residing in the Co-ops.

CHURCH AND STUDENT CENTERS

Adventist: *Seventh Day;* 2236 Parker Street.

Bahai: *Assembly of Berkeley;* 2925 Ellis Street.

Baptist: *First Club and Roger Williams Club for Students;* 2345 Channing Way; *Thousand Oaks;* Colusa Avenue and Catalina Street; *Calvary;* 1908 Addison Street; *Baptist Student Center;* 2601 Channing Way.

Catholic: *Newman Hall Student Center;* 2700 Dwight Way.

Christian: *Christian Church of Berkeley;* 2401 LeConte Avenue.

Christian Science: *Joint Reading Room;* 2142 Center Street; *First Church;* 2619 Dwight Way; *Reading Room;* 2440 Bancroft Way; *Second Church;* 1521 Spruce Street; *Reading Room;* 892 Colusa Avenue.

Congregational: *First;* 2345 Channing Way; *North;* Walnut and Cedar Streets; *Plymouth House Student Center;* 2340 Durant Avenue.

Episcopal: *All Souls,* Spruce and Cedar Streets; *St. Mark's and Canterbury Club for Students,* Bancroft Way and Ellsworth Street; *St. Clement's;* Russell Street and Claremont Avenue;

Greek Orthodox: *Russian St. John;* 1900 Essex Street.

Jewish: *B'nai B'rith Hillel Foundation,* 2736 Bancroft Way; *Congregation Beth El;* Arch and Vine Streets.

Latter Day Saints: *Church of Jesus Christ;* Walnut and Vine Streets; *Institute of Religion;* 2368 LeConte Avenue.

Lutheran: *Church of the Cross;* 1744 University Avenue; *Bethlehem;* Prince and Telegraph Streets; *St. Michael's;* 2516 Durant Avenue; *Student Center;* 2311 Bowditch Street; *University Lutheran Chapel;* 2425 College Avenue.

Methodist: *Trinity and Wesley Foundation Student Center;* 2320 Dana Street; *Epworth University and Epworth Club for Students;* 1953 Hopkins Street.

Nazarene: *First Berkeley Church,* Bancroft Way and McKinley Street.

Nondenominational: *Northbrae Community Church;* The Alameda.

Presbyterian: *Calvary,* 1940 Virginia Street; *Covenant;* 1623 University Avenue; *First Calvin Club for Students;* Dana Street and Channing Way; Knox; Lorina and Russell Streets; *St. John's and St. John's Club for Students;* 2640 College Way; *Westminster House Student Center;* Bancroft Way and College Avenue.

Unitarian: *Channing Club for Students,* 2425 Bancroft Way; *First Unitarian Church of Berkeley,* 1 Lawson Road, Kensington.

United Presbyterian: *St. Paul's;* 2024 Durant Avenue.

Vedanta Society of Northern California; 2455 Bowditch Street.

FACTS

*Many educators regard the University of California as one of the best in the United States, and one of the best in the world. These are among the criteria: the University ranks first in the nation for its Nobel Laureates: it has twenty, twelve of whom are at Berkeley. It ranks first in the number of Guggenheim Awards given its faculty members. The American Council on Education twice rated American universities by asking 100 specialized authorities to assess the departments with which they were familiar. In every case, the University was either tied for first or was second only to Harvard. The University commonly ties or equals Harvard in the number of its faculty who are members of the National Academy of Sciences.

*In 1959, the Nobel Prize in Physics was shared by Professors Emilio Segré and Owen Chamberlain of the Berkeley campus. They discovered the anti-proton and so opened the world of anti-matter to experimental physics. In 1960, Professor Donald Arthur Glaser of the Berkeley campus won the Nobel Prize in Physics. He is the inventor of the Bubble Chamber, in which atomic matter may be studied. In 1961, the Nobel Prize in Chemistry was awarded Professor Melvin Calvin of the Berkeley campus for his work in photosynthesis. Cszelaw Milosz won the the Nobel Prize in 1980 for Literature, proving that Berkeley excels in the Humanities, as well as in the physical sciences.

Other Nobel Laureates at the University, their fields, campus, and the year in which they won the prize:

Year	Name	Field	Campus
1980	Cszelow Milosz	Literature	Berkeley
1975	Renanato Dulbecco	Medicine	San Diego
1972	J. Robert Schrieffer	Physics	Santa Barbara
1970	Hannes Alfven	Physics	San Diego
1968	Luis Alvarez	Physics	Berkeley
1965	Julian Schwinger	Physics	Los Angeles
1964	Charles H. Townes	Physics	Berkeley
1963	Maria Goeppert-Mayer (deceased)	Physics	San Diego
1961	Melvin Calvin	Chemistry	Berkeley
1960	Willard F. Libby (deceased)	Chemistry	
1960	Donald Arthur Glaser	Physics	Berkeley
1959	Emilio Segré	Physics	Berkeley
1959	Owen Chamberlain	Physics	Berkeley
1951	Glenn T. Seaborg	Chemistry	Berkeley
1951	Edward McMillan	Physics	Berkeley
1949	William F. Giauque (deceased)	Chemistry	Berkeley
1946	John H. Northrop (deceased)	Chemistry	Berkeley
1939	Ernest O. Lawrence (deceased)	Physics	Berkeley
1934	Harold C. Urey (deceased)	Chemistry	San Diego

Government
Systemwide Administration
President: David S. Saxon
Chancellors:
Berkeley: Ira Michael Heyman
Davis: James H. Meyer
Irvine: Daniel G. Aldrich, Jr.
Los Angeles: Charles E. Young
Riverside: Tomas Rivera
San Diego: Richard C. Atkinson
San Francisco: Julian Krevans
Santa Barbara: Robert A. Huttenback
Santa Cruz: Robert L. Sinsheimer

Directors of Major Laboratories:
Lawrence Berkeley Laboratory: David A. Shirley
Lawrence Livermore National Laboratory: Robert E. Batzel
Los Alamos National Scientific
  Laboratory: Donald M. Kerr, Jr.
Laboratory of Biomedical and Environmental Sciences:
  (U.C.L.A.): Owen R. Lunt

Campuses: Dates founded, acres
Berkeley: 1868 (1,232 acres)
Davis: 1905 (3,600 acres)
Irvine: 1965 (1,510 acres)
Los Angeles: 1919 (411 acres)
Riverside: 1907 (1,200 acres)
San Diego: 1912 (2,040 acres)
San Francisco: 1873 (107 acres)
Santa Barbara: 1944 (815 acres)
Santa Cruz: 1965 (2,000 acres)

University work–force: (full- and part-time) (1980)
Faculty (assistant, associate and full professors): 6,253
Other academic personnel: 21,673
Staff and management: 66,618
Total workforce: 94,544
An additional 18,385 employees work at four U.C.-managed Department of Energy Laboratories.

Students come from every county in California, all other 49 states, and some 100 foreign countries. About 90% are California residents.

Fees and expenses
Fees for undergraduate California residents: (Fall 1982)

Registration: $170.00/quarter
Education fee: $208.33/quarter
Berkeley campus fee: $12.50/quarter
Total: $390.83/quarter

Personal expenses: $600–1,065
Total: $4,093–5,217
Fees are somewhat higher at graduate and professional schools.

Non-resident students pay an additional $2,400 tuition fee yearly.
Financial aid to students in 1978–79 amounted to $128.9 million
and went to 46% of the student body.

Libraries
Main libraries on each campus are supplemented by over 100 spe-
cialized branches throughout the University. Holdings in millions
of volumes (1981):
Berkeley: 5.75
Los Angeles: 4.23
San Francisco: .48
Davis: 1.60
Santa Barbara: 1.37
Irvine: .93
San Diego: 1.37
Santa Cruz: .61
Riverside: .98

Housing at Berkeley:
50 Sororities and Fraternities
15 Residence Halls
14 Co-ops
1,022 Married Student Apartments
580 rooms for international students

Campus Staff at Berkeley:
5,929 academic
9,023 staff personnel
Enrollment: (1980)
128,000 on nine campuses
30,462 full-time registered students at Berkeley.
21,277 Undergraduate enrollment
9,185 Graduate enrollment at Berkeley.
Alumni:
85,000 active members in the California Alumni Association.

Libraries at Berkeley:
5.75 million books
200,000 maps
850,000 current serials

35,000 recordings
22 branch libraries
8 major departmental libraries
40 million manuscripts

Major Divisions:

14 Colleges and Schools
72 Departments of Instruction
43 Institutes, Bureaus, and Laboratories
15 Center Stations and Research Units
100 undergraduate majors
85 languages taught

Enrollment by Campus (Fall, 1980)

Campus	U.G.	G.	H.S.	Total
Berkeley	21490	8596	793	30879
Davis	13677	3137	1948	18762
Irvine	7794	1469	1023	10286
Los Angeles	21882	8189	3961	34032
Riverside	3282	1369	56	4707
San Diego	9049	1332	1037	11418
San Francisco	—	—	3779	3779
Santa Barbara	13363	2088	—	15451
Santa Cruz	6001	471	—	6472
TOTAL UNIVERSITY:	96538	26651	12597	135,786

Key: U.G. = Undergraduate; G. = Graduate; H.S. = Health
Sciences.
University Extension offered courses to 387,000 enrollees on each
of the nine campuses in 1979–80.

TRADITIONS
(Mostly dead)

The Stanford Axe
Like the Little Brown Jug, the Old Oaken Bucket, and the Cigar Store Indian, the Stanford Axe came to surpass symbolism in some memories. In 1899, Stanford students forged it, painted it red, and branded it with with an "S." The year before they'd lost a track meet and their first Big Game with U.C., both by humiliating

The Axe Procession, 1899

scores. They had also lost the 1899 track meet to U.C. The Axe was their psychological weapon for the coming Big Game, to the winner of which Senator James Phelan was scheduled to give an important trophy, The Football Players, by the distinguished deaf sculptor Douglas Tilden (see *University: Plan*).

On April 15 they took the Axe to the game in San Francisco. There, whenever their Indians scored a point they brought the 10-pound weapon down noisily onto blue and gold ribbon, symbolizing U.C. The Berkeley team won the game 9–7. Then some of its supporters rushed forward, grabbed the Axe, and smuggled it, running, to the nearest ferryboat by way of a Chinese butcher shop.

Stanford students searched Berkeley for days. They used hammers and crowbars to investigate furniture in the Chi Phi Fraternity House, but they ignored the grand piano and so missed the Axe.

For 31 years the Berkeleyans kept it in a vault of a local bank. On April 3, 1930, a group of young men who said they were from an important newspaper arrived in Berkeley. One of the interviews they requested was of the armored car crew carrying the Stanford Axe from a public display back to the bank. As they hurled their questions and blazed away with their photographer's lights the "Immortal 21," as they were later called, seized the Axe and raced for their rooms at Stanford. U.C. men followed. They made for the San Mateo Bridge hoping to be able to cut off the Indians between San Jose and Palo Alto. They found the drawbridge raised. The toll taker was from Stanford.

In 1933, the Stanford Axe became the prize of the annual Big Game. The winner was permitted to keep it for the entire year, and U.C. normally kept it on display in its Student Union when it was entitled to possession. After U.C. stole it in 1946, the administration of each school ordered students to let their teams have the glory. Nevertheless, the Axe was stolen recently as 1960, and students spend considerable pre-Big Game time plotting other symbolic overthrows of their rival.

The Big C: "Labor Day"

Since 1896, February 29 has been a day on which some major task must be done at the University. On occasion, the day of actual performance has been Charter Day, March 23, during a Leap Year, however, and the Big C was built on that day at the turn of the century. The trail to it was built in 1916. The letter is periodically and mysteriously painted with Stanford's dominant color, red, before Big Games, and there have been occasional attempts by Berkeley's undergraduates to change its luminous gold to something more to their liking. The tradition has become stronger on the Davis than Berkeley campus, where it is almost forgotten.

Blue and Gold

At the first UC class reunion Joseph C. Rowell, who later was University librarian for 44 years, suggested that blue become one of the University's colors. He and other supporters of the idea evidently were influenced by the fact that many early students in Berkeley were the sons of graduates of Yale, whose dominant color also is blue. Rowell's class was 1874. It had one woman member, Elizabeth Bragg (later Mrs. Elizabeth Bragg Martenstein). She is credited with the suggestion that gold be the second color to characterize California.

Dress as Status Symbols

Hats once symbolized University classes and still are occasionally seen, though more often in print than as clothing. There was the freshman beanie, sophomore cap, junior plug, and the taller senior plug. When worn in modern days they are likely to be seen at the Freshie Glee, Soph Hop, Junior Prom, and Senior Ball.

Other clothing customs of the last century are vestigial: there was a "Pajamarino" or "Pajamahoolo" held annually at the Greek Theatre so that students would be privileged to see one another in pajamas, a desire that seems to have abated or gone underground;

Fraternity life, ca. 1925

the sophomores distinguished themselves by carrying canes with bear's heads carved into them, which of course led freshmen to try to take them forcibly.

The general informality of dress on the Berkeley campus is a style that does not pass out of fashion. In the 1906 *Blue and Gold Year-book* Philip M. Carey wrote, "The thousand ways that this Western student rough-house spirit finds for venting itself are not in wrecking property and disobeying the law. . . . It comes perhaps of our Western free and easy ways, of our Western manner of dress, miner's boots and corduroy trousers, blue shirts and battered plugs, all evidence of the type. . . ."

Oski Bear
In 1901 there was a "Pajamahoolo" on campus. The crowd wanted to hear a certain campus monologuist, Jack Butler, but he was in Sacramento where his wife had just given birth. The crowd learned this and decided to name the baby. Someone yelled, "Let's call him Oski Wow!" People applauded that, and although they relented and voted by acclamation to name the baby John California Butler, Oski was a name used afterward—and probably less publicly before— when referring to the baby bears that were campus mascots in stuffed or real form.

The Senior Pilgrimage
Members of the Class of 1898 had a vaguely Chinese sounding yell: "Ki Yi—Ki Yi, Ki Yippee—Ki Yi, 98, 98, Hi Hi Hi." This caused its members, upon graduating, to put on Chinese mandarin clothing and to affect the Oriental courtesy of bowing to one another. That same day they trooped the campus to bid each building goodbye. There are more buildings and more students, but some graduating seniors still make this sentimental tour.

Pedro
Along fraternity row on College Avenue the cry "Pedro," uttered as a siren-like wail, often is sent up while most students are working for their final examinations. One of the many explanations of the customs is that it was started by someone who imagined a story of a beautiful Spanish girl, daughter of the former owner of the campus, who fell in love with an Indian named Pedro. Her father had the Indian murdered, according to the mostly forgotten story, and she

has been wandering the campus for him ever since. Another explanation is that Pedro is a professor's long-lost dog whose return will end all finals.

Charter Day

Charter Day takes place each April in the Greek Theatre, commemorating the day the University received its charter from the State Legislature. It is tradition to have an important speaker at the ceremonies. Students have heard Teddy Roosevelt, William Taft, George Marshall, Earl Warren, and John F. Kennedy at ceremonies, which include professors in full academic regalia. Traditionally, the oldest alumni of the University is honored at the ceremonies.

(Left to right) Governor Edmund G. Brown, Regent Edward Pauley, and President John F. Kennedy, at Charter Day, 1961.

Museums

Essig Museum of Entomology
211 and 311 Wellman Hall
The collection at the Essig Museum contains four million specimens, primarily from the western hemisphere. The insects of California and of Mexico are well-represented. Groups and individuals desiring tours of the museum should call to make an appointment to visit the collection. For tour reservations, call 642-4779. For general questions about insects, call 642-5565.

Jepson Herbarium
3010 Life Sciences Building
Complementing the Botanical Gardens, this facility enables botonists to identify California native plants. It also maintains a card file of California place names and a collection of color photographs of California plants and plant communities. Call 642-2465 for information.

Lawrence Hall of Science
Centennial Drive near Grizzly Peak Boulevard
One of the most creative, widely-noted museums of modern science, the Lawrence Hall offers exhibits which encourage active participation, and, in addition, classes in such subjects as basic computer sciences. Open daily 10 a.m. to 4:30 p.m., Thursdays 10 a.m. to 9 p.m. Admission: $2.50 for adults; $1 for children 7–18; $1.50 for senior citizens. Free transportation to the Hall originates at Center and Shattuck streets, Berkeley, every half hour. (Also see page 56.)

Lowie Museum of Anthropology
Kroeber Hall, Bancroft Way and College Avenue
Call 642-3681 for Exhibit Hall hours and information on admission charges. (Also see page 87.)

Museum of Geology
Third and fourth floors, Earth Science Building
Open to the public at no charge, the Museum of Geology displays photographs, mineral and rock specimens, and maps that examine the earth and its components.

Museum of Paleontology
Earth Sciences Building

A reconstructed skeleton of a saber-tooth cat, dinosaur skeletons, and other fossils are on display to illustrate the development of life through history. Other exhibits include fossils of the type geologists use in the search for oil. Open house occurs every April, early in the month, when adults and children are encouraged to become paleontologists for a day, picking through rock samples and fossils. Group tours of the museum may be arranged by calling 642-1821.

Museum of Vertebrate Zoology
2593 Life Sciences Building

This museum contains an extensive collection of vertebrate animals, and is open for research purposes to scientists and students by prearrangement. Information on California wildlife is also available from the staff. Call 642-3567 to arrange laboratory time.

Sather Tower ("The Campanile")

The best-known landmark of the Berkeley campus, Sather Tower offers a panoramic view of the San Francisco Bay Area from its top story. For a small charge (25 cents) a friendly and knowledgable elevator operator will take you to the top. Concerts on the 48-bell carillon are offered three times each day on weekdays. On Sundays at 3 p.m., a more extensive concert is given. (See *No. 14 of Campus Buildings.*) In the floor lobby of the tower, a window display offers a photographic history of the university, including memorabilia.

Seismographic Station
475 Earth Sciences Building

The Berkeley Seismographic Station is one of the two oldest earthquake observatories in the western hemisphere. It constitutes the center of a network of earthquake observatories throughout Northern California and the Pacific Northwest. Geologists working at the station are trying to learn how to predict earthquakes, which are ever present in California. Groups may arrange tours of the station by calling 642-3977. A recorded message detailing recent seismic activity is available by calling 642-2160.

The University Art Museum
2626 Bancroft Way
Berkeley, California 94720
(Directly across the street from the central campus.)
In 1934, faculty members of the Art Department at Berkeley were relegated to mounting paintings in an unused power house behind Sproul Hall. Not until 1963, when the Modernist painter Hans Hofmann donated $250,000 and 45 paintings to the University, were comprehensive plans made for a full-size museum. Mario Ciampi, a San Francisco architect, with design associates Richard L. Jorasch and Ronald E. Wagner, won a national competition with their proposal for an exposed, reinforced concrete structure of five fanned levels, including 31,000 square feet of exhibition space, a sculpture garden, and on the lower level, a film theater, a bookstore, a restaurant, administrative and curatorial offices, storage rooms, a carpentry shop, matting room, lumber storage, a conservation studio, and a photography studio.

Construction of the museum began in 1967, and took three years to complete. The construction cost of $4.85 million was met primarily with funds from student registration fees. No state funds were used.

The Museum offers programs in film, painting, drawing, sculpture, architecture, performance, video, and photography to Berkeley students and Bay Area residents and visitors. Average annual attendance is about 400,000.

The permanent collection includes Greek vases, Asian scrolls, and historic European and American works of 47 canvasses by Hans Hofmann.

The Pacific Film Archive, (denoted as "PFA") housed in the lower level of the Museum, is a major center for screening and research of film. It offers a showcase for the entire history of film, screening an average of two films nightly. The Museum Theater seats 199 people. The Pacific Film Archive also has a 10-seat screening room and 16mm and 35mm viewing tables. The non-circulating study collection of Japanese feature films is the largest of its kind outside of Japan. The PFA also has a collection of American independent and avant-garde films, an international selection of animation classics, and rare Soviet silent films in 35mm prints. The PFA offers a public service media program, including research screening, a "ready reference hotline" for questions about films, and a film program for local schools.

Telephone numbers for the University Art Museum:
 Galleries: For current gallery and general information, call 642-0808 for a 24-hour recorded message.
 Theater: See *Calendar* for schedule.
 For daily Pacific Film Archive schedule, call 642-1124 for a 24-hour recorded message.
 Museum Offices:
 Administrative Offices: 642-1207
 Pacific Film Archive: 642-1412
 Public Affairs: 642-1438
 Membership/Council: 642-1209
 Bookstore: 642-1475
 The Swallow Restaurant: 841-2409

University Herbarium
2010 Life Sciences Building
This Herbarium contains collections of native, exotic, poisonous, and rare and endangered plants. A reference library is also available. Call 642-2465 for further information.

The Wood Collection
Forest Products Laboratory, Richmond
Field Station
This collection contains more than 10,000 wood specimens from throughout the world. It is open to the public, 8 a.m. to 5 p.m. Monday through Friday, except for University holidays. For more information, call 231-9456. A shuttle bus to the Richmond Field Station is available from the campus. Check with the information desk in the Student Union for schedules.

Worth-Ryder Art Gallery
116 Kroeber Hall
This museum serves both as a public gallery and as a teaching facility for the Department of Art. There are continuous showings of recognized artists, as well as student works, of paintings, sculpture, drawings, and graphics, throughout the year. Call 642-2582 for more information.

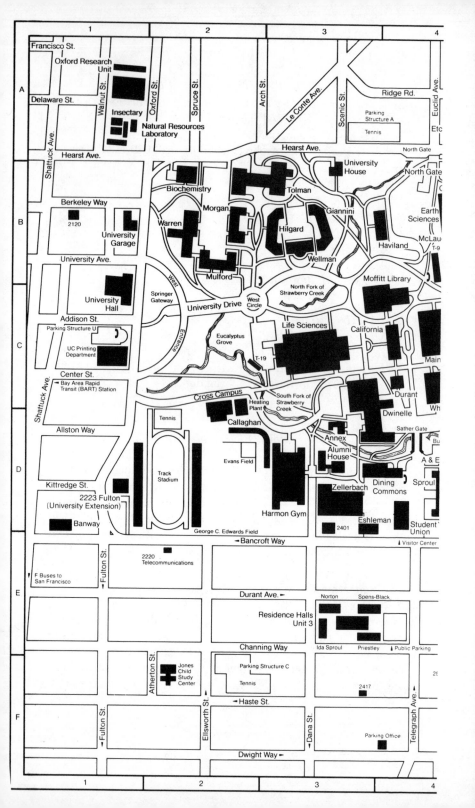

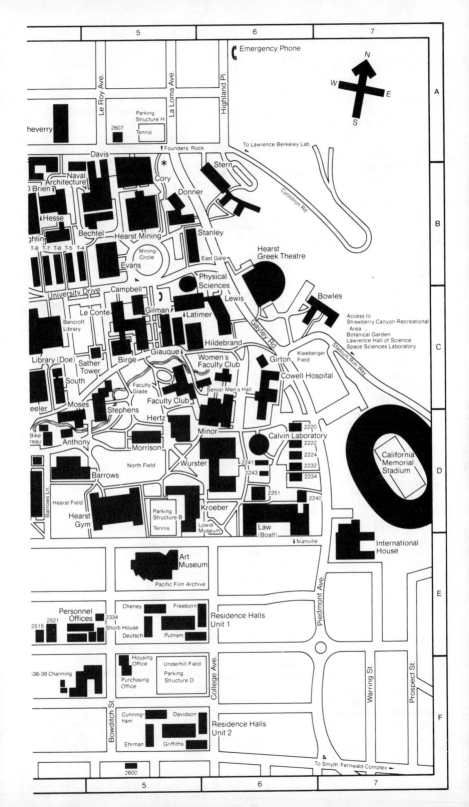

Points of Interest

Art Museum (11-5 Wednesday-Sunday). The major campus art center, its facilities include 11 exhibition galleries, a sculpture garden, the Pacific Film Archive (more than 800 film programs annually), a bookstore, and the Swallow Restaurant. In addition to displaying traveling exhibitions, the Museum houses a permanent collection of Asian and Western art as well as video and film collections. One gallery is devoted to the world's largest collection of Hans Hofmann paintings donated by the artist.

Bancroft Library (9-5 Monday-Friday; 1-5 Saturday). Paintings of early California and the first nugget of the 1849 California Gold Rush are on permanent display, in addition to changing exhibits of rare books and manuscripts.

Botanical Garden (9-5 daily). Located in Strawberry Canyon, this ranks among the world's leading gardens in the variety and quality of its plants.

California Memorial Stadium. Completed in 1923 in time for the traditional Big Game with Stanford University, it seats over 76,000.

Cory Hall (8-5 Monday-Friday). Electrical equipment, historical and modern, 2nd floor.

Earth Sciences Building (8-5 Monday-Friday; 1-5 Saturday-Sunday). Paleontology Museum, ground, 1st, and 2nd floors; earthquake recorder, 1st floor; rock collection, 3rd floor; map collection, 5th floor.

Hearst Greek Theatre (South entrance open 1-4). Patterned after the amphitheatre at Epidaurus, Greece, it seats 8,500, and was presented in 1903 as a gift by newspaper publisher William Randolph Hearst. The Theatre is used for annual Charter Day ceremonies, University meetings, rallies, music festivals, and dramatic productions.

Hearst Mining Building (8-5 Monday-Friday; 8-noon Saturday). Historical displays; mineral, metallurgy, ceramics, and mining engineering exhibits.

Hilgard Hall (8-5 Monday-Friday). Soil cross-sections from California and tropical areas.

Kroeber Hall—Lowie Museum of Anthropology (10-4 daily, 12-4 weekends). The Museum is a major research facility with 500,000 catalogued items. Changing exhibits on the peoples of the world: art, artifacts, ethnological graphics, and archaeological examples from the Museum's collection.

Worth Ryder Art Gallery (12:30-3:30 Tuesday-Friday). Contemporary art works by students and faculty.

Lawrence Hall of Science (10-4:30 MTuWF; 10-9 Th; 10-5 Sat, Sun). A public science center where all ages can participate in astronomy, computer, and biology activities. Planetarium programs, films, and lectures weekly. Call 642-5132 for schedule. Admission: $2.00 adults, $1.50 students and senior citizens, $1.00 children 7-18, children under 7 and LHS members free. For a group of 10 persons or more, admission is $1.00 per person.

Mulford Hall (8-9 M-Th; 8-5 F; 1-5 Sat, Sun). Woods of the United States and other nations.

O'Brien Hall (8-5 Monday-Friday). Operating pushbutton hydraulic models in the breezeway.

Sather Tower (popularly known as the Campanile) is the best-known landmark of the University. Erected in 1914, it is modeled after St. Mark's Campanile in Venice. Open 10-4:15 daily except University holidays. The elevator takes you to the observation platform (last trip at 4:15) for 25 cents.

Student Union (8-10 Monday Friday; 10-6 Saturday). Shops, restaurants, travel center, meeting rooms, lounges, art displays, crafts studio, box office, and recreation center.

Wellman Hall (8-5 Monday-Friday; 9-5 Sat). Insect displays.

Wurster Hall (8-5 daily). Exhibitions by students on 1st and 2nd floors. Special exhibitions displayed in Room 106.

Information

Campus Police (2 Sproul Hall, basement—open 24 hours daily);
Emergency 911, 642-3333; other police calls 642-6760.

Visitor Center: (Lobby, Student Union; 8-5 Monday-Friday, closed 12-1 p.m.). Weekday tours are given by students, starting at 1 p.m. When Center is closed, the Information Desk in the Student Union can help.

General:
101 Sproul Hall

Admissions:
120 Sproul Hall

Student Information:
102 Sproul Hall

University Extension:
2223 Fulton Street

Other Campuses

Los Angeles (UCLA)

"We must divide the University though we divide the state to do it!" a Los Angeles judge once declared The Alumni Association at the University of California, Los Angeles, which he was addressing, did not consider his position radical, nor would it have, possibly, until the beginning of World War II, when it became evident that there was a need for more unity between UCLA and Berkeley.

Royce Hall, UCLA

There are basic differences between the University's two largest campuses. UCLA was begun in 1882 as the State Normal School in Los Angeles. It became the "southern branch" of the University in 1919. It moved to land that nearby cities gave to it in the Westwood Hills near the Santa Monica Mountains in 1929, and there it served a community two or three times the size of the one around Berkeley. Under great pressure to grow, it was restrained by its association with Berkeley, its members thought: the administration seemed remote and conservative. The administrators at Los Angeles, on the other hand, were affected by the quickening pace of their city. Local pride kept urging them to independence.

In 1934, a UCLA dean led a group of southern alumni to Sacramento. They asked the Legislature for a separate graduate school. The Graduate Division became statewide with two sections: northern and southern. When budgeting was under way, similar groups from the south tried to raise UCLA's share of the the general appropriation. Competition for financing became almost frantic as UCLA's region developed. The arrival of war veterans made more building urgent.

Then came a reversal of attitude. This occurred in part because UCLA got at least some of its goals of representation. More members of the Board of Regents were appointed from Southern California. It also occurred because UCLA itself had changed. First, it had matured as an institution. Second, it recognized intrinsic problems that it could solve only by preserving and strengthening its bond with the "mother campus" at Berkeley.

State colleges arose around the campus at UCLA. Nearby, the value of real estate increased to a point higher than either the faculty or students could afford to pay. UCLA became a campus of commuters. Every day many of its students passed junior and state colleges more accessible than UCLA. Having to travel from such communities as Los Angeles proper and Santa Monica each day, most students had little time for campus life. Not even those who could afford cars could afford to spend time parking near the campus. Most undergraduates had to go 10 miles or more to a point near the campus. If they drove they parked a mile away and walked for 30 minutes to class. They carried their lunch to save time and money; they studied in the library between classes.

UCLA grew rapidly while these problems were developing. The rate of growth made them critical. In 1945, the campus opened a College of Engineering, and within the next few years opened schools of public health, social welfare, law, nursing, and medicine. It gained recognition for its teaching of psychology, architecture, social welfare, public health, urban planning, library and information sciences, management, nursing, education, dentistry, history, political science, chemistry, mathematics, art, music, theater arts, medicine and law. It pioneered the applications of data processing to business after installing one of the first large computers in its Western Data Processing Center, in which it invested $4 million. UCLA's own popularity turned it into the site of a traffic jam.

When legislators began to wonder whether some other form of campus or educational system might not be superior and less expensive, UCLA and Berkeley drew closer together psychologically. A plan was established for UCLA in which 25 per cent of its students, at minimum, would be able to live on the campus. Only a small percentage live near the campus now. They are mostly in fraternity and sorority houses that were built before the surrounding area, Westwood Village, became as costly as it is.

A second wave of growth arrived. This one was calculated to relieve congestion rather than to add to it. Additional dormitories and a Student Union went up. The campus matured academically and in its extracurricular performances. These new dormitories, classrooms, and research buildings brought a small army of steel-helmeted contractors and workers to the campus. UCLA began to allow private financiers to build parking lots on its campus by leasing sites.

With the help of the statewide administration at Berkeley, UCLA toughened its courses. Clark Kerr announced, after he became president of the University in 1958, that his central policy would be to raise educational standards despite coming growth (see *University: Kerr*). He opposed many "practical" courses as irrelevant to the nature of universities. At UCLA, this ended the School of Applied Arts by 1960. It eliminated most of the trade-school courses at the campus' Department of Business Education. There are no longer courses in how to give typing tests.

UCLA's School of Applied Arts was replaced with the School of Fine Arts. The reorganized faculty held that UCLA should continue to teach the techniques of acting for which it had become famous, and which plainly answered some of the needs of its community. It maintained that scientists have laboratories and that actors must have stages. As a result, the School of Fine Arts includes music, art, and the "dramatic arts," which are defined at UCLA as radio, television, and film acting as well as acting for the stage. The dramatic arts faculty became established and is expanding. It students write and produce their own plays, television shows, and movies. One short film, *Time Out of War*, won an Academy Award in 1957.

The dramatic arts are being used to help draw students back into the campus life of UCLA. There are increasingly more plays, and there are more concerts, films, and lectures. A Center for the Study of Comparative Folklore and Mythology, with faculty members from 11 different fields, was established. It publishes widely in folklore and assists in the presentation of highly popular folk music. Crowds of students have been appearing for campus events, where once there would never be more than 100.

Thus, the campus at Westwood Boulevard and LeConte Avenue, Los Angeles, is being changed rapidly. The open space in its 411 acres is fast disappearing. Austere new buildings are being added to its basic Lombardic Romanesque design. Its wide central plaza is busy through the day and evening.

Josiah Royce Hall, containing the Auditorium and some classrooms and offices, is on the north of the plaza. It is named for the American philosopher who at 15 was enrolled in the early University, and is modeled after the Church of St. Stephan's at Bologna, Italy. The Powell Library is on the south of UCLA's plaza. It is in the early Italian Romanesque style and has a canopied entrance, striped coursing on the lower story, arched loggia over the portal, brick ornaments in the Byzantine tradition, and above all an arcaded tower. To the east and south are Chemistry-Geology, Physics-Biology, Administration, and Education buildings. Down the hill to the west, leading to the gymnasiums, are Romanesque terra cotta balustrades. The UCLA skyline is one of pinnacled towers and the deep red-tile rooftops of the Italian Renaissance or of Spain.

Due to the large metropolitan area which it serves, UCLA has grown to the point of overtaking Berkeley. In 1980, it had 34,032 students, and it is still growing rapidly.

Special resources at UCLA include: the Institute of Geophysics and Planetary Physics (also at Riverside and San Diego), the Institute of Social Science Research, the Molecular Biology Institute, the Laboratory of Biomedical and Environmental Sciences, the Center for African Studies, the Jules Stein Eye Institute, the Mental Retardation Research Center, the Brain Research Institute, and the Institute of Industrial Relations.

Davis

Davis was begun in 1906 on 778 acres that the Legislature bought
with $104,250, and on which it placed a dormitory and a dining hall.
It did not plan classrooms; it wanted to teach agriculture there and
nothing more—student farmers seemed to want nothing more. The
three-year course took place mostly in the fields and in a shop that
was later built near the dormitory.

Over the years, agriculture became more scientific, technical,
mechanical—and rewarding. The campus at Davis reflected this
change. On its site 13 miles west of Sacramento, it developed 3,000
acres on which farming has been increasingly improved in laboratories and fields, and where the teaching of farming has become as
technical as any other course at the University.

Davis now offers the full range of arts and sciences instruction,
but is still identified with agriculture. It is often credited with
bringing the post-World War II revolution in California's farming.

The Davis campus

It helped develop mechanical cotton pickers for the long-staple crop, an improvement that changed the state's entire agricultural economy. It produced chemicals to make the leaves of cotton plants fall off before harvesting, flame throwers safe enough to burn the weeds out of fields, machines to harvest sugar beets, asparagus, tomatoes, nuts, fruit, and grapes.

Davis students are proud of a distinguished agricultural heritage, their role and their future. They tend to symbolize their work in farming whenever they can. They have the only flat campus at the University, and many of them own bikes and treat them the way ranchers treat horses—riding them casually or even brilliantly, and tethering them like animals outside of classes. Their other important form of campus transportation is a kind of wagon train drawn by a tractor.

They have a milking contest every year. It takes place during a Picnic Day, an annual open house begun on the campus in 1909, when a few hundred people came for it. Recent Picnic Days have attracted thousands of people from every campus: there are intercollegiate swims, a soccer match, horse, fashion, and air shows, band competitions, exhibits, aquacades, melodramas, and dances. The even is held in April. In fall, Davis students hold their annual Little International Livestock Show.

They insist on rural courtesies, honor, and humor. They have "Howdy Days," take tests under the Oxford System of self-discipline, and call their women students "Cow-eds." They have a symbolic cry, a version of a traditional one at Berkeley, that they offer at most major events:

"Bossiee Cow Cow, Honey Bee Bee, Oleomargine, Oleo Butterine, Alfalfa—Hey!"

Davis has historically won top honors in viticulture, enology, nutritional sciences, and veterinary medicine. (The acclaimed School of Veterinary Medicine is the only such school in California.) The campus is especially noted for several research centers, including the Institute of Ecology, the Food Protection and Toxicology Center, the Center on Administration of Criminal Justice, the Crocker Nuclear Laboratory, the California Primate Research Center, and the University's Energy Extension Service.

Riverside

The University paid $60,000 for a field station at Riverside in 1907. As the Imperial Valley grew and orchards became its major industry, the station became essential to its prosperity, and famous throughout the world. A powdery mildew almost destroyed cataloupe growing in the Valley, for example, until members of the station isolated the blight and developed a cantaloupe that would resist it. During a single year they also developed five new varieties of peach so that the fruit could be adapted to specific climates.

The increasing population of Southern California caused the University to open a College of Letters and Science at Riverside in

Riverside

When it began to teach liberal arts the new campus had 60 faculty members, and 127 students turned up for classes at the new park-like campus in the desert at the foot of the Box Spring Mountains. The ratio was unequalled anywhere in the United States. Currently, Riverside has 4,707 students.

Because of its proximity to the famous orange groves of Southern California, Riverside became a natural center for research in agriculture and environmental studies. It also has several joint programs with UCLA, including programs in biomedical sciences, medicine, engineering, and a large internship program which places hundreds of students as interns with government agencies and with private industry.

Special resources of the Riverside campus include: the Citrus Research Center and Agricultural Experiment Station, the International Center for Biological Control (also at Berkeley), the State-wide Air Pollution Research Center, the Dry Lands Research Institute, the Center for Social and Behavioral Science Research, and the California Museum of Photography.

San Francisco (UCSF)

Dr. H. H. Toland left his practice in South Carolina in 1852, and he went to work in the Gwin Mine at Calaveras County, California. He was rich by the time he went back to medicine in San Francisco. The Civil War passed. In the war's last years, Dr. Toland invested his money in a medical school. Within five years he was offering it to the University; within eight years the Regents accepted. They valued Toland's building at Stockton and Chestnut streets, with its laboratory, museum, and library, at $100,000. Toland went back to private practice, treated hundreds of poor people without charge, and died rich, famous, and contented in 1882.

The doctor's gift was the beginning a University campus. There were no University controls at first; the medical faculty made policy and financed it through tuition. In the 1890's the school became a four-year college and moved to Parnassus Heights. There it was given 13.5 acres by Adolph Sutro, an early banker and real estate 1954. This development was opposed by some of the station's scientists who thought that their work might become restricted by the expansion; but they agreed ultimately with Provost-Emeritus Gordon S. Watkins, the fourteenth son of a Welsh coal miner, the architect of the new policy, who insisted that Riverside was destined for growth and should control it.

holder who owned most of the slopes north of Twin Peaks.

The Legislature paid for new buildings, and the University placed medicine, dentistry, and pharmacy on the heights overlooking the Bay on one side. The shaggy, fragrant eucalyptus trees that Sutro had seeded were on the other. By 1902, it became clear that the medical faculty would be unable to finance the school they had planned, and the Regents assumed full control; they turned the campus' main building into an out-patient clinic and hospital. Both of these were necessary for the school, it developed, after the earthquake and fire of 1906. In 1915, the trustees of Hahnemann Medical College of the Pacific voted to join it to the University, which, for its part, added homeopathy to its curriculum and began to use the hospital, a San Francisco institution for many years. The University also soon added nursing, biochemistry, and pharmacology to its curriculum, and by 1919 it had gifts of $750,000 with which it was able

U.C. San Francisco: The Schools of Medicine, Dentistry, Nursing, and the Langley Porter Psychiatric Institute

to construct a new hospital building. Langley Porter Clinic, named for a San Francisco pediatrician, is used for research and treatment of mental illness. It is operated jointly with the state.

UCSF's major research institutes are: the Cardiovascular Research Institute, the Hooper Foundation, which works in epidemiology, the Cancer Research Institute, the Proctor Foundation, the Hormone Research Laboratory, the Langley Porter Psychiatric Institute, the Metabolic Research Unit, the Laboratory of Radiobiology, and the Reproductive Endrocrinology Center, and several international exchange programs.

There are two general acute-care hospitals (soon to be merged into one), and an Ambulatory Care Center. The campus has affiliated programs with 150 institutions throughout California, the largest being at San Francisco General Hospital Medical Center and at the Veteran's Administration Hospital Medical Center in San Francisco.

In a recent survey of peer opinion, the School of Medicine was ranked among the top three in the United States. It was first in the National Institutes of Health's funding for research and teaching. Other recent surveys have ranked the School of Pharmacy first in the country and the School of Nursing third.

Only one-fourth of UCSF's $285 million annual budget (1981 figures) comes from state funds. Approximately one-fourth comes from federal grants, one-fourth from the teaching hospital, and one-fourth from bequests.

With over 1,200 professionals, UCSF is one of San Francisco's largest employers.

UCSF provides care for 20,000 inpatients annually and care for 600 psychiatric inpatients at the Langley Porter Psychiatric Institute. Its outpatient service is one of the largest in California, serving more than 300,000 patients in medicine, surgery, dentistry, and psychiatry.

UCSF has earned an international reputation as a biomedical research center. Major research accomplishments have been in the fields of: cardiovascular disease and cardiac surgery, cancer, genetic diseases, brain tumors (UCSF has the nation's only brain tumor research center), liver disease, neurobiological sciences, prenatal, infant, and child maternal care, hormones, endrocinology, and metabolic diseases, oral cancer, cleft palate rehabilitation and reconstructive surgery for orofacial anomalies.

Tours of UCSF

General public tours are offered every Tuesday (except holidays). The walking tour starts at the Information/Visitor Center in the lobby of the Medical Sciences Building, 513 Parnassus Avenue, San Francisco, at 1:00 p.m. The tour terminates at the same location at 2:30 p.m. Student and special group tours are also available for community groups, health professionals, foreign visitors, and entering students. There is a shuttle bus which runs between the Berkeley and San Francisco campuses. Call the Visitor's Centers of either campus for more information.

A series of noon-time programs is offered each Wednesday until 1:00 p.m. for visitors. The programs cover common health problems in such fields as arthritis, obesity, diabetes, hypnosis, cancer research, human sexuality, and medical ethics. Visitors are encouraged to bring their lunch for the program. For subjects and location, telephone (415) 666-4394, or write to: UCSF Campus Tours, University of California San Francisco, San Francisco, California 94143.

The UCSF Visitor/Information Center is in the lobby of the Medical Sciences Building. The Center has campus and San Francisco maps, as well as public transportation information. White courtesy phones are placed at each major campus building entrance which provide direct access to the Center for assistance. For weekend and evening campus events, call (415) 666-2119 from off-campus after 5 p.m., or from extension 2119 on the campus.

Speakers' Bureau

Speakers from UCSF faculty and staff are available to address community groups and schools on health science topics and on current research, teaching, and patient-care programs at UCSF. Interested groups should contact the UCSF Speakers' Bureau, University of California, San Francisco, San Francisco, California 94143. Telephone (415) 666-4394.

Santa Barbara (UCSB)

The University acquired a state college in Santa Barbara, and in 1954 moved it into a 408-acre former Marine base near the municipal airport at Goleta, 12 miles north of the city. Students moved into barracks while the campus was being installed into the abandoned military structures and two new buildings, one a library, the other a research and training center.

U.C. Santa Barbara

By U.C. standards, Santa Barbara ranks as a "medium-sized" campus, with its 15,431 students in 1980. The 815-acre campus, at the foot of the Santa Ynez Mountains on the beach of Goleta, has an almost country-club atmosphere and refreshing sea breeze.

U.C.'s Santa Barbara campus became internationally famous in 1970 when its students rioted in protest of American involvement in Southeast Asia. The world heard of Santa Barbara again in 1972 when a massive oil spill struck the coast.

Santa Barbara is noted for its School of Education and for its comprehensive undergraduate program in engineering. It has the nation's only Master's Degree program in scientific instrumentation and offers one of the most comprehensive environmental studies majors in the nation. This latter program was inspired by the 1972 oil spill. UCSB publishes a journal of undergraduate research and writing called "Discovery." A marine sciences program includes fifty researchers working in a dozen specialized disciplines, ranging from microscopic plankton to underwater earthquakes.

Special campus resources include: the Marine Science Institute, the Center for Chicano Studies, the Computer Sytems Laboratory, the Institute of Environmental Stress, the Institute of Religious Studies, the Social Processes Research Institute, the Quantum Institute, and the Computer Systems Laboratory.

Santa Barbara headquarters the University's offices for its foreign study programs. The Education Abroad Program administrates programs in 15 countries in association with 39 universities in Europe, the Middle East, Africa, Latin America, and the Far East.

San Diego (UCSD)

U.C. San Diego, formerly known as the Scripps Institute of Marine Biology, originated in 1912, when zoologists at Berkeley, seeking to establish a marine station on the Pacific Ocean chose La Jolla, the present campus of U.C. San Diego. Land was given to the Institute by Mr. E. W. Scripps and by Miss E. B. Scripps, who also founded Scripps College, one of the Claremont Colleges, 120 miles northeast of La Jolla.

The first faculty appointment was made in 1957 when the Legislature authorized the creation of a campus at La Jolla in response to the projected expanding enrollment. The emphasis on graduate work in science, technology, and engineering resulted from the special needs of the San Diego civic and industrial community. In 1960 the Regents selected the University of California, San Diego, as the offical campus name. The School of Medicine was established in 1968.

U.C. San Diego

The 1,200-acre campus is located on a bluff overlooking the Pacific Ocean, and is wooded with fragrant eucalyptus trees. Much of the land was purchased with a $1 million grant from the General Dynamics Corporation, whose Atomic Laboratory is nearby. La Jolla (Spanish for "jewel") is a suburban beach community thirteen miles north of the center of San Diego. Both San Diego and Santa Cruz are unique among the U.C. system in that they both have a system of independent cluster colleges, modelled on Oxford University, in which each college has its own particular emphasis. San Diego has four such colleges: Revelle, John Muir, Third College, and Earl Warren. They offer similar subjects, but differ substantially in educational philosophy.

The Scripps Institution of Oceanography is internationally known as a center of research and teaching. Other special resources include: the Institute of Marine Resources, the Center for Developmental Biology, the Energy Center, the Center for Human Information Processing, the Center for Music Experiment and Related Research, and the Institute for Pure and Applied Physics. San Diego does not exclusively teach the sciences, however. There are strong programs in economics, history, languages, linguistics, literature, philosophy, and psychology.

Santa Cruz (UCSC)
In 1957, it became clear to the University that the effects of the baby-boom of the 1950's would severely strain the facilities of the Berkeley campus. In that year, the Regents selected the south central coast counties area as a suitable location for a new campus which would relieve some of the strain at Berkeley. In 1961, the 2,000-acre Cowell Ranch, overlooking Monterey Bay, was donated to the University for the new campus.

In 1962, architect John C. Warnecke and landscape architect Thomas D. Church were selected as planners. They chose the present Spanish-style architecture to blend with that found in the historic Monterey Bay region, which was the Mexican capital of California.

In 1962, the University community established a set of educational principles for Santa Cruz, primarily in response to agitations of students who were seeking reform in the traditional educational structure. The following seven principles were settled on for Santa Cruz: 1) The "college" (in the Oxford sense) as the basic unit of planning and of student and faculty identification; 2) initial concentration on undergraduate liberal arts education; 3) the residential nature of the campus; 4) early distinction in the arts and sciences; 5) a restricted curriculum, designed to serve the needs of students, instead of those of the faculty; 6) stress on tutorials, seminars, and independent study; and 7) a sports program on an intramural basis, de-emphasizing the traditional competitive aspects of the University.

Santa Cruz is composed of eight independent colleges where students may cross-enroll to gain different academic emphases: Cowell, Stevenson, Crown, Merrill, Benjamin F. Porter, Kresge, Oakes, and College Eight. There is also a graduate division. The grading system at Santa Cruz is unique in that it stresses the development of the individual over the institution. Accordingly, a narrative evaluation system was instituted, replacing the traditional letter grading system. Letter grades are offered on request, and are assigned in upper divsion science courses. Eighty percent of Santa Cruz graduates who apply to graduate and professional schools are accepted by such schools.

Santa Cruz is one of the most beautiful of the nine campuses; it is nestled among tall redwood groves which punctuate rolling farmland overlooking Monterey Bay. Cows still roam the foothills at the entrance to the campus, which is patrolled by police on horseback.

The Santa Cruz Campus

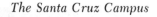

The Irvine Campus

Irvine (UCI)

Opened in the fall of 1965, Irvine is one of the smaller campuses, with 10,286 students in 1980. Irvine occupies 1,510 acres above Newport Bay, 40 miles south of Los Angeles on property given to the University adjacent to the Irvine Beach.

Irvine has three professional schools; the Graduate School of Administration, the School of Engineering, and the College of Medicine. The school for Criticism and Theory, a national summer program in literary criticism, attracts students from all over the United States.

Irvine's special resources include the Institute of Transportation Studies (with Berkeley), the Center for Pathobiology, the Public Policy Research Organization, the Alcohol Research Center, and the Fine Arts Village.

Other Divisions

Los Alamos National Scientific Laboratory

This site was the Los Alamos Ranch for Boys until 1943, when the University, acting for the Atomic Energy Commission under the Manhattan Project, took control of its 48,700 acres in order to develop the most powerful force in the history of man. During World War II, it was one of the world's largest secret laboratories and testing grounds. In the pre-dawn hours of July 16, 1945, its scientists were at Alamagordo, New Mexico. There they saw the dark sky aflame with the world's first nuclear fission bomb, which they had helped to create.

After the war, the University continued to control research at Los Alamos, but did so under the terms of the McMahon Atomic Energy Act of 1946. The Atomic Energy Commission prepared atomic tests on the laboratory's land near Las Vegas, and in the succeeding years it continued to use the site for underground testing of atomic weapons. The University has worked intensively here on peacetime uses of atomic energy. It produced the first controlled thermonuclear reaction at Los Alamos in 1958. Among other achievements at the laboratory were the first homogeneous reactor, fast reactor, visible plutonium, neutrino detection, conversion of nuclear heat to electric power, use of uranium phosphate in reactors, and fueling reactors with molten plutonium. All of Los Alamos' 13,000 people are in some way associated with the laboratory, where more than 3,200 of them are employed.

Mount Hamilton

James Lick lived the complete century beginning 1796. He was a powerful man, spare, with a craggy face, and black-bearded. He moved from his native Fredericksburg, Pennsylvania, to Buenos Aires, and then in 1847 to San Francisco. He preceeded the gold rush by one year and succeeded in making at least $3 million as merchant to the immigrants. During the course of his career he sold a number of things: flour, pianos, timber, and land.

Lick was not well during the 1870's. One day when he was sick and bored he received a visitor from the California Academy of Sciences. He had given the Academy a small lot on Market Street in

San Francisco, and one of its professors wanted to thank him. The professor bought a small telescope. With it, he said, Lick could amuse himself by looking at the heavens through his two north windows. Lick, fascinated, could scarcely stop looking at the magnified heavens; and soon he decided to build an observatory.

He wanted it to be on Market Street. Astronomers raised such an uproar, claiming that an urban telescope was out of the question, that he proposed another site: the hillside over his farm in Santa Clara County. Again, the scientists told him they would need fogless skies. Then Lick, after hiring and firing assorted trustees, and choosing and unchoosing sites, made a will designating $1.2 million for the observatory and "the world's largest and most powerful telescope." (The will also left $60,000 for a memorial to Francis Scott Key, $1000,000 for a statue of three historical California epochs that he wanted in front of San Francisco's City Hall, $100,000 for an "Old Ladies Home," $150,000 for free public baths, and $450,000 for a California Institute of Mechanical Arts.)

These were not his first choices. "Mr. Lick's own idea," wrote the editor of the *Overland Monthly* afterward, "from which he was dissuaded with difficulty, was to build a marble pyramid, bigger than those of Egypt, in his memory."

The observatory was decisively planned for Mount Hamilton (4,209 feet above sea level, 90 miles southwest of Berkeley) when Lick lay on his deathbed. The mountain became his pyramid. His body was buried in the base of the pier of the great telescope.

Land for the project was assembled from a number of owners: chiefly the U.S. government, and also the State of California and private donors including Lick. There are more than 3,000 acres. The main building has offices, computing rooms, a library of 14,000 books, and the great domes for the 36-inch Equatorial and the 12-inch Equatorial. Under the bigger telescope there is a moveable floor that was the first of its kind; it brings the observer within reach and eyesight of the telescope's elevation. The refractor's magnifying power may be changed from 270 times. The Observatory also has a 20-inch astrographic telescope with a focal length of 12 feet. Its newest and largest instrument is a 120-inch reflecting telescope, the sixth at the station, and second in the world only to Mount Palomar's. It was built at a cost of $2.8 million. Its largest accessory is a semi-subterranean spectograph.

Soon after the Observatory was opened one of its directors, Professor Edward E. Barnard, discovered Jupiter's fifth moon. (Galileo discovered the first four in 1610.) Since Barnard's success, the Observatory has racked up many others: additional satellites of Jupiter, many comets, and thousands of visual double stars. It studied planetary and irregular gaseous nebulae, and the dimensions of the earth's galaxy, and with light-absorbing materials that make objects around the Milky Way seem fainter than expected. Mount Hamilton's scientists, working in an almost ideal climate for star gazing, have a long-range project in which they are trying to find the radial velocities of all of the brighter stars. The Observatory has a corresponding branch, the D. O. Mills Observatory in Santiago, Chile, which enables its scientists to observe astral events of the southern hemisphere.

Lick Observatory is open to the public every day but Sunday.

AFFILIATED UNITS OF SAN FRANCISCO

Hastings College of Law

Serranus Clinton Hastings was a New Yorker who was the principal of an academy at 20 and a midwestern lawyer running for the Iowa Legislature at 24. That was 1838. He won. He became a Congressman, served beside Lincoln and Douglas, and at 33 became Chief Justice of the Supreme Court of Iowa. But he saw no future in that and quit a year later. He moved overland to California where he was elected a legislator again, and where by the end of his term in 1851 he had become attorney general of the state. Hastings was a banker during the gold rush. He became rich. He went back to politics and was elected California's first Chief Justice of the State Supreme Court.

Hastings' talents in education, money-making, politics, and the law brought the Regents of the University to his side. They asked him how they might help to break the apprenticeship system by which lawyers were made in those days, and how to install formal education instead. He had a simple method: he would buy them a school. He insisted, however, that the school have its own board of directors headed by the Chief Justice of the State, and that its dean be an ex-officio member of the University faculty. They agreed. He gave them $100,000. They assigned the school an annual appropriation of $7,000.

Then Judge Hastings jolted his profession. He insisted that the school train good students who had no money. Lawyers attacked him with charges that he wanted to cheapen their work. He con-

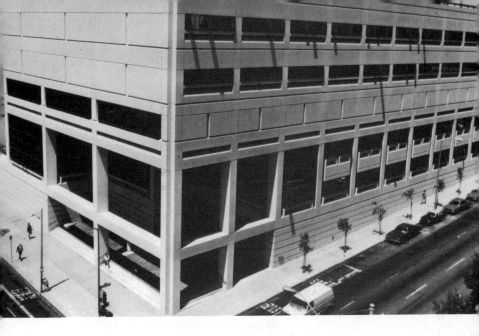

Hastings College of the Law

vinced the Legislature to keep its contract with him, though, and became the first dean of the school. His two sons succeeded him after he retired in 1885. "The desire of the founder," he announced, "is to diffuse a knowledge of the great principles of jurisprudence, not only among those who propose to devote themselves to the noble profession of the law, but also among all classes of society. . . . Without this, civilized government cannot exist."

His principles stuck. They are the reason that Hastings College of the Law, 198 McAllister Street, San Francisco, possesses one of the most remarkably accomplished faculties in the history of American law. This faculty was organized by David E. Snodgrass, a former dean. Its regulations are that no full-time member of the faculty may be less than 65. The provision has enabled it to enlist dozens of men who have reached international eminence at other institutions, but who are nonetheless retired by them because of regulations that separate age from talent. Although the part-time teaching staff is comprised of younger members of the San Francisco Bar, the full-time one has a median age above 72; and yet it has a vigor and skill that led Roscoe Pound, Dean Emeritus of Law at Harvard University, to characterize it as "the strongest law faculty in the country."

The 65-Club, as it has been called, first became possible in 1940, when Dean Snodgrass succeeded William M. Simmons. Snodgrass then became the faculty's only full professor as well as its dean; the

College had fewer faculty members than were required for accreda-
tion. Simultaneously, Snodgrass learned that Orrin K. McMurray,
Dean of Law at Boalt Hall, on the University's Berkeley campus,
had been compelled to retire. McMurray was 67; the retirement
rule that stopped him in Berkeley could not affect him at Hastings,
whose attachment to the University, by the original demand of
Judge Hastings on the Regents, was incomplete. Afterward the 65-
Club recruited some of the best unemployed legal talent in the
country. Many were in their 70's and 80's but had been deans and
full professors and had written the standard texts of the legal world.

Hastings College has been moved more than 15 times since it was
founded. In 1953, it occupied its own $1,750,000, glass-sheathed
building. Recently a new law center has been established in a refur-
bished building across from the building at 198 McAllister Street,
which borders on Golden Gate Avenue; this has expanded Hastings'
capacity to the point where it can now claim to have the third largest law class in the United States. (Harvard and the University of
Texas at Austin are larger.)

San Francisco Art Institute

The Civil War uprooted many American artists; many chose to become rootless after it. San Francisco, forming in violence, attracted
them; it was excessive, tolerant, and dramatic. Some of these artists
formed an association there in 1871. Most of them had jobs and no
place to draw; they agreed to work for an art school and museum.

The California School of Design held its first classes in 1874. It
taught drawing, painting, and sculpture. It rented rooms for 20
years, and in 1893 occupied the former mansion of Mark Hopkins,
the railroad millionaire, on Nob hill. Edward Searles gave the
building to the University so that the Association could teach "the
fine arts, music, and literature." But the Mark Hopkins Institute of
Art was destroyed by the fire and earthquake of 1906.

The association's art collection, gained by gifts and purchases,
went on display at the Panama-Pacific Exposition of 1915. It was
kept in the Palace of Fine Arts, a structure that was intended to be
temporary that was designed by Bernard Maybeck for the exposition. These pictures became the core of the San Francisco Museum
of Art when it was opened in the Civic Center in 1935. The school,
having moved to 800 Chestnut Street in San Francisco in 1926,
became known as the California School of Fine Arts, and in 1961, it
was renamed the San Francisco Art Institute. Fine work and many

famous artists appear in it regularly.

The school has become identified with abstract expressionism since Hans Hofmann taught at the University in the 1930's, but accommodates many shades of art, sculpture, and ceramics.

OTHER FIELD STATIONS AND MAJOR LABORATORIES

Radio Astronomy Laboratory

At Hat Creek, Shasta County, California, the University has been using and developing the relatively new branch of astronomy in which heavenly messages that take the form of radio waves are received and analyzed. It maintains an 85-foot radio telescope that was financed on its land in 1956 by the Office of Naval Research. This instrument is a bowl-shaped antenna; it is one of the largest of its kind in the United States (although about one-third the size of counterparts in Australia and England), and has supplemented visual telescopes in clarifying hypotheses relating to the birth of stars and the tendencies of nebulae.

Presently, the University is involved in a project in Hawaii to construct the world's largest telescope, scheduled for completion in 1984.

Naval Biological Laboratory, Oakland

The staff of this laboratory is comprised of civilian and naval personnel whose research is directed by the University through the School of Public Health; it was organized to study highly infectious diseases affecting the Navy, particularly those that are air-borne. Its disciplines include physiology, biochemistry, biophysics, and genetics. Members of this laboratory design, engineer, and build many of the precision instruments used in it for the special study of microorganisms. During World War II, the Laboratory tested biological and chemical warfare techniques developed at the lab in San Francisco Bay.

Richmond Field Station

The work of this large center is research in engineering and forestry. It includes a division of the Hydraulic Engineering Laboratory, most of which is situated in Hesse Hall, Berkeley Campus. There Hydraulic Engineering maintains a model basin for the study of rivers, harbors, waves, winds, tides, and sediments. Forestry studies such problems as how California's six million feet of hardwoods—tan oak, black oak, madrone, chinquapin and others—may be used.

Another laboratory at Richmond is for research in soil mechanics and bituminous materials: soil properties, mechanics, foundation engineering, and the behavior and properties of asphalts and asphaltic mixtures. Faculty members of the Department of Civil Engineering and of the Institute of Transportation Studies research in it.

The Sea Water Conversion Laboratory is also at Richmond. Its scientists are slowly bringing down the cost of conversion within economic bounds.

There are other laboratories: Air Pollution, Algae, Institute of Transportation and Traffic Studies, Institute of Engineering Research, Highway Patrol Testing, Sanitary, and Waves.

White Mountain Research Station (Mono County)
Here, scientists are studying nature and men at high altitudes.

Bodega Bay
The station here includes 320 acres for the study of marine biology, and for summer classes in invertebrate animals, marine plants, and fishes.

Agricultural Field Stations
Antelope Valley County; Deciduous fruit, Santa Clara County; Hopland, Mendocino County; Imperial Valley, Imperial County; Sierra Foothill Range, Yuba County; South Coast, Orange County; Tulelake, Siskiyou County; West Side, Fresno County.

Department Experimental Areas
Blodgett Forest, El Dorado County; Lindcove, at Riverside; Napa Experimental Vineyard, Napa County; Wolksill Experimental Orchards, Solano County; Boyd Desert Research Center, Orange County.

BERKELEY

(Alt. 0-1,300, pop. 111,500)

José, the son to whom Don Luis Peralta gave the northernmost part of the Rancho San Antonio, went with a brother in 1818 to the bank of a stream running through the property. There, he wrote later, they found a nest of quail's eggs (*cordorniz*, "quail"). "We ate the eggs and called the creek Codornices Creek," he wrote. In 1841, he built an adobe, the first house in Berkeley, near that place.

Eleven years later, squatters were claiming most of the region. They asserted rights of lease, purchase, and occupancy. The Treaty of Guadualupe Hidalgo, which ended the Mexican War, guaranteed the legality of Mexican land grants, but it could not prevent claimants from glutting the courts and so putting justice aside. The four Peralta brothers sold their inheritance, always under the pressure of squatters. They of course gained more than the Costanoan Indians had from Don Luis Peralta.

Although much East Bay land changed ownership through false surveys and harassing raids on cattle, houses, and persons, the site of Berkeley was transferred into Yankee hands through the legal payment of $8,200. A settlement at the Bay caused a need for a stagecoach to Oakland by 1852. Most East Bay towns grew from the waystations of this line, which was the future San Pablo Avenue. One of them north of Oakland was Jacob's Landing, where a sea captain began a ferry and freight service. The place named for him became Ocean View. It was the origin of Berkeley, into which it was later absorbed. It boasted such businesses as Captain Jacob's, a grocery owned by a retired sea captain named W. F. Bowen; and a starch and wheat factory that was moved from San Francisco because the water it needed had to be imported from Sausalito for $1 for 250 gallons. Thus the shoreline was first to be developed.

Berkeley's hillside area was established when the College of California, having been developed for six years in Oakland, became surrounded by an urban community that seemed inimical to quiet scholarship. In 1856, the College's first teacher and manager, the Reverend Henry Durant, went to Strawberry Creek. He was invited there by its owner, his friend Captain Orrin Simmons, a retired sea captain who had sold his hardware business in San Francisco to settle in the East Bay two years earlier. Durant, according to the quotable Victorian prose of William Carey Jones, a Professor of Jurisprudence who was the University's biographer, was overcome:

"And he came to the spot where . . . rising calmly from the sunlit Bay, the soft green slope ascended, gently at first, and then more abruptly, till it became a rugged storm-worn mountain and then disappeared in the sky. As he gazed upon the glowing landscape he knew he had found it. He had found what he sought through life. Not alone the glory of the material landscape drew from him the cry, 'Eureka, I have found it!' Before him, on that beautiful spring morning, other scenes, invisible save to him, passed before his mental vision . . . Standing on the heights of Berkeley he bade the distant generations 'Hail!' and saw them rising 'demanding life impatient for the skies' from what were then fresh, unbounded wilderness on the shore of the great tranquil sea."

By whatever emotion he was himself convinced, Durant succeeded in logically persuading the trustees of the college that Captain Simmon's land was excellent for a school. They rejected dozens of other proposals (see *University: Plan*); they agreed to negotiate for the land three miles north of Oakland. They made their decision a short time before the state offered to merge its still unorganized university with the college, and so before the College of California officially left Oakland for its new 160-acre campus, it became the University of California.

A regional debate to name the new town followed. Many of the formal suggestions came from Frederick Law Olmsted, the first American landscape architect, who had been hired to plan the campus and some of the streets surrounding it.

What might Berkeley have been called? Olmsted proposed that the name of some great man be used with an English termination. He offered a list of terminations: -burne, -lea, -mead, -mere, -croft,

-wood, -lynne, -cot, -home, -val, -stock. Nobody seemed eager. He tried Spanish. He liked *Verano,* meaning, "summer," because it "is a good name by itself, being significant, so near to the climate of San Francisco, where there is no summer." He also reasoned for *La Cuinza,* which means "the nursery garden" or "place of training," neither of which would have pleased modern students.

After almost two years of labor the naming and planning committee, on May 7, 1866, came in with its report ". . . recommending that there should be scientific streets and literary ways—the streets to run north and south, the ways east and west; that the streets be called in alphabetical order after the names of American men of science, and the ways in like order after American men of letters; that the town shall be called Peralta. The streets, beginning on the east: Audubon (now College Avenue), Bowditch, Choate (now Telegraph Avenue), Dana, Ellsworth, Fulton, Guyot (now Shattuck Avenue), Henry, Inman, John Jay, Kent, Lieber, Mitchell. The ways, beginning on the north: Allston, Bancroft, Channing, Dwight, Everett, Felton, Goodrich, Hawthorne, Irving, Jarvin, Knapp, Lowell, Motley."

There were more names than either ways or streets, it turned out, but the scheme was useful.

Members of the same committee, on May 24, 1866, resumed the more difficult job of naming the town, for there was no support for their suggestion that it be called Peralta. They met in San Francisco in the office of the Reverend Samuel H. Willey, the moving force of the University. They included a founder of the Pacific School of

Religion, a pastor of the first Unitarian Church, pastor of the new school of the Presbyterian Church of Oakland, and some San Francisco bankers and businessmen.

One of these last was Frederick Billings. He was a lawyer who helped the Northern Pacific become transcontinental; the Montana town is named for him. (There is a debate over whether Billings was or was not at this particular meeting. It does not matter.) Somewhere he ran across the line, "Westward the course of empire takes its way." It was appropriate, he thought one day while sitting near Founder's rock, looking at the Golden Gate. It came from the poem, *Prospect of Planting Arts and Learning in America:*

> *There shall be sung another golden age*
> *The rise of empire and of arts*
> *The good and great inspiring epic rage*
> *The wisest heads and noblest hearts.*

> *Not such as Europe breeds in her decay*
> *Such as she bred when fresh and young*
> *When heavenly flame did animate her clay*
> *By future poets shall be sung.*

> *Westward the course of empire takes its way*
> *the four first acts already past*
> *A fifth shall close the drama with the day*
> *Time's noblest offspring is the last.*

The poet was George Berkeley, an eighteenth-century Irish philosopher who once proposed to start a college in Bermuda. "The reformation of manners among the English in our Western plantations and the propagation of the Gospel among the American savages," he wrote, "are two main points of high moment." The English government failed to appropriate the money it had promised him for the school, and so after a long wait in Rhode Island he returned to his home and became Dean of Dromore, then of Derry, then Bishop of Cloyne. His books influenced some of philosophy's greatest minds: Hume, Reid, Kant, and Mill.

The new West Coast college town among the American savages was named for the bishop on May 24, 1866. Afterward, a San Francisco newspaper reminded Californians of another Berkeley, Sir William, British colonial governor of Virginia in 1642. "Thank

God," Sir William once told a Royal Commission, "there are no free schools nor printing presses in Virginia, and I hope we shall not have them these three hundred years; for learning has brought heresy and disobedience and sects into the world, and printing hath divulged them, and libels against the best government. God keep us from both."

The newspaper suggested that a footnote under the name of the town on maps: "This is not Berkeley the Tory, who anathematized free schools and printing presses, but Berkeley, the friend of education, who wrote the famous treatise on tar water."

Development
The founders of the University recognized that Berkeley's plans would affect their own. They hired Frederick Law Olmsted to design both the campus and part of the community around it.

Olmsted proposed winding, tree-shaded streets instead of the usual linear ones forming rectangular blocks. He drew a central axis "in the line of the Golden Gate" to unite Berkeley and its university. Developers used the axis, University Avenue, but almost nothing else of the Olmsted Plan. The physical appearance of Berkeley adjacent to the University was detemined by the amateur planners who laid out that section's streets for homesteading. Westward at the bay shore, Jacob's Landing developed into a community that also used the familiar grid pattern for street-making.

Berkeley incorporated in 1878. It planned a government for its 2,000 people. The first election ballot had farmers and merchants on one side and University faculty and other workingmen on the other. The Workingmen's Ticket won because its supporters, finding few of their people at the polls, went on horseback to round up voters in the hills.

Ferryboats were busy, and horsecars moved along Telegraph Avenue. They took an hour to reach Oakland, and often more because commuting students tipped the cars off tracks. The hazards of transportation drew commuters to the University. Berkeley had 10,000 people by 1894. It developed a character, one important factor of which was the impressive number of churchmen. They came to teach and to serve students and in time influenced government. They permitted no liquor sales within one mile of the University, for example. Later the state legislature enacted this into law for all institutions of higher learning. This caused a clustering of saloons just beyond the limit. It also caused a serious shortage of successful restaurants, which depend on liquor sales for income. Other schools located around the University, whose faculty they often employed part-time. These included a European-style prepratory school called the Berkeley Gymnasium, the Anna Head School and one whose owner, George Bates of Cambridge, claimed it had "a generous cuisine, a . . . feature considered absolutely essential to the well-being of studious and growing youth." But having a full range of private schools caused Berkeley to neglect its public ones. It taught 300 pupils in a two-story frame building in 1882. As late as 1895 a member of the School board could safely demand that all high schools be abandoned. He seems to have won his point temporarily, for the city had no adequate high school until 1901. Within 40 years it developed a high school system nationally famous for the quality of its teaching.

Berkeley underwent sudden growth during the first decade of the twentieth century. The two major causes were Phoebe Apperson Hearst's sponsorship of an international architectural competition for the campus (see *University: Plan*), which both developed and won attention for the University, and the earthquake and fire of 1906, which caused thousands of San Franciscans, or potential San Franciscans, to move to the East Bay. Berkeley's population was 13,214 in 1900. It rose to 40,434 in 1910.

It had a need to control its growth. In 1915, California passed a city planning enabling act. Soon afterward Berkeley appointed an Art Commission headed by Duncan McDuffie, a real estate man. Under the commission's guidance it moved toward becoming a residence suburb forever. It agreed that 25 percent of the owners on the frontage of any street could install one of eight zoning classifications. More than 90 percent of Berkeley's structures were single-family residences at the time. These individual owners usually chose to permit only new occupants like themselves. Ever since, Berkeley has called itself, "The City of Homes."

Berkeley avoided a completely suburban character because there were no residences near the highway, at the old stage routes beside the Bay, when zoning elections were held. There and in industrially specialized Emeryville nearby, manufacturing became established. Between this region and the campus thousands of industrial workers built homes. Many became oriented toward jobs and culture around the rim of the Bay, in Berkeley and elsewhere, rather than toward the University.

The rate of growth persisted through depressions and wars and the major local disaster, a wind-whipped fire that destroyed 130 acres of frame residences and stores in September, 1923. The population of 1910 was redoubled by the 1930's when, surveys showed, the new San Francisco-Oakland Bay Bridge enabled 11,000 Berkeleyans to commute to San Francisco every day. By then each neighborhood had a specific character. Houseowners to the north of the campus were building on the remaining lots of the hills, designing for informal gardens and views of the Bay and San Francisco. Naples was the city to which North Berkeley was most often compared. The older neighborhood to the south of the campus contained many of the larger and more costly houses, particularly on or near Claremont Avenue.

World War II caused an increase of 40 percent of Berkeley's population. People who came to work in burgeoning shipbuilding projects often chose the "City of Homes" if they were employed anywhere in San Francisco or north and south on the industrial ways of the East Bay. In a city of 121,000 people, 50,000 were employed, according to estimates in the early 1950's. More than one-fourth of them worked for the University, and more than one-fifth were classified as professional. Berkeley's educational level and per capita income were among the highest in the state. Still, the 1960 census indicated that Berkeley experienced some of the decentralizing that cheap credit, automobiles, and new highways had caused among cities throughout the country. It population declined, slightly but significantly, to 111,268. While its private enterprise was building for more density around the University, the city was slowly coming to recognize the need of redevelopment elsewhere within its parts; some of its leadership was moving into the valleys beyond the Berkeley Hills, or up the chain of cities off The Arlington: Kensington, El Cerrito, and Richmond. Schools and neighborhoods had declined. The city was physically ready for a new stage of growth, and was approaching psychological readiness.

Government
After the incorporation of its three separate districts—Ocean View or West Berkeley; the Shattuck business district; and Berkeley itself, the region around the University—the city prepared to write its own charter. The motive was to gain a school system. Berkeley met resistance to taxation, however. A strong faction continued from that time onward to resist higher expenditures demanded of them by increased urbanization. In 1895, Berkeley reframed its

charter to increase the tax limit to 75 cents per $100 assessed valuation. Then it began to brood about the possibility of political corruption. Control of state government by railroad owners had generated this feeling among many voters, and later caused the reforms of Hiram Johnson. In Berkeley, it caused the first municipal nonpartisanship government in the United States. This was made possible by a redrafting of the charter by Professor William Carey Jones, Dean of Jurisprudence at the University, in 1909.

Under this charter, policies are determined by a mayor and eight councilmen who receive no salary but are paid for official meetings that they attend. They are elected, and so is an auditor. They appoint a city manager who makes all administrative appointments, five library trustees, and the members of all boards and commissions. The charter also insures the rights of initiative, referendum, and recall. Its present form dates from 1923, when the city manager was installed.

Berkeley, 1958–

Berkeley, a city world famous for its university, has a stereotype attached to it. Although the University itself is widely respected, the City of Berkeley conjures up images of a place where anything goes, where radicalism is not merely tolerated, but is encouraged. The mere mention of Berkeley is enough to stir a vigorous debate at many social gatherings. In fact, the city has come to be so strongly identified with certain social trends that its name is used as an adjective as well as a noun: ". . . that's very 'Berkeley' of you," one might exclaim. Where else but Berkeley could a millionaire heiress, Patty Hearst, be kidnapped by a revolutionary gang, only to convert to her captors' philosophy? When one thinks of Berkeley, one thinks of the original beatniks and their underground culture, of obscure poets and musicians, of Angela Davis and the Black Panthers, of Jerry Rubin and the Yippies, of student unrest, and, of course, of riots. Berkeley, it seems, is synonymous with revolution. "I'm from Berkeley," said one famous bumper-sticker of the 1960's, "but I'm not revolting."

How did a small town (pop. 111,500) accquire this world-wide reputation? Several factors combined to make Berkeley one of the most unique cities in the United States. First, the State of California, with its large and relatively wealthy population, poured money into the University of California, beginning with the influx of students who arrived after World War II. As a result, the University began to attract many of the best professors in America. Students from across the United States and from many foreign countries were also drawn to the University for its unequalled facilities, its scientific research, and its fine humanities programs. But people also came to Berkeley because it seemed to be a center of new ideas.

Social consciousness at Berkeley was fostered at the end of World War II because of the University's leadership in the development of the most destructive force the world had ever known—the atomic bomb. Ernest O. Lawrence, Owen Chamberlain, and J. Robert Oppenheimer were only a few of the Berkeley scientists who helped to make the University either an instrument for progress or for war. Every Berkeley student felt, somehow, profound responsibility for the deaths at Hiroshima and Nagasaki; most became determined to avoid future guilt. A campus famed for its impractical idealism suddenly moved toward political involvement. Students knew that with heavy financial support and cooperation from the federal government, the University had become inextricably linked with the military and with American industry. It was revealed in the early 1960's, for example, that Berkeley economists, political scientists, and administrators had cooperated with the CIA to train government forces in the Indonesian revolution. With this knowledge, the stage was set for a highly socially aware, politically active, and educated community evolving out of a staid, conservative, university town.

At this point, another key American event heightened the political consciousness of Berkeley students. In the late 1950's and 1960's, the Civil Rights Movement rocked the country. It was a period of changing social and cultural values, and many Berkeley students went to the South to participate in voter registration programs for Blacks. They returned from bruising struggles against Southern bigots, exciting Berkeley with a strong commitment to political action. Berkeley students were among the leaders of the fight against racism in Northern California's schools, restaurants, and clubs.

The Berkeley School District, reacting to these changes, became one of the first in the nation to achieve racial integration in its schools. Millions of federal dollars were sent to Berkeley to support experimental educational programs; during the 1960's, flushed with these grants, Berkeley became one of the richest school districts in the United States. The city had incorporated long before in order to gain its own school district. Now it was determined to use this district as a model for the nation. It was able to provide this model chiefly because, unlike most other California cities, its school district covered the entire city and because its people had become largely united in their social aims.

Berkeley's high level of social consciousness was powerfully affected by the Communist Scare of the 1950's. The Board of Regents instituted a Loyalty Oath which required all faculty members to swear that they were patriots at a time when the definition of patriotism had come into question. Many professors resigned from the University rather than permit state intrusions into academic freedom. Thus the Loyalty Oath, which lasted from 1950–56, had a profound impact on Berkeley, politicizing the town to a degree never seen before in its history.

By 1961, the struggle between the left and the right forever changed the character of Berkeley city politics. Downtown business interests, who were Republicans, had controlled the city for over 50 years. Berkeley had awakened to the fact that the "non-partisan" local elections in California chiefly benefited the conservatives. In the wake of this new consciousness a left-wing slate was swept into power in Berkeley's City Council and School Board, demolishing conservative power in Berkeley for the next twenty years.

The extreme left brought a new style to political debate in Berkeley: confrontation. Accusations of racism, which occurred frequently, polarized the community as much as the accusations of Communism did in the 1950's.

The 1961 election also resulted in the establishment of local political parties which stayed alive in between elections. Berkeley Citizens Action, for example, maintained an office all year long. This in itself was unusual in American politics.

Continuing the new trend of radicalism and political activism, Mario Savio and other students led the Free Speech Movement of 1964, which declared Berkeley the harbinger of radicalism in America. Reversing their neutrality, students became activists, protesting the University's dehumanizations, which increased with its growing size. At last, after they seized Sproul Hall, they were suppressed by the armed forces of law enforcement authorities. The State appeared to have won a battle, but it could not win the war. Docility would never again be a characteristic of Berkeley students.

From the Loyalty Oath and the Free Speech Movement onward Berkeley was profoundly affected by political developments. Political consciousness was solidified in Berkeley by the Viet Nam war. Leadership of the community was seized by anti-war protesters, who for the first time in American politics, used local governmental forums to protest national policy. The City Council was asked to endorse resolutions opposing the war in Viet Nam; proponents of the resolutions were refused. In one dramatic event, protesters marched on the Oakland Army Terminal in an attempt to prevent Army troop trains from sending troops to Viet Nam. They were met by a wall of heavily armed Oakland policemen, and some of the most violent riots in America ensued.

Local developments, too, brought about student involvement in politics. In 1969, the University continued its expansion into the City of Berkeley by tearing down a number of houses on University-owned property to make room for research institutes and park-

An incident during the People's Park riots

ing facilities. Students raged at what they perceived as the encroachment of the University on the living space of the town. They demanded the one square block area be preserved as a "People's Park." The "Park" became a symbol of non-conformist resistance to the State. Violent confrontations resulted as the University tried to evict recalcitrant squatters from the property. Governor Ronald Reagan called out the National Guard, but this time the "police action," in contrast to that of the response to the Free Speech Movement five years earlier, was more like a military invasion. Troops bivouacked at the Berkeley dump, from which they flew helicopters to tear gas on protesting students. Tanks and platoons of troops with fixed bayonets and loaded rifles were used to prevent students from camping at People's Park.

But Governor Reagan's success was only temporary. In 1970, People's Park became a staging area for all student protests. Students rallied there to protest the bombing of Cambodia, and American military involvement in Southeast Asia in general. In true

National Guard helicopters, spraying students with tear gas during the disturbances

Students, confronted by bayonet-wielding National Guardsmen who were called out by Governor Reagan

Berkeley form, People's Park was renamed Ho Chi Minh Park to symbolize resistance to the Viet Nam War. These movements established Berkeley as the most political city in America.

Still, despite the image many Americans have of Berkeley, violence was rare in the city. Political debates and community movements are far more prevalent. Nearly every form of social activity in Berkeley became politically tinged. Vegetarianism, Asian religions, Yoga, meditation, martial arts, Feminism, the Gay sub-culture, pop-psychology, art, and even housing in Berkeley are all expressions of distinct political and cultural beliefs. It is safe to say that any new way of life is likely to be pioneered in Berkeley.

A visitor reading local papers will immediately notice hundreds of advertisements for self-help groups (there are over 300 of them in Berkeley, an astounding number for a community its size) and for self-employed writers, artists, musicians, masseurs and masseuses, carpenters, craftsmen, architects, researchers, solar engineers, and teachers of all kinds. Each one of these people considers him or herself to be an innovator and is likely to disclaim interest in material advancement.

These and many other elements make Berkeley a unique community. It is a small town, a place of contradictions and of urban problems. Berkeley is not thought of as being a religious city, but there are one-hundred churches within the city limits. There are forty bookstores in Berkeley, a huge number for a city of 111,500. In addition to the University of California, there are hundreds of educational institutions, ranging from a lively adult education program sponsored by the City of Berkeley, to psychic institutes, to an Open Education Exchange, which is a clearinghouse for independent teachers in all conceivable fields, to drama and art studios, to accupressure and massage workshops. There are artists' collectives, including the influential Berkeley Cooperative, and several others in the South Berkeley area. There are craftspeople who market their work on Telegraph Avenue near the University, making the street a colorful and exciting place. The general air of permissiveness in Berkeley attracts the "Street People," who form a drug culture, and who live in People's Park, undisturbed by the police. "The Avenue," as it is sometimes called, is a fascinating microcosm of Berkeley; academics, students, tourists, artists, and Street People all share the one small place.

Berkeley is afflicted with many urban planning problems. The housing crisis, which is prevalent in many cities, is particularly acute in Berkeley. The University enrolls 30,000 students each year, but provides housing for only 14% of that number. This places a strain on the city and its services. Students have to search for months to find housing, and eventually the latecomers wind up as far away as San Francisco, Oakland, El Cerrito, or Albany. There are many shared houses, where the nuclear family has been replaced by communal-style households of unrelated dwellers. The construction of the Bay Area Rapid Transit (BART) system added to the housing difficulties. Almost no houses have been built to replace the ones torn down during the construction of the system.

Neighborhoods in Berkeley, as they do in many other cities, seem to reflect class divisions. Blue-collar workers chiefly live in the Oceanview and South Berkeley areas. Small factories, laboratories, and repair shops provide jobs for residents of this area. Laborers, one of whose largest segments is that 14 percent of the population which is Black, are removed from the intellectual, largely white middle class community which surrounds the University. But the Black community is relatively active politically, contributing the last two mayors, a county supervisor, and a congressman. Berkeley is not nearly as concentrated with minorities as are neighboring Oakland and Richmond however; these latter two cities now are 60% Black. Berkeley also has many Asians and Latin Americans, which also contribute to an ethnically diverse city. Many people live in Berkeley but work in Oakland and San Francisco. They live in the exclusive Berkeley hills, with spectacular views of the Bay. The Claremont District, south of Ashby Avenue at the base of the hills, contains some of the most expensive and beautiful homes in California.

Public administrators in Berkeley are frustrated by an aloof university which is preoccupied with national and international issues. The University occupies a huge island at the center of the city. It has a tremendous impact on city services, yet it pays no taxes to support these services. The city government is run by a city manager who is employed by the City Council and the Mayor. Though he or she is supposedly non-partisan, the job is inherently political, and the city manager is subject to diverse sets of constituencies; these include the University, the minority community, various neighborhood groups (they are highly organized in Berkeley) and business interests.

If Berkeley were more homogenous, as is true of other suburban communities, the political battles would take on a different character. While proclaiming an altruistic interest in the general welfare of the city as a whole, individual residents oppose changes if they are affected personally. They favor low-cost housing, for example, but they oppose it in their own neighborhood because they want park lands. They oppose shopping malls, but centers such as Walnut Square and the North Berkeley Center are booming. Berkeleyans traditionally resist the establishment of businesses such as banks and department stores which draw outside traffic. Urban congestion, then, is acceptable elsewhere, but not in Berkeley!

Berkeleyans have been accused of being parochial because of their anti-growth attitudes. This is dramatically evident to any motorist, who will notice that the city streets simply are not large enough to accommodate the increased traffic flow. The snarled traffic is paradoxical. Although the city's population has declined in recent years, it has seen a dramatic increase in the number of people coming into the city to take advantage of its many restaurants, specialized shops, (it has the only sake factory outside of Japan, for example) and its varied educational institutions.

Berkeley reacted to the congestion by establishing an anti-automobile policy. It put up barriers to divert traffic from residential neighborhoods, established a network of bicycle lanes, and discouraged the development of public parking.

It remains an open question whether Berkeley will seek to solve its social problems through its confrontational style of politics, or whether it will mature into a system which can resolve its pressing quality-of-life issues. Berkeley will remain unique. It is neither completely suburban, nor is it totally urban. But with its beautiful scenery and weather, its proximity to open space and parks, its fine educational institutions, its excellent public transportation, and its varied culture, it has the feel of a small suburb, and the sophistication of an urban center. Berkeley well deserves its own self-definition, the "Athens of America." Like the ancient Greek democracy, it is full of wonders and innovations, of destructive bickering and creative impulses, of a way of life over which the whole world may marvel.

PLACES OF INTEREST AND IMPORTANCE

Aquatic Park
University Avenue and East Shore Freeway
Built by the WPA in 1935–40, this mile-long lagoon extends to
Ashby Avenue where there are tidal gates to control its water level.
Sailboats are rented here; sailboat lessons are given to children and
adults for fees. Apart from these concessions, there are public
model-yacht contests and miniature sailboat races in the lagoon.
The water is three to fifteen feet deep.

Berkeley Tennis Club
Domingo Avenue and Tunnel Road
Berkeley, a nationally known center of tennis since "Pop" Fuller
trained Helen Willis Moody and Helen Jacobs here, is the site of
the many tournaments. The city has 18 public courts.

Berkeley Marina
The Marina, crowded with sailing and fishing boats, is known for its
fishing pier, which was once used for ferryboats. Fishermen need
no license to fish from it. There is a wide variety of restaurants with
spectacular Bay views.

Botanical Gardens (See University: Plan)

California Schools for the Deaf and Blind
Parker and Warring Streets
This was begun with a school for children whose physical handicaps
disqualified them from public education, but who learned best
when together. Women volunteers chipped in funds for its original
lot in San Francisco; later, by act of the State Legislature, it became
a state organization. It was renamed and moved to Berkeley. In
1875 its $175,000 building was destroyed by fire, and as a precau-
tion the administration redesigned the school into separate structures on one campus. Bartlett Hall was occupied in 1894. In 1980,
the buildings were declared unsafe for blind and deaf children in
the event of an earthquake and the school was closed. The University will take over the site for student housing.

Campanile
(See *University: Plan—Sather Tower*)

Codornices Park
Euclid Avenue and Bayview Place
On a ledge midway up the Berkeley Hills, this park commands fine
views of the Bay and of San Francisco. It also has tennis courts and a
playground; but is famous for the Municipal Rose Garden that
blooms brilliantly, attracting many thousands of people, bees,
humingbirds, and aphids, mostly in late summer and fall. The park
follows the canyon of Codornices Creek.

Community Theater
Civic Center, between Milvia and Grove Streets
Concerts, lectures, readings, and some plays are offered in this
3,500-seat auditorium, which is operated by the Berkeley School
System but is open to the public.

Co-op (Consumers Cooperative of Berkeley, Inc.)
In 1937, members of the University and of church groups organized
to establish a food store. Their policies were the "Rochdale Principles" declared by weavers of Rochdale, England in 1884, and first
practiced in a shop in Toad Lane: "1) open membership, 2) democratic control, 3) sales for cash at prevailing competitive prices, 4)
patronage refunds in proportion to purchases, 5) limited interest on
invested capital, 6) neutrality in politics and religion, and 7) con-
stant education and expansion." The Consumers Cooperative
merged in 1947 with the Berkeley Cooperative Union, which had
been started in 1938, largely by members of Finnish ancestry, and
which was operating a service station and hardware store.
    The Co-op now has nine stores in Berkeley, Oakland, El Cerrito,
Walnut Creek, San Francisco, and Corte Madera in Marin County.
In addition to the food center stores, Co-op offers a wide variety of
consumer services, including a wilderness supply shop, a natural
foods store, a recycling center (for bottles, cans, and newspapers)
hardware-variety stores, service stations, a credit union, an insurance service, a health plan, a book co-op, a pharmacy, a respected
arts and crafts shop, a funeral society, and a legal collective. Con-
sistent with cooperative principles, it also fosters cultural activities
such as classes in arts, languages, and social sciences; lectures and

concerts; and a summer camp. Membership exceeds 120,000, and patronage and patronage refund rate about three percent. The Co-op is therefore one of the few grocery cooperatives to have progressed despite the evolution of competitive supermarket chains, and is an effective social as well as economic activity.

Cragmont Park
Cragmont Avenue at Hilldale Street
This rocky park, formed epochs ago during a subterranean explosion of volcanic ash, has a desert-like beauty. It offers fine views of San Francisco. It surrounds a lookout station that is the site of annual Sunrise Ceremonies at Easter.

Greek Theatre
Campus Drive near Hearst Avenue
(See *University: Plan*)

John Hinkel Park
Southhampton Avenue and San Diego Road
This park is the site of popular performances put on by the Berkeley Shakespearean Festival each summer.

Hotel Claremont
Tunnel Road and Domingo Street
In 1914 an architectural explosion, costly, intricate, and instantly fashionable, was announced open as a hotel. Since then the Claremont, clearly visible from San Francisco, has rivaled the nearest hills, dominating the heights of what may be the wealthiest neighborhood of the East Bay. A landmark grown more important with the years, it has a 20-acre garden and the Berkeley Tennis club at its base; most of the hotel is in Oakland, but it keeps a Berkeley address. The hotel is a residential one, used as a resort and for conferences and for large meetings. It has an Olympic-size pool and its own tennis club. The Terrace Lounge is famous for its panoramic view of the Bay.

International House
(See *University: Plan—Off Campus*)

KPFA
2207 Shattuck Avenue
This uniquely non-commercial radio station (94.1 FM) offers a wide range of programming as well as a series of discussions and interviews daily. Founded in 1949, it has a companion station (KPFB, FM 89.3) and associated ones in Los Angeles and New York. Its listeners finance it.

Live Oak Park
Berryman Street at Shattuck Street
This popular Berkeley city park has a rich and ancient beauty because of a woman who left a Missouri plantation to come west with her husband, four children, mother, sister, and two freed slaves. Some of the oaks east of here were planted at the urging of or by the hand of Mary Byrne; many others, and many other kinds of trees and shrubs, have been planted since. The park has a clubhouse in which Berkeley offers classes ranging from chess to judo; it has freeform play equipment, sandpiles, and a little theater in which young people and adults have play productions.

Indian Rock
San Diego Street near The Arlington
Indian women once ground food in the pits of the rocks of this park; the signs are still visible. The rock is a popular site for both technical and non-technical rock climbing among adults and children. It has a fine view of the Bay.

Pacific School of Religion
1789 Scenic Street (the neighborhood is known in Berkeley as "Holy Hill.")
After Congregationalists helped to begin the University, the American Association of Congregational Churches concluded that a seminary would be of value in California. The Pacific Theological Seminary was opened in San Francisco in 1869, was moved to Seminary Hill, Oakland in 1871, and was moved to Berkeley in 1901. The school, developed out of Berkeley's first church, a nondenominational, Congregationalist-sponsored chapel at Dwight Way and Telegraph, has taught students of many denominations. Its first graduating class included two Methodists, three Congregationalists, and one Baptist. Great men have addressed its membership: James

Bryce, Teddy Roosevelt, Booker T. Washington, and James Henry Breasted among them. It is a graduate school and so has been able to conduct widely respected research into religious questions. It has a Palestine Institute (tours are available) that in recent years has won it particular recognition for their discovery of Biblical places in Israel. To honor a new president in 1939, it gave Palestinian lamps their first flames in more than 3,000 years, thus demonstrating its posssessions and their antiquity.

The school includes the Holbrook Memorial Library, a Gothic structure of gray cut stone having more than 30,000 books, Babylonian cuneiform tablets, the "Breeches" Bible (Geneva, 1560), fourth-century Biblical inscriptions on papyrus, and rubbings of the Nestorian Monument in China.

Tilden Park
(Berkeley—2,065 acres)

Severe water shortages caused the forming of the East Bay Municipal Utilities District in 1922, and within 14 years this led to the East Bay Regional Park System. Tilden Park was named for Major Charles Lee Tilden, one of the first supporters of the park, and was made up of the first 2,200 acres in the system.

Park facilities include: 50 miles of hiking and bridle trails and scenic drives, a nature study area, developed picnic grounds, the Northern California Botanical Gardens (which includes every native species of plants and animals in California), a Junior Museum, Scout camps, fishing, swimming at Lake Anza, the Environmental Education Center, a Nature Area, nature programs and hikes with rangers, naturalists, and geologists, an 18-hole golf course, an historic Merry-Go-Round, a miniature steam railway, an archery range, camping grounds, tennis and volleyball courts, places for social meetings, places for weddings, play fields, equestrian trails, and horse shoe pits. Its meeting place, the Brazilian Room, is so called because it was originally Brazil's exhibit at the Exposition and Fair on Treasure Island in 1939.

The Little Farm

This miniature barn and corral were built in 1955 by the Vocational Carpentry Class at Berkeley High School with materials provided by the Berkeley Kiwanis club. The barn is 5/8 the size of real barns and is worked in the same way that they are. It has Mexican burros, sheep, a pig, goats, rabbits, pigeons, chickens, geese, and peacocks. The naturalist is almost always nearby to answer questions. His cabin is to the left of the farm.

Nature Trail

Beginning near the Nature Area, the trail follows Wildcat Creek for one-half mile through foothill chaparral to Jewel Lake across the bridge at the end of the lake, and back to the main entrance. At several places it branches off and affords side trips over more rugged terrain. At the start of the trail are bay trees. They give moist shade for a section called Fern Glen, where there are wood ferns, sword ferns, and bracken ferns at the end of the section. The wood and sword ferns are evergreen; the bracken is not. Oaks and madrones are farther up the trail.

Jewel Lake

This small lake has many forms of waterlife—cattails, ducks, turtles, fish, and frogs. Ducks, particularly mallards, are common, and are eager to be fed. The lake is covered with duckweed, and they dive for underwater plants and insects. Mallards are not among the divers, but they do take an occasional dips to feed off the bottom of the shallow lake. In early spring red-winged blackbirds build nests in the cattails. At sundown they come in great flocks to spend the night, offering a brilliant evening sight until winter begins.

Jewel Lake Meadow

The clover meadow near the lake is a feeding place of birds and other animals: deer, quail, flickers, sparrows, and raccoons. They may be seen from the nearby eucalyptus grove.

Woodland Camp

This small region is reserved for groups of children. It is large enough for 150. It has washrooms, drinking fountains, fireplaces, and tables in the rough. It and other campus in Tilden Regional Park may be reserved for groups at the park office.

Wildcat Peak

There are 10 miles of untamed land between the road and the peaks. The trail begins near Jewel Lake and goes up the mountainside for 1.5 miles. There, it offers a magnificent view of San Francisco, the Bay, and the bridges. To the southeast, Mt. Diablo is visible, as is the San Pablo reservoir north-east of the Peak. On extremely clear days hikers can see the Sierra Nevadas. The fire trail at the base of Wildcat Peak is a popular spot for runners.

Cricket (Miniature Train)

At the end of the main road in Tilden Park to the south there is a narrow-gauge railway that has survived occasional bad weather, landslides, and adults: it consumes coal at the rate of one-quarter ton a month, breathes smoke, and pulls hundreds of children and some older ones around a scenic route having views of San Pablo Bay and Wildcat Canyon. Then it draws realistically into a miniature station where there are refreshments.

The Cricket was designed and built by Erich Thomsen when he was a young mechanical engineer for the Western Pacific Railroad in 1952. Thomsen bought a chassis and boiler from a locomotive builder and made the Cricket's Victorian stack himself. The rail is 12-pound flat-bottomed, making a double-loop line, known as the Tilden, South Gate and Pacific Railway.

ARCHITECTURE

These are historical elements of East Bay architecture:

SPANISH-AMERICAN

The adobe was the most influential style of the Spanish-Mexican period. The word, which comes from the Egyptian through the Arabic and Spanish, refers to the fine-grained, black soil that can be mixed into a thick, sticky paste and baked under sunlight. The Spanish and Mexicans made adobe by spading, or more often having Indians spade, level places near creeks, and by tramping straw binder into the mud before shaping blocks of it. They used about 1,000 blocks in a small one-room house. In the two counties of the East Bay, the Spanish and Mexicans built 182 adobe houses and church buildings, mostly in 1777–78 and at the end of the Mexican rule. Surveyors in 1942 found 20 of them still standing. The designs were simple; the occupants were usually the builders and architects too. Most adobes were built squarely on the earth, without foundations. Better structures that had foundations, though, were given style by the arrangement of supporting rocks in adobe cement, and by grillwork in front. Their builders often widened the eaves to throw shade and to keep rain from washing the adobe away.

MONTEREY COLONIAL

A Boston merchant, Thomas Oliver Larkin joined the Spanish Colonial and Yankee styles, and so created a uniquely California house. His plan, built in Monterey in 1835, included two rooms on either side of a central passageway, in the manner of American Colonial houses. The redwood frame carried a second story for which there was an interior staircase. The house had a double veranda and a hipped, shingled roof, which, in later Monterey Colonials, was tiled.

BALLOON AND WESTERN PLATFORM FRAME

Builders who used multiple studs instead of heavy, widely spaced posts during the Civil War were making houses that would "blow away like balloons in the wind," their more conservative colleagues said. But the innovation, made possible by the development of the nail, distributed weight and stress at many points throughout the frame. It proved as durable a method as any its critics were using. A modification of the balloon frame was the western platform frame. Its studs ended at each floor level.

CLASSICAL REVIVALS

Successful '49ers recalled, when they had safely stowed their fortunes, that Greek and Roman buildings characterized the most cultured families of the South and East. Many of their architects had recently come from Europe, where eclecticism, or revivalism, was important to the design of residences for the last two-thirds of the nineteenth century, beginning with England's Sir John Soane in the 1820's. California's builders closely followed and slightly modified the patterns of the East, which took its styles from Europe. In the East Bay, many houses built much later were given stray classical elements whose fashion began about 1790 and lasted at least until

1860, when a Romanesque revival gave way to Italianate and then French designs.

BOARD-AND-BATTEN

A triad of boards, when nailed to a frame, affords great strength. Series of them will support a house. Pioneers used the simple board-and-batten method often, and in Berkeley as late as 1920. The term survives: there is a kind of exterior siding popular in the East Bay in which two boards are placed parallel to one another, and a batten over their seam.

"ELIZABETHAN"

For 30 years beginning about 1880, the Bay Area adapted a number of specifically English forms to its own needs, terrain, and materials. Two of the most important of them were the Queen Anne and the Eastlake.

The Queen Anne was given its name during the late 1870's. It referred to the English ruler of the early eighteenth century. It was, however, an English cottage form of Elizabeth I's day in California shingles. An influential American architect named Henry Hobson Richardson brought it to Staten Island, and it was widely copied in California. Its plan is asymmetrical. It has small-paned windows, including bay windows (*oriels*), and gabled Dutch roofs. Its most characteristic feature is a round tower.

The Eastlake Cottage was developed in the East Bay simultaneously with the Queen Anne, while there were Gothic and Romanesque revivals roughly from 1875–1900. It evolved into what is often called the San Francisco Style. Its survivals remain as prominent as a cartoon built on a painstakingly drawn landscape; it is the "row house" commonly built in San Francisco during the early twentieth century. The most prominent feature of the design is the wide bay window that overlooks the street—and other wide bay windows. Beginning as projecting rectangles, this bay became substantial and involved, and is associated with extensive millwork ranging from delicate to ponderous on the same house, in columns, balustrades, and pediments.

When he saw pictures of the Bay Area houses whose design bore his name, Sir Charles Eastlake of London sputtered, "I now find, to my amazement, that there exists on the other side of the Atlantic an 'Eastlake Style' of architecture, which, judging from the (California) specimens I have seen illustrated, may be said to burlesque such doctrines of art as I have ventured to maintain . . ." But however less than architecturally pure, the East Bay's Eastlake Cottages have a character and serviceability unmatched by many other styles.

"MEDITERRANEAN"

Houses similar to those in Spain were thought in the 1890's to be the means by which California could express its colonial past. This desire came to include architectural fashions from other Mediterranean countries, for many Californians thought, too, that Mediterranean solutions were completely adaptable to the West Coast. A low, symmetrical house made of adobe, with projecting end beams and terraced roofs was one result.

CALIFORNIA BUNGALOW
"Early Berkeley"

The source of the word bungalow is *bengali*, a tent that British colonial administrators used in the Far East. The British placed their tents on raised foundations to cause a flow of air. The California bungalow is similarly often raised and then covered with shingles or board-and batten. Its materials are usually natural ones, with natural finishes. In this and other ways the bungalow proved adaptable to California's climate and terrain.

In Berkeley, the simple, informal bungalow attracted Bernard Maybeck, an architect whose personal history was the source of the style of architecture called "Early Berkeley." His father came from Germany in 1848 and became a woodcarver in New York. His mother died before he was three. She wished him to be an artist. His father made him draw, study philosophy, and languages, and when he was 17 apprenticed him to a woodcarver on Broadway in

Maybeck went to Paris to become a furniture designer and there, passing the *Ecole des Beaux Arts*, saw, he later wrote, a model for the rest of his life, "a wonderful individual who was wearing a pot hat and gloves. He was an architect." The young American eventually enrolled in the school, became an architect himself, and returned home to work in Florida, Missouri, and then California. After substantial designing in San Francisco he joined the faculty of the University of California, where, because there was no school of architecture, he taught drawing.

Maybeck's chance to return to architecture occurred when, in 1894, Mrs. Phoebe Apperson Hearst offered the University a building in memory of her husband, a gold, silver, and antimony miner who had also been a U.S. Senator. Within minutes after she left his office the University's president, Martin Kellogg, was asking Maybeck, the only architect he knew on the campus, to produce a sketch. The sketch was on Kellogg's desk the next day. Mrs. Hearst accepted it (although it was never built), and was so impressed that she later commissioned Maybeck to advise an international competition for the design of the Berkeley campus. (See *University: Plan*.)

In time, Maybeck planned and often personally built dozens of houses in the East Bay. He used local materials, allowing them to weather naturally and to be seen under light which he sculptured with narrow windows, arabesques, and massive plants. Exposing textures and shapes previously hidden, he asserted values which remain implicit in his region today. When he died in 1957, Maybeck was 95. He had become a major influence on California architecture during his own lifetime.

AN ARCHITECTURAL TOUR

Many visitors to Berkeley enjoy taking walking tours of the town to get a feel for the flavor of the place. What follows is a selected list of the major buildings of Berkeley, in an attempt to express what is meant by the architectural style of Berkeley.

Some of the material is reprinted with the permission of the Berkeley Architectural Heritage Association. Since its incorporation, the Berkeley Architectural Heritage Association has established an annual tradition of sponsoring neighborhood architectural walking tours. These tours have often been researched and led by a resident of the featured neighborhood. Some of these tours are presented here for your own architectural discovery of Berkeley. For more information contact BAHA at the following address: P.O. Box 1137, Berkeley, CA 94701.

The buildings listed are broken down by district. The name of the architect, the date of construction, and in some cases, the architectural style are noted following the address. Enjoy your walk!

CLAREMONT DISTRICT

1. California School for the Deaf and Blind (unoccupied)
Derby Street at Belrose
George B. McDougall. 1934
Mediterranean; Art-Deco

2. Claremont Court Gates

John Galen Howard. 1907
Neo-classic, Palladian arched motif. The gates delineated the
Mason-McDuffie tract.

3. Claremont Heights Outdoor School
54 Vincente Road
John Carson. 1912

4. Claremont Hotel
Russell Street at Domingo Boulevard
Charles W. Dickey. 1906–15
French Chateau and Spanish-Renaissance tower. Frank Lloyd
Wright once remarked that the Claremont Hotel was "one of the
few hotels with grace and charm in America."

5. Claremont Park Company Gates and Pavillions
Claremont Avenue at The Uplands
William C. Hays. 1905
Art-Nouveau

6. Judah L. Magnes Museum of Jewish Art
2911 Russell Avenue
D.J. Patterson. 1914
The lot was designed by John McLaren, who designed Golden Gate
Park.

7. Seldon Williams House
2821 Claremont Boulevard at Avalon
Julia Morgan. 1928
Mediterranean Revival

DOWNTOWN
1. Berkeley High School
Grove Street and Milvia
Grove Street buildings, 1938. Auditorium, 1940–46
Streamlined Modern. The Florence Schwimley Auditorium is late
WPA Moderne with bas relief panels. The "A Building" was de-
signed by William C. Hays in 1920. It is Mediterranean Neo-Clas-
sic.

2. Berkeley Main Post Office
2000 Allston Way at Milvia
Oscar-Wederoth. 1914
Roman Renaissance Revival

3. Berkeley Public Library
Kittredge Street and Shattuck
James W. Plachek. 1930
Art-Deco

4. Berkeley Unified School District (formerly Berkeley City Hall)
2134 Grove Street near Center
Blackwell and Brown. 1908
This was the same firm which designed the San Francisco City Hall.
The style is Beaux Arts.

5. Tupper and Reed Music Store
2277 Shattuck Avenue
William R. Yelland. 1926
Elizabethan ("Hansel and Gretel" style)
Note the wrought-iron "Pan" on the top of the building.

HOMESTEAD AREA (south of Telegraph)

1. Berkeley City Club
2315 Durant Avenue
Julia Morgan. 1929
Italian-Renaissance palazzo. This building is a National Historic
Landmark.

2. McReary House
2318 Durant Avenue
1904
Colonial Revival

3. Town and Gown Club
2401 Dwight Way at Dana Street
Bernard Maybeck. 1899
Early Brown Shingle First Bay Tradition. The building is a Berkeley
City Landmark.

NORTH BERKELEY

1. Captain Boudrow House
1536 Oxford Street at Vine
1889
Queen Ann Revival

2. 1301 Oxford Street
Built by Napoleon Byrne. 1868
An Italianate villa, this was one of the first American settlements in Berkeley.

3. John Galen Howard House
1401 LeRoy Avenue
John Galen Howard.

4. Maybeck residential
Buena Vista and LaLoma
Bernard Maybeck. 1916–31

5. Rose Walk
Connects LeRoy Street and Euclid Avenue
Bernard Maybeck and Henry Gutterson. 1913–1936

NORTHGATE (Including Holy Hill)

1. Benjamin Ide Wheeler House
1820 Scenic Avenue
1900
Neo-Classic

2. Graduate Theological Union
2465 LeConte Avenue
1925
Georgian Revival

3. Phoebe Apperson Hearst House
2368 LeConte Avenue
Ernest Coxhead. 1900
Mediterranean Revival

NUT HILL

1. Hume Castle
2900 Buena Vista Road
John Hudson Thomas. 1928
Romanesque, done in the style of a Gothic French monastery.

2. "Temple of the Wings" Boynton House
2800 Vista Road
A. Randolph Monroe. 1914, remodelled in 1924 after the 1923 fire.
Beaux Arts Neo-Classic

OCEANVIEW

1. Conestoga Wagon Wheels
Vacant lot at 4th Street between Virginia and Cedar
The wheels are embedded in the trunk of an old tree. ca. 1890

2. Church of the Good Shepard
1823-9th Street at Hearst
Charles Bugbee. 1878
Victorian "Carpenter Gothic"

3. Finn Hall
1819-9th Street
1908 The building is on the National Register of Historic Places.

4. Pioneer store
834 Delaware Street
1855–65
This is one of the oldest buildings in Berkeley.

SOUTH CAMPUS

1. Anna Head School
Bowditch Street between Haste and Channing
Edgar S. Fisher. 1892. Auditorium Addition 1923

2. First Church of Christian Science
Dwight Way at Bowditch
Bernard Maybeck, 1910. The Sunday School Addition was designed

by Henry Gutterson 1927.
The building incorporates many styles, including Gothic, Renaissance, Neo-Classic, Japanese, Mediterranean, and Modern-Industrial. It is regarded as Maybeck's masterpiece and is registered as a National Historic Landmark. There are guided tours every Sunday at 12:30 p.m.

3. International House
Piedmont Avenue at Bancroft
George Kelham. 1928
Mediterranean Revival

4. Julia Morgan Center for the Arts
College Avenue at Derby
Julia Morgan. 1908
Brown Shingle First Bay Tradition.
The building is registered as a National Historic Landmark, and is open to the public, Monday through Friday, 9 a.m. to 5 p.m.

SOUTHWEST

1. China Station Restaurant
Third Street at University
1913
Mission Revival
This was the old Southern Pacific Depot.

2. Niehaus Villa
Seventh Street and Channing, northwest corner
1889
Stick-Eastlake

Selected listings are reprinted, by permission, from *24 Walking Tours of Berkeley, California*, copyright 1980 by The Berkeley Architectural Heritage Association. (P.O. Box 1137, Berkeley, California 94701.)

EAST BAY REGIONAL PARK SYSTEM

After a drought caused the forming of the East Bay Municipal Utilities District (denoted as "EBMUD") in 1922, the district established reservoirs at Lake Chabot and upper San Leandro Creek; the Pardee Dam, named for the physician who was the moving force behind the district, was put over the Mokelumne River in 1925, with a 98-mile aqueduct.

By the late 1920's EBMUD had extensive reservoirs at the top of the Berkeley Hills. This included 40,000 acres that had been owned by the East Bay Water Company, which it bought. Conservationists demanded its use as a park. Irving Kahn, an Oakland merchant, financed a University study showing in 1930 that the 150 square miles (then containing 450,000 people) of the region had less than 900 acres of parks. That was less than one percent of East Bay land.

Voters of Alameda County approved a regional park system in 1934; the cities included Oakland, Berkeley, Alameda, Piedmont, Albany, Emeryville, and San Leandro. People of Contra Costa County, however, were not permitted to vote; their supervisors kept the measure off the ballot. In 1936 the district began to buy 2,200 acres in the Berkeley Hills, chiefly on the Contra Costa side. The district now includes 8,300 acres that are in their free state except for a few developments designed to encourage understanding and pleasure in natural things.

Including parklands under development, there are nearly thirty parks in the East Bay Regional Park District throughout Contra Costa and Alameda Counties. Most parks are well-developed, and include places for hiking, swimming, boating, horseback riding, and other recreational facilities. The East Bay Regional Park District central office is at 11500 Skyline Boulevard in Oakland.

The East Bay Regional Park District publishes a free monthly news-letter and calendar of weekend programs in its parks. To order the calendar, call 531-9043.

Reservations and Other Information:

For group picnic areas, youth group day and overnight camping, meeting rooms. 531-9043
General Information 531-9300
Naturalist Services:
Tilden Environmental Education Center, Nature Area . . 525-2233
Robert W. Crown Memorial State Beach (Alameda) 525-2233
Golf Reservations:
   Tilden. 848-7461
   Willow Park (Chabot) 537-2521
Equestrian Center
   (Chabot) 569-4428
Marksmanship Range
   (Chabot) 569-0213
Merry-go-round
   (Tilden) 524-6283
Pony Rides
   Tilden. 525-8022
   Chabot. 569-4428
Little Train (Tilden). 531-9300
Public Safety Department. 531-9300
   Business. 531-9300
   Emergency. 531-3122
Disabled Access to EBRPD Parks 531-3122

Public Transportation to Parks:

A.C. Transit serves several East Bay Regional Parks all year. During the summer, bus service is expanded to reach the more remote parks. All lines have BART connections on weekdays. Phone A.C. Transit for information on routes and schedules. Telephone: 653-3535 (Oakland and San Francisco); 582-3035 (Hayward); 232-5665 (Richmond)

ALAMEDA COUNTY

Alameda Creek Trail
The trail originates in the Alameda Creek Quarries Regional Park (under development) near Union City, and continues for 24 miles to the Bay. The trail is suited for hiking, jogging, and bicycling.

Camp Ohlone
Located 7 miles southeast of the Sunol Regional Park in southern Alameda County, Camp Ohlone has facilities for horseback riding, group camping, and backpacking. Reservations are required for backpackers.
Telephone: 862-2244

Chabot Regional Park
Redwood Road
San Leandro
Chabot is a highly developed and popular park with facilities for fishing, boating, hiking, archery, riflery, horseback riding, picnicking, and for family camps.

Coyote Hills Regional Park
Patterson Ranch Road
Fremont
Take the Jarvis Avenue turn-off from State Highway 17, continue west to the traffic light at Newark Boulevard; continue right one half mile beyond the railroad crossing to the park sign. Park rangers offer a variety of interesting programs, including a guided walk through an ancient Ohlone tribal village, and weekend walks on the marshlands.
Telephone: 471-4967

Cull Canyon Regional Recreation Area
Southeast of Chabot Regional Park near Castro Valley. From Highway 580, take Crow Canyon Road, then left on Cull Canyon Road. Cull Canyon has hiking and equestrian trails, a swimming lagoon, a sandy beach and lawn, lake fishing, jogging trails, picnic facilities,

and horseshoe pits.
Telephone: 357-2766

Crown (Robert W.) Memorial Beach
8th and Westline Drive
Alameda
Crown is a popular sandy beach because of its proximity to East Bay
cities. Picnic facilities, volleyball nets, snack bar, showers and restrooms.

Del Valle Regional Park
10 miles southeast of Livermore in southern Alameda County.
There are hiking and equestrian trails, boat rental and ramp, and
fishing in the 750-acre lake. 80,000 trout are stocked annually.

Garin and Dry Creek Pioneer Regional Parks
On Garin Avenue off Mission Boulevard south of Hayward.
2,000 acres of foothill country, with hiking and equestrian trails,
playfields, and picnic facilities. Spectacular view of the Bay from
Garin Park.

Hayward Regional Shoreline
At the foot of West Winton Avenue in Hayward.
This is a restored tidal lagoon for birdwatching, hiking, and observa-
tion of tidal life.

Redwood Regional Park and Roberts Recreational Area
Off Skyline Boulevard
Oakland
Hiking, equestrian and jogging trails. Sports fields, archery range,
and a swimming pool at Roberts Recreation Area.

San Leandro Bay Regional Shoreline (under development)
Take the Hegenberger Road exit off Highway 17 in Oakland, then
turn right at Doolittle Drive. Hiking, bicycling, and jogging trails.
Picnic grounds and places for birdwatching.

Shadow Cliffs Regional Recreation Area
Located east of Pleasanton. Take the Santa Rita Road exit off Highway 580.
Swimming, fishing, and boating in the 74-acre lake. Volleyball and picnic facilities. The Alameda County bicycle trial is along Stanley Boulevard.

Sunol Regional Wilderness
East of Fremont in southern Alameda County. Go south on Highway 680 to the Calaveras Road exit. Turn left on Calaveras Road, and left again on Geary Road (east) to the park entrance. Backpacking and group camping only. Trails are along Alameda Creek into "Little Yosemite."

Temescal Regional Recreation Area
At the junction of Highways 24 and 13 in Oakland.
Swimming and fishing in Lake Temescal. Hiking and jogging trails, meadows, playgrounds, and picnic areas.

CONTRA COSTA COUNTY

Black Diamond Mines Regional Preserve
On Somersville Road off of Highway 4 just south of Pittsburg.
U.C. Berkeley has a continuing dig which explores the remnants of a 19th century coal mining town. Tours of the mines are available by arrangement. Hiking and equestrian trails.
Telephone: 757-2620

Briones Regional Park
On Bear Creek Road off San Pablo Dam Road. Just west of Pleasant Hill. Hiking, jogging, and equestrian trails. Picnic facilities.

Contra Loma Regional Park
South of Pittsburg and Antioch. Take Highway 4 to the Lone Tree Way exit, and continue south to Fredrickson Lane and the park entrance. Swimming and fishing in the lake. Hiking, bicycling, jogging, and equestrian trails. Solar energy display.

George Miller, Jr. Regional Shoreline (see Miller Regional Shoreline)

Las Trampas Regional Wilderness
Just east of Danville. From Highway 680 take Crow Canyon south at San Ramon to Bolinger Canyon Road. From Highway 580, take the Crow Canyon exit north at Castro Valley. Hiking and equestrian trails and picnic sites. There are interesting geological formations of water-carved caves and rock spires.

Kennedy Grove Regional Area
El Sobrante
From San Pablo Dam Road, turn right (east) on Castro Ranch Road, and then turn right again on Hillside Drive to the park entrance. Lawn area in a eucalyptus forest. Picnic facilities, volleyball courts, and horseshoe pits. Group reservations only.
Telephone: 531-9043

Martinez Regional Shoreline *(under development)*
Take the Alhambra Valley Road exit off Highway 4 in Martinez. Facilities for picnicking, fishing, bocci ball, baseball and softball. Birdwatching in the salt marshes.

Miller Regional Shoreline
Point Richmond
Picnic facilities, fishing. Swimming at the north end of the shoreline on Keller's Beach.

Morgan Territory
At the eastern boundry of Contra Costa County.

Point Isabel Regional Shoreline
Richmond
At the foot of Central Avenue. Facilities for fishing, picnicking, bicycling, sports, birdwatching. Spectacular views of Marin County and the Golden Gate Bridge.

Point Pinole Regional Park
Pinole
Take Interstate 80 north to Hilltop Road. Continue to San Pablo Avenue. Continue north, then turn left (west) on Atlas Road to the park entrance. A.C. Transit line #78 serves the park from the Richmond BART station. 4 miles of shoreline with views of Marin County and San Francisco. Eucalyptus groves, marshes, and meadows. Facilities for fishing, bicycling, picnicking, and birdwatching. A shuttle bus is available to the fishing pier.
Telephone: 237-6896

Wildcat Canyon Regional Park
Richmond
Take Arlington Avenue and turn right on McBryde Avenue toward Alvarado Park, then left on Wildcat Canyon Parkway. Picnic facilities along the creek, and a 4-mile hike to Jewel Lake in Tilden Regional Park.
Telephone: 531-9300

A GUIDE TO STATE AND NATIONAL PARKS IN THE BAY AREA

Note: except where specified, the area code for all telephone numbers in this guide is 415.

State Park permits are reservable through Ticketron.
Telephone: 788-2828
Permits are also obtainable through the University Box Office in the Student Union building of the Berkeley campus.
Telephone: 642-3125
The State Parks and Recreation Department sells a list of all 225 state parks in California for $1. Write to: Department of Parks and Recreation, P.O. Box 2390, Sacramento, California 95811.

STATE PARKS

Big Basin Redwoods State Park
Big Basin Highway
Felton
51 campsites
Telephone: (408) 338-6132

Butano State Park
Cloverdale Road
Pescadero
21 campsites

Castle Rock State Park
1500 Skyline Boulevard
Los Gatos
23 campsites for backpackers only
Telephone: (408) 867-2952

Cowell Redwoods State Park
State Highway 9
Felton
235-foot tall redwoods. The Roaring Camp and Big Trees Narrow-Gauge Steam Railroad is nearby. 113 campsites
Telephone: (408) 335-4598

Half Moon Bay State Beach
At the end of Kelly Avenue
Half Moon Bay
51 campsites

Henry Cowell State Redwoods Park (see Cowell State Redwoods Park)

Mount Diablo State Park
26 miles east of Oakland. 60 campsites.
Telephone: 939-2059

Mount Tamalpais State Park
7 miles west of Mill Valley
18 campsites and picninc areas. There are well-marked trails all over the mountain.
Telephone: 338-3770

Portola State Park
Alpine Road
La Honda
52 campsites
Telephone: 948-9098

Samuel P. Taylor State Park
Sir Francis Drake Boulevard

Lagunitas
65 campsites, picnic areas along the creeks. There is a beautiful drive through the redwoods on Sir Francis Drake Boulevard. *Telephone:* 448-8897

NATIONAL PARKS
Golden Gate National Recreation Area (GGNRA)
Park headquarters are in Fort Mason of the Marina District in San Francisco.
Telephone: 556-0560, 561-7162
Frequent nature programs offered by park rangers in the Marin Headlands section of the Area. Backpacking camps. Maps are available from the Marin Headlands Ranger Station at Fort Cronkite. For information, call 561-7612. *Muir Woods* is also a part of GGNRA. For information, call 388-2595. The San Francisco Municipal Railway operates connecting buses (line 76) between San Francisco and the Marin Headlands of GGNRA on weekends and holidays. For information on schedules, call MUNI at 673-6864.

Point Reyes National Seashore
Point Reyes Station
Telephone: 663-1092 (Administrative Offices and campsite reservations)
There are picnic facilities, a Morgan horse farm, and 146 miles of hiking and equestrian trails. Reservations are necessary for overnight camping. During the summer months, two months advance booking is often necessary. There is a free shuttle bus which runs from the Park Headquarters to Limantour Beach during the summer months. Another bus runs from Drake's Beach to the Point Reyes Lighthouse for whale-watching in December, January, and February, weather permitting. Golden Gate Transit operates buses between San Francisco and Point Reyes, Olema, Bolinas, and Stinson Beach. For information on routes and schedules, call Golden Gate Transit at *332-6600*.

A GUIDE TO BAY CRUISES

Out-of-town visitors should be cautioned that the weather may turn cold and windy on the Bay.

Blue and Gold Fleet
Leaves from Pier 39 in San Francisco.
Telephone: 781-7877

Golden Gate Ferry (Golden Gate Transit District)
Leaves from Pier 1 at the Ferry Building in San Francisco for Sausalito and Larkspur.
Telephone: 332-6600, 453-2100, 982-8834

Harbor Tours
Leaves from Pier 43 1/2 from Fisherman's Wharf in San Francisco. Harbor Tours offers trips to Angel Island (25 cents admission to the Island; call 435-1915 for Island information); Alcatraz Island, which includes a tour of the island the the prison museum; a "Bar-B-Que on the Bay," and a "Sunday Brunch Cruise."
Telephone: 546-2810

Red and White Fleet
Leaves from Pier 43 1/2 at Fisherman's Wharf in San Francisco.
Telephone: 546-2810

PUBLIC TRANSPORTATION

Alameda Contra Costa Transit District (A.C. Transit)

Timetables and route maps are available from any driver. They can also be obtained from A.C. Transit Customer Services: 508-16th Street, Oakland 94612. Or call Transit Information at 653-3535.

Monthly passes are available at a discount to riders for $24 for East Bay routes $45 for Transbay service. These passes entitle the rider to an unlimited number of rides on all local East Bay bus lines. On Intercity express buses, the pass reduces the fare by 10 percent.

Local passes are available the last week of the preceeding month and the first week of the effective month at the Co-op, Emby Foods, Fry's, Lucky's and Safeway stores throughout the East Bay (west of the hills), and from A.C. Transit Customer Services Office by mail, or from the Ticket Office at the Transbay Transit Terminal in San Francisco.

Transfers

When you board a bus and are not using a Monthly Pass, ask for a transfer. Then "stop off and go again" as many times as you like, within the printed time limit, as long as you don't reverse your direction. You may ride the same line again, or adjacent lines. Simply present your transfer to the driver for validation. BART stations have free transfer dispensers to all AC Transit lines.

Lost and Found

Articles inadvertently left on the bus, when found by the driver, are turned over (usually the following day) to the Customer Services Center, Lobby, 508-16th Street, Oakland, where they may be recovered upon proper identification by the owner. Call 654-7878 extension 250, between 9:30 a.m. and 5 p.m. Monday through Friday.

A complete system route map is available from A.C. Transit, and can also be found on page A6 of the Oakland Telephone Directory.

Alameda Taxi and Van Service

This is a subsidized service which provides transportation for handicapped and senior citizens 24 hours a day, seven days a week. Passengers in wheelchairs ride seven days a week, 7 a.m. to 12 a.m. Twenty-four hour advance reservations are requested. A $20 taxi script book is sold for $4; a trip voucher is sold for $1.
Telephone: 552-4100

Bay Area Rapid Transit District (BART)

800 Madison Street, Oakland 94607 General offices: 465-4100
For information concerning BART and connecting bus service, call BART'S phone information center:
Fremont/Union City area: 793-BART
Hayward/San Leandro area: 783-BART
Livermore/Pleasanton area: 462-BART
Oakland/Berkeley/Orinda area:
 465-BART
Richmond/El Cerrito area: 236-BART
San Francisco/Daly City area:
 788-BART
South San Francisco/San Bruno area:
 873-BART
Lafayette/Walnut Creek/Concord area:
 933-BART
Antioch/Pittsburg area: 754-BART
For the Hearing Impaired: 839-2220
Bikes on BART
If you ride your bike to BART you can lock it a bike rack with your own lock. Racks are available at all stations except downtown Oakland, San Francisco and Berkeley. A BART permit allows riders to take their bikes on BART during the non-commute hours. For information regarding the permit, call BART's Office of Passenger Service, at 465-4100.
Tourist Ride
A $1 BART ticket for each tourist buys unlimited rides for up to three hours as long as the rider enters and leaves at the same sta-

tion. The best time to take the tourist ride is from 9 a.m. to 3 p.m. or after 7 p.m.

BART and the Airports

It is a 10-minute drive from the Coliseum Station to the Oakland International Airport by way of A.C. Transit bus #57 or taxicab.

The Airport Connection offers a convenient shuttle van from the Durant Hotel in Berkeley to Oakland International Airport. For reservations, charters and information, call 841-0150.

Oakland Air-BART

This is a shuttle which connects the Oakland International Airport with the Coliseum station. The service operates Monday through Saturday, 6 a.m. to 12 a.m., and Sunday, 9 a.m. to 12 a.m. One bus is accessible to passengers with wheelchairs. The fare is 75 cents. Senior citizens, handicapped passengers, and children through age 12 ride free.

Telephone: 444-4200

The Powell Street BART station is only a few blocks from the Downtown Airline Terminal and the Airporter bus to San Francisco International Airport. The Airline Terminal is at 301 Ellis Street, San Francisco. From the Daly City BART station the airport is only 20 minutes away on Sam Trans (San Mateo Transit District) bus #3B.

Special Fares

Discount tickets are sold only at participating banks, and are not available at BART stations. The banks also sell regular fare blue tickets worth $10 and $20.

Children 4 and under ride BART free. Discount tickets available for senior citizens 65 and older and children 5–12 years of age. Handicapped persons with a Bay Region Transit Discount Card can purchase a discount ticket for BART as well as discounts on local buses.

The minimum fare on BART is 50 cents; the maximum fare is $1.75. The one-way fare from Berkeley to San Francisco is $1.10.

Things to See and Do with BART

1. *Golden Gate Park*—from Civic Center Station, take #71 or #72 MUNI (San Francisco Municipal Railway), from Glen Park Station take #10 bus.
2. *Union Square*—3 blocks from Powell Street Station.

3. *Ferry Building*—4 blocks from Embarcadero Station.
4. *Fisherman's Wharf*—from Powell Street Station take #59 or #60 cable car.
5. *Chinatown*—from Powell Street Station take #59 or #60 cable car.
6. *Oakland Museum*—1 block from Lake Merritt Station.
7. *Knowland Park and Zoo*—from Coliseum Station take A.C. Transit bus #56.
8. *Jack London Square*—from Oakland City Center-12th Street Station take A.C. Transit #11, #33, #34, #59 or #76 or walk 10 blocks.
9. *Lake Merritt*—from Oakland City Center-12th Street Station take A.C. Transit bus #12, #18, or #34.
10. *Oakland Coliseum and Arena*—Coliseum Station via walkway.
11. *Paramount Theatre*—1 block from 19th Street Station in Oakland.

BART and Buses
In San Francisco stations and the Daly City Station, white MUNI machines sell a two-part transfer for 25 cents. Passengers should purchase the transfer before leaving the fare gates. One part is used for a a MUNI ride away from BART and the other part is used for the ride back to BART.

In East Bay stations served by A.C. Transit, passengers may obtain a free transfer from the white A.C. Transit dispenser before leaving the fare gate. Passengers pay the regular bus fare to return to BART.

BART Express Buses connect five BART stations (Walnut Creek, Hayward, Bay Fair, Concord and El Cerrito Del Norte) with outlying communities.

BART Express Bus fares for adults are 75 cents.

Berkeley Taxi and Van Service
This is a subsidized service, similar to Alameda Taxi and Van Service, which provides continuous transportation to senior citizens and handicapped passengers. Handicapped ride Berkeley Taxi seven days a week, 7 a.m. to 12 a.m. A $20 book of scrip is sold from $4-10, depending on income; a trip voucher is $1.
Telephone: 644-6534

Lawrence Berkeley Lab Shuttle

This is a shuttle van which operates between the University campus, the downtown Berkeley BART station, downtown Berkeley, and the Lawrence Berkeley Laboratory. The shuttle runs Monday through Friday, 6:40 a.m. to 6:50 p.m., at seven minute intervals during the morning and noon rush hours, and at 10 minute intervals during the rest of the day. The service is free to visitors, lab workers, and students. The shuttle is accessible to passengers with wheelchairs.

Telephone: 486-4165

"Regional Transit Guide"

Complete public transportation information for the entire San Francisco Bay Area is available in a small but useful book called the "Regional Transit Guide." The book is available for $2 from the Metropolitan Transportation Commission, Hotel Claremont, Berkeley, California 94705.

COMMUNITY RESOURCES GUIDE

Berkeley Information Network
For visitors or new residents, the Berkeley Public Library offers a "Berkeley Information Network," which is a telephone number one can call to get information on every conceivable activity for orientation purposes in Berkeley. The service covers parks, legal services, politicians, government offices, women's groups, newspaper clubs, medical services, swimming pools, religious organizations, libraries, draft counseling, environmental groups, theaters, adult courses, senior services, football games, business organizaions, and carpools. *Telephone: 540-0666*

Jazz Concert Information
For current jazz concerts and events in the Bay Area, call the Jazz Line at radio KJAZ in Alameda.
Telephone: 521-93FM

Oakland Events Message
The Oakland Convention and Visitors Bureau has a 24-hour recorded message on concerts, dance, theater, cultural events, sports events, tours, childrens activities, and special events. Call the "Great Time Line."
Telephone: 839-9008

Foreign Visitors Events Message
The San Francisco Convention and Visitor's Bureau has a 24-hour daily recorded message in five languages. Telephone numbers:
English: 391-2000   *Deutsch:* 391-2004   *Español:* 391-2111
Français: 391-2003   *Japanese:* 391-2101

HOTELS IN AND AROUND BERKELEY

Bed and Breakfast International
(Lodging in private homes)
151 Ardmore Road
Kensington 94707
Telephone: 525-4569

Best Western Berkeley House Motor Hotel
920 University Avenue
Berkeley
Telephone: 849-1121

The Boatel Motor Lodge
21 Jack London Square
Oakland
Telephone: 836-3800

California Motel
1461 University Avenue
Berkeley
Telephone: 848-3840

Campus Motel
1619 University Avenue
Berkeley
Telephone: 841-3844

Capri Motel
1512 University Avenue
Berkeley
Telephone: 845-7090

Carlton Hotel
2338 Telegraph Avenue
Berkeley
Telephone: 845-5964

The Claremont Resort Hotel and Tennis Club
41 Tunnel Road
Berkeley
Telephone: 843-3000

Coliseum Motel
4801 Coliseum Way
Oakland
Telephone: 532-4084

The Durant Hotel
2600 Durant Avenue
Berkeley
Telephone: 843-8981

Flamingo Hotel
1540 Shattuck Avenue
Berkeley
Telephone: 548-9930

The French Hotel
1540 Shattuck Avenue
Berkeley
Telephone: 548-9930

Golden Bear Motel
1620 San Pablo Avenue
Berkeley
Telephone: 525-6670

Hyatt Oakland
455 Hegenberger Road
Oakland
Telephone: 562-6100

Jack London Inn
Nimitz Freeway and Hegenberger Road
Oakland
Telephone: 562-5311

Hilton Hotel
Oakland International Airport
Oakland
Telephone: 635-5000

Lake Merritt Hotel
1800 Madison Street
Oakland
Telephone: 832-2300

Lake Merritt Lodge and Residence Club
2332 Harrison Street
Oakland
Telephone: 893-3130

Marriott Hotel
200 Marina Boulevard
Berkeley
Telephone: 548-7920

Shattuck Hotel
Shattuck Avenue at Allston Way
Berkeley
Telephone: 845-7300

A GUIDE TO RESTAURANTS

Here are 104 selected restaurants in and near Berkeley. They range from simple vegetarian places to several that are nationally famous for the haughtiest of *haute cuisine*. Many compilers, boasting such titles as "Restaurant Critic," rush into print pretending that quality, price, and service will remain obligingly unchanged until their next annual visit. Here we state that all of these *must* change; we offer no critiques, but rather the community's consensus about restaurants that have proven themselves over the long haul. The restaurants are likely but not certain to persist; the prices, hours of service, and menus are not. For the latest information, phone. We welcome your additions or corrections to our list. Write: Diablo Press, Inc., P.O. Box 7042, Berkeley, CA 94707.

Addison Court
Address: 1919 Addison Street
Berkeley
Telephone: 841-3927
Hours: Monday through Friday, 8 a.m. (breakfast), 11:30 a.m.-5 p.m. (lunch), 5:30 p.m.-10 p.m. (dinner). Friday, Saturday, soon Sunday 5:30-11 p.m.
Price Range: $4.25-11.95
Specialty: Soup, salad, fresh breads
Comments: Excellent value; fine, fresh foods and environment; refills on soup permitted

A La Carte
Address: 1453 Dwight Way
Berkeley
Telephone: 548-2322

Hours: Tuesday through Sunday 6 p.m. to 9:30 p.m. Sunday
   brunch: 10 a.m. to 2 p.m.
Price range: $9.50–11
Reservations: Yes
Specialty: Gourmet French
Comments: Parties to 25 people

Armenian Village, The
Address: 1593 Solano Avenue
Berkeley
Telephone: 524-7838
Hours: Tuesday through Saturday 5:30 p.m. to 9 p.m.
Price range: $5.95–8.50
Reservations: Yes
Specialty: Shishkabob
Comments: Simple decor, laudable food.

Au Coquelet Cafe-Restaurant
Address: 2000 University Avenue
Berkeley
Telephone: 845-0433
Hours: 6 a.m. to 2 a.m, 7 days a week Sunday Brunch: 9 a.m. to 4
   p.m.
Price range: $9.95 prix fixe for the full-course meal; moderate to
   expensive salads and soups are also served in front
Reservations: Yes
Specialty: Full-course French meals; Basque pastries, specialty cof-
   fees
Comments: Au Coquelet is a popular Berkeley hang-out.

Ay Caramba
Address: 1901 University Avenue
Berkeley
Telephone: 843-1298
Berkeley
Hours: 11 a.m. to 9 p.m. daily.
Price range: $2–4
Reservations: No
Specialty: Mexican

Comments: Inexpensive, fast food

Balabosta, The
Address: University Avenue and 6th Street
Berkeley
Telephone: 548-0300
Hours: 5 p.m to 11 p.m. six nights a week; 4 p.m. to 11 p.m. Sundays
Price range: $4.95–30
Reservations: For three or more; for singles and couples there is a waiting list.
Specialty: Unusual shellfishes, smoked fowl, lamb sausage, meats
Comments: During the day, the restaurant is open only to groups

Bay Wolf Cafe and Restaurant
Address: 3853 Piedmont Avenue
Oakland
Telephone: 655-6004
Hours: Open daily 11:30 a.m. to 2 p.m.; 6 p.m. to 9:30 p.m.; 11:30 a.m. to 2 p.m. weekends; Saturday, 10 a.m. to 3 p.m.; Sunday brunch, 10 a.m. to 3 pm., 3:50 p.m. to 11:50 p.m.
Price range: $9–11.50
Reservations: Yes
Specialty: Mediterranean
Comments: Fine quality

Beggar's Banquet
Address: 1428 San Pablo Avenue
Berkeley
Telephone: 525-9466
Hours: Lunch: Monday through Friday, 11:30 a.m. to 2 p.m. Dinner: Sunday through Thursday 5:30 p.m. to 9 p.m. Friday and Saturday, 5:30 p.m. to 10 p.m.
Price range: $5.95–9.25
Reservations: Yes
Specialty: Continental
Comments: Banquet facilities for groups of up to 50

Bertola's
Address: 4659 Telegraph Avenue
Oakland
Telephone: 547-9301
Hours: Monday through Friday, 11:30 a.m. to 2:15 p.m., 5 p.m. to
9:45 p.m.; Saturday, 4 p.m. to 11 p.m.; Sunday, 2 p.m. to 9:45
p.m.
Price range: $3.45–5.45
Reservations: No
Specialty: Prime rib, veal, baked chicken
Comments: Noisy atmosphere, but reasonably priced, good food

Best Western Berkeley House—Wellington's Dining Room
Address: 920 University Avenue
Berkeley
Telephone: 849-1121
Hours: Monday through Friday 11:30 a.m. to 2 p.m.; 5 p.m. to 10
p.m.
Price range: $7.25–15.50
Reservations: Yes
Specialty: Rack of lamb, Beef Wellington, Prime Rib
Comments: Entertainment Tuesday through Saturday. Banquet facil-
ities for groups of up to 500

Bishop G. Berkeley's Bar and Grill
Address: 2181 Shattuck Avenue
Berkeley
Telephone: 841-9030
Hours: Monday through Saturday, 11:30 a.m. to 3:30 p.m.; 5:30
p.m. to 10:30 p.m. Closed Sunday
Price range: $7.95–10.65
Reservations: Yes
Specialty: Hamburgers, steaks, seafood
Comments: Outside patio for lunch

Brennan's
Address: 720 University Avenue near 4th Street
Berkeley
Telephone: 841-0960
Hours: Open daily 10 a.m. to 10 p.m. The bar is open from 10 a.m.

to 2 a.m.
Price range: $3–4.50
Reservations: Only for groups
Specialty: American
Comments: Hof-brau—serve yourself

Cafe Del Sol
Address: 2181 Solano Avenue
Berkeley
Telephone: 525-4927
Hours: Open Monday through Friday, 10:30 to 11 p.m., Friday and
    Saturday, 10:30 a.m. to midnight. Open Sunday 10 a.m. to 11
    p.m.
Price range: $5–8
Reservations: Yes
Specialty: Drinkᵣ, quiches, sandwiches
Comments: Solid healthy food and a pleasant deck.

Cafe Romano
Address: 2914 College Avenue
Berkeley
Telephone: 841-6871
Hours: Open Tuesday through Sunday, 5 p.m. to 11:30 p.m.; 'till 12
    a.m. Friday and Saturday
Price range: $3.35–11.80
Reservations: No
Specialty: Pizza and pasta
Comments: A popular hang-out in the Elmwood District

Cafe Vin
Address: 1889 Solano Avenue
Berkeley
Telephone: 527-9313
Hours: 8 a.m. to 10 p.m. daily
Price range: $3.25–11.50
Reservations: No
Specialty: Pizza and pasta
Comments: Self-service

Cafe Venezia
Address: 1903 University Avenue (near Grove)
Berkeley
Telephone: 849-4681
Hours: Monday through Saturday 11:30 a.m. to 10 p.m. Sunday 4
   p.m. to 10 p.m.
Price range: 3.95–7.95
Reservations: No
Specialty: Italian, fresh pesto, coffees, pastries
Comments: Some of the freshest pasta around

Carlos Murphy's
Address: 5901 Frontage Road
Emeryville
Telephone: 547-6766
Hours: Open Monday through Thursday, 11 a.m. to 11 p.m.; Fri-
   day and Saturday, 11 a.m. to midnight. Open for brunch on Sun-
   day with complimentary champagne from 10 a.m. to 2:30 p.m.
   and for dinner from 4:30 p.m. to 10 p.m. The Cocktail Lounge is
   open daily from 11 p.m. to 2 a.m.
Price range: $3.95–8.95
Reservations: For parties of ten or more only
Specialty: Mexican, Irish, Smoked meats, quiches, crepes,
Comments: Includes a 72-item menu. Fine view of the Bay and the
   Berkeley Marina

Casa De Eva
Address: 2826 Telegraph Avenue (near Derby)
Berkeley
Telephone: 540-9092
*Hours:*Monday through Friday, 11 a.m. to 10 p.m. Saturday, 5 p.m
   to 11 p.m. Closed Sunday
Price range: $4.35–6.65
Reservations: For groups of six or more
Specialty: Mexican
Comments: Authentic cooking at reasonable prices

Celia's Mexican Cuisine
Address: 2040-4th Street
Berkeley

Telephone: 549-1460
Hours: Monday through Friday 11:30 a.m. to 11 p.m. Saturday,
4 p.m. to 11 p.m. Sunday, 4 p.m to 10 p.m.
Price range: $3.70–8.75
Reservations: Yes
Specialty: Mexican
Comments: This restaurant is one of a chain with other locations in
San Francisco, San Mateo, and Palo Alto.

Charley Brown's
Address: 1890 Powell Street
Emeryville
Telephone: 658-6580
Hours: Monday through Thursday, 11:30 a.m. to 2:30 p.m.; 5 p.m.
to 10 p.m. Sunday, 4 p.m. to 9 p.m.
Price range: $7.95–16.95
Reservations: Yes
Specialty: Prime rib and lobster
Comments: American fare

Chez Panisse
Address: 1517 Shattuck Avenue
Berkeley
Telephone: 548-5525
Hours: Downstairs Restaurant: Tuesday through Saturday by reser-
vation only, at 6 p.m., 6:30 p.m., 8:30 p.m., and at 9:15 p.m.
Upstairs Cafe: Monday through Saturday, 11:30 a.m. to 12 a.m.
Price range: Downstairs Restaurant: Prix fixe of $30. Upstairs Cafe,
$5.75–15
Reservations: Required in the Restaurant. Not necessary in the
Cafe
Specialty: Formerly known for country French coooking, Chez
Panisse now offers gourmet food from selected California locali-
ties. The upstairs Cafe specializes in an a la carte version of the
Restaurant's menu, as well as pizzas, specialty desserts and cof-
fees.
Comments: Chez Panisse has a well-deserved reputation for excel-
lence.

China House
Address: 1113 Solano Avenue
Albany
Telephone: 527-9911
Hours: Daily 11:30 a.m. to 10 p.m.
Price range: $4.25–6
Reservations: Yes
Specialty: Mandarin, Szechuan and Hunan
Comments: Banquet facilities for groups of up to 50

China Station
Address: 700 University Avenue near 3rd Street
Berkeley
Telephone: 548-7880
Hours: Daily 11:30 a.m. to 1 a.m. Cocktails 'til 2 a.m.
Price range: $4–9
Reservations: Yes
Specialty: Cantonese
Comments: A popular restaurant. The noise level is high. A bar adjoins the restaurant.

Choyce's
Address: 2725 San Pablo Avenue
Berkeley
Telephone: 848-4023
Hours: Monday through Friday, 7 a.m. to 9 p.m. Weekends, 8 a.m. to 8 p.m.
Price range: $4.10–6.10
Reservations: No
Specialty: Soul food
Comments: A bargain, but expect no more.

Concina De Los Andes
Address: 3105 Shattuck Avenue (adjacent to La Pena Cultural Center)
Berkeley
Telephone: 843-0662
Hours: Tuesday through Sunday 6 p.m. to 10 p.m.
Price range: $3.50–6
Reservations: For six or more

Specialty: Latin American

Comments: Entertainment nightly in La Pena Cultural Center, which adjoins the restaurant. La Pena is nominally attached to Concina, but is financially independent. La Pena frequently sponsors cultural and political events on Latin America.

Colonel Lee's Mongolian Bar-B-Q

Address: 1373 Solano Avenue
Albany
Telephone: 526-7200
Hours: Daily 11:30 a.m. to 4:30 p.m.; 5 p.m. to 9 p.m. Friday and Saturday, 5 p.m. to 9:30 p.m.
Price range: $6.25 for all you can eat (complete dinner)
Reservations: Yes
Specialty: Mongolian
Comments: Buffet style. Customers are allowed to watch the chef as he cooks the meals.

Dock of the Bay

Address: 235 University Avenue (Berkeley Marina)
Berkeley
Telephone: 845-7656
Hours: Lunch: Monday through Saturday, 11 a.m. to 2 p.m. Dinners: Monday through Thursday 5 p.m. to 10 p.m. Sunday Brunch: 11 a.m. to 2 p.m. Early bird dinners, Sunday 4 p.m. to 6 p.m. Fishermen and early risers: Monday through Saturday 4 a.m. to 2 p.m. Breakfast, Monday through Saturday, 4 a.m. to 11 a.m.
Price range: $8.95–12.95
Reservations: Yes
Specialty: New Orleans seafood
Comments: Fine view of the Bay; cocktail lounge; live entertainment Wednesday through Saturday. Banquet facilities are available.

Don Paquin's

Address: 2428 Telegraph Avenue
Berkeley
Telephone: 843-7739
Hours: Monday through Saturday 11:30 a.m. to 8:30 p.m.

Price range: $2.75–5.60
Reservations: Yes
Specialty: Mexican
Comments: No fuss, but central location

Dragon Garden, The
Address: 2811 Telegraph Avenue
Berkeley
Telephone: 841-6806
Hours: Monday through Friday, 11:30 a.m. to 9 p.m. Weekends 5
  p.m. to 9 p.m.
Price range: $4–11.50
Reservations: Yes
Specialty: Cantonese and Mandarin
Comments: For South campus Chinese food

Dynasty, The
Address: 1841 Euclid Avenue
Berkeley
Telephone: 841-8363
Hours: Daily 11:30 a.m. to 9:20 p.m.
Price range: $2.50–5.50
Reservations: Yes
Specialty: Cantonese and Mandarin
Comments: For North campus Chinese food

Fatapple's
Address: 1346 Grove Street near Rose Street
Berkeley
Telephone: 526-2260
Hours: Daily 6 a.m. to 11 p.m.
Price range: $2.50–5
Reservations: No
Specialty: Fresh hamburgers, pies
Comments: A popular restaurant

Fondue Fred's
Address: 2556 Telegraph Avenue
Berkeley
Telephone: 549-0850

Hours: 5 p.m. to 11 p.m.

Price range: $4.50–7.00. 90-cent cheesecake, all you can eat

Reservations: Yes

Specialty: Fondue, cheesecake

Comments: Quick, inexpensive

Fourth Street Grill

Address: 1820-4th Street

Berkeley

Telephone: 849-0526

Hours: Lunch: Monday through Friday 11:30 a.m. to 2:30 p.m. Closed Sunday for lunch. Dinner: Monday through Saturday 5:30 p.m. to 10 p.m. Sunday, 5 p.m. to 10 p.m.

Price range: $3.50–6

Reservations: No

Specialty: Grilled fish; fresh pasta daily; sirloin steaks

Comments: Patrons consider it worth a wait.

Fu Lu Shou

Address: 2115 Kittredge Street

Berkeley

Telephone: 548-7544

Hours: Monday through Friday 11:30 a.m. to 2:30 p.m.; 5 p.m. to 9 p.m. Weekends 5 p.m. to 9 p.m.

Price range: $4–6

Reservations: Yes

Specialty: Mandarin and Szechcuan

Comments: Small place, few seats

Fugetsu

Address: 1776 Shattuck Avenue

Berkeley

Telephone: 548-1776

Hours: Lunch: Monday through Friday, 11:30 a.m. to 2 p.m. Dinner: 5:30 p.m. to 9:30 p.m. Weekends, 5:30 p.m. to 10 p.m.

Price range: $5.95–10.95

Reservations: Yes

Specialty: Japanese seafood, duckling

Comments: Western and traditional Japanese seating is available. Uses no MSG

Genghis Khan Bar-B-Que
Address: 2556 Telegraph Avenue
Berkeley
Telephone: 644-1359
Hours: Monday through Saturday 11:30 a.m. to 3 p.m. Weekends,
  5 p.m to 10 p.m.
Price range: $4.50–7.90
Reservations: Yes
Specialty: Mongolian Barbeque
Comments: Inexpensive protein

Gingerbread House, The
Address: 741-5th Street
Oakland
Telephone: 444-7373
Hours: Tuesday through Saturday, 11 a.m. to 12:30 a.m.
Price range: $9.95–32.95
Reservations: Yes
Specialty: Traditional Creole and Cajun. Lobster, Pheasant, ginger-
  bread, pasteries
Comments: This is a family business which is known for its superb
  home-style cooking and warm hospitality

Giovanni's Cafe
Address: 2420 Shattuck Avenue near Channing Way
Berkeley
Telephone: 843-6678
Hours: Sunday through Thursday, 11 a.m. to 12 a.m. Friday and
  Saturday, 11 a.m. to 1 a.m.
Price range: $7–15
Reservations: Yes
Specialty: Italian
Comments: Noisy atmosphere; extensive wine list

Good Earth, The
Address: 2175 Allston Way; branch at 2598 Telegraph Avenue
Berkeley
Telephone: 841-2555
Hours: Monday through Friday, 8 p.m. to 10 p.m. Weekends 8
  p.m. to 12 a.m.

Reservations: For groups of over eight persons
Price range: $3–8
Specialty: Natural foods minus processed sugar, ten-grain breads, large salads, vegetarian dishes. Meat dishes available
Comments: A popular health-food restaurant

Granata's
Address: 2730-9th Street near Pardee Avenue
Berkeley
Telephone: 845-9571, 540-9297
Hours: Tuesday through Friday, 11:30 a.m. to 3 p.m. Tuesday through Thursday and Sundays, 4 p.m. to 10 p.m. Friday and Saturday 4 p.m. to midnight. Closed Monday
Price range: $4.75–11
Reservations: No
Specialty: Italian
Comments: One of the longest-running

Guerrero's
Address: 2504 Shattuck Avenue
Berkeley
Telephone: 548-9830
Hours: Monday through Friday, 11 a.m. to 10 p.m. Saturday, 5 p.m. to 9 p.m.
Price range: $1.50–8.95
Reservations: No
Specialty: Mexican
Comments: Unpretentious

Heidelberg
Address: 2366 Telegraph Avenue
Berkeley
Telephone: 841-4200
Hours: Daily 11 a.m. to 12 a.m.
Price range: $1.89–3.99
Reservations: No
Specialty: International
Comments: For budget conscious

H's Lordship's
Address: 199 Seawall Drive (on the Berkeley Marina)
Berkeley
Telephone: 843-2733
Hours: Monday through Friday, 11:30 a.m. to 3 p.m.; 4:30 p.m. to
10 p.m. Weekends, 10 a.m. to 11 p.m.
Price range: $5.95–10.25
Reservations: Yes
Specialty: Prime rib, fresh fish
Comments: There is a fine view of the Bay. Dancing, cocktails,
banquets, catering

Hunan Palace
Address: 1556 Solano Avenue
Albany
Telephone: 525-2330
Hours: Tuesday through Saturday, 11:30 a.m. to 9:30 p.m. Closed
Sunday
Price range: $8–13
Reservations: Yes
Specialty: Hunan
Comments: Hunan Palace offers over 160 items on its menu.

India Kashmir Restaurant
Address: 1888 Solano Avenue
Berkeley
Telephone: 525-1122
Hours: Daily, 5:30 p.m. to 9:30 p.m.
Price range: $7–12
Reservations: Yes
Specialty: Curries, Tanduri, Shishkabob
Comments: Good quality, well prepared, spicy

Indonesia Village
Address: 2006-9th Street (near University)
Berkeley
Telephone: 841-9667
Hours: Wednesday through Monday 5:30 p.m. to 10 p.m. Sunday
5:30 p.m. to 9 p.m.
Price range: $5.25–7.50

Reservations: Yes
Specialty: Indonesian
Comments: Strong flavors, inexpensive

Jade Pagoda
Address: 1923 University Avenue
Berkeley
Telephone: 843-1535
Hours: Tuesday through Friday, 11:30 a.m. to 10 p.m. Weekends,
12:30 p.m. to 10 p.m. Closed Monday
Price range: $3–10
Reservations: Yes
Specialty: Cantonese
Comments: Plain but filling

Joshu-Ya
Address: 2556 Telegraph Avenue
Berkeley
Telephone: 848-5260
Hours: Monday, Wednesday through Friday, 2:30 p.m. to 5 p.m.
Weekends, 5 p.m. to 9:30 p.m. Closed Tuesday
Price range: $5.80–10.75
Reservations: Yes
Specialty: Japanese
Comments: Banquets for 20 people

Juan's Place
Address: 941 Carleton Street

Berkeley
Telephone: 845-6904
Hours: Monday through Friday, 11 a.m. to 10 p.m. Weekends, 2
   p.m. to 10 p.m.
Price range: $1.85–6.25
Reservations: For groups of six or more
Specialty: Flautas and enchiladas, Mexican beer and wine
Comments: Popular prices

Kimchee Cabana
Address: 938 San Pablo Avenue (south of Solano Avenue)
Albany
Telephone: 525-1350
Hours: Monday through Saturday, 5:30 p.m. to 9:30 p.m. Closed
   Sunday. Lunch for groups by reservation
Price range: 4.50–10.95
Reservations: Yes
Specialty: Korean
Comments: Agreeably ethnic

King Tsin
Address: 1699 Solano Avenue, near Tulare Street
Berkeley
Telephone: 526-3536, 525-9890
Hours: Monday, Wednesday through Saturday, 11:30 a.m. to 2:30
   p.m., 4:30 p.m. to 9:30 p.m. Sunday 4:30 p.m. to 9:30 p.m.
   Closed Tuesday
Price range: $5–8
Reservations: For six or more
Specialty: Northern Chinese
Comments: King Tsin is always popular. The service is efficient; for
   a leisurely dinner, tell the waiter to stagger the courses

King Yen Restaurant
Address: 2984 College Avenue
Berkeley
Telephone: 845-1286
Hours: Daily 11:30 a.m. to 9:30 p.m. Weekends 11:30 a.m. to 10
   p.m. Sunday 12 p.m. to 9:30 p.m.
Price range: $3.95–6.95

Reservations: Yes
Specialty: Hunan, Szechuan, Mandarin
Comments: Banquet facilities for 10 to 50 people

La Casita
Address: 1549 Shattuck Avenue
Berkeley
Telephone: 549-0396
Hours: Monday through Friday, 11:30 a.m. to 2:30 p.m., 5:30 p.m.
  to 9:30 p.m. Sunday, 5 p.m. to 9 p.m.
Price range: $4.75–8.50
Reservations: Yes
Specialty: Mexican
Comments: Banquet facilities for up to 30 people

La Tolteca
Address: 1723 University Avenue
Berkeley
Telephone: 841-0921
Hours: Monday through Saturday, 11 a.m to 8 p.m.
Price range: $3.70–4.95
Reservations: Yes
Specialty: Mexican
Comments: Long established

Landing, Restaurant and Lounge, The
Address: Marriott Inn—Berkeley Marina
Berkeley
Telephone: 548-7920
Hours: Monday through Friday, 6:30 a.m. to 10 p.m. Weekends, 7
  a.m. to 10 p.m.
Price range: $7–12
Reservations: Yes
Specialty: Seafood
Comments: A fine view of the Bay

Larry Blake's
Address: 2367 Telegraph Avenue near Durant Avenue
Berkeley
Telephone: 848-0886

Hours: Monday through Friday, 11:30 a.m. to 1 a.m. Saturday,
10:30 a.m. to 1 a.m. Sunday, 10:30 a.m. to 12 a.m.
Price range: $6.95–12.95
Reservations: For groups of five or more. For groups of less than
five, there is a priority waiting list.
Specialty: Hamburgers, steaks, New Orleans oyster loaf, stuffed
mushrooms Bordelaise
Comments: Larry Blake's has been a campus hang-out for over forty
years. The downstairs Rathskeller has entertainment nightly,
usually Rhythm and Blues. Banquet facilities for groups of up to
50 persons.

Le Bateau Ivre Restaurant and Coffee House
Address: 2629 Telegraph Avenue
Berkeley
Telephone: 849-1100
Hours: Weekdays, 4 p.m. to the last meal. Closed Monday
Price range: $9.25–13.25
Reservations: Yes
Specialty: Orange duck, New York steak with cognac sauce, veal
sweetbreads with champagne sauce
Comments: High quality continental

Lion of India
Address: 2025 Telegraph Avenue
Berkeley
Telephone: 549-1535
Hours: Daily, 11 a.m. to 9 p.m.
Price range: $3–7
Reservations: Yes
Specialty: North Indian
Comments: Banquets for up to 60

Long Life Vegi House
Address: 2129 University Avenue (near Shattuck)
Berkeley
Telephone: 845-6072
Hours: Tuesday through Sunday 11:30 a.m. to 9:30 p.m. Closed
Monday
Price range: 2.95–6.50

Reservations: Yes
Specialty: Vegetarian Chinese
Comments: Uses no MSG

Maiko
Address: 1629 San Pablo Avenue near Cedar Street
Berkeley
Telephone: 525-1575
Hours: Monday, Tuesday, Thursday, and Friday, 11:30 a.m. to 2 p.m. Thursday to Tuesday, 5 p.m. to 10 p.m. Closed Wednesday
Price range: $5.75–10
Reservations: Yes
Specialty: Japanese Tempura and Teriyaki, Sushi
Comments: Traditional Japanese seating available

Mandarin Garden
Address: 2025 Shattuck Avenue
Berkeley
Telephone: 848-4849
Hours: Daily, 11:30 a.m. to 2:30 p.m.; 4:30 p.m to 9:30 p.m.
Price range: $3.75–18
Reservations: Yes
Specialty: Mandarin and Szechuan
Comments: Banquet facilities up to 300

Mandarin House
Address: 2519 Durant Avenue
Berkeley
Telephone: 549-1877
Hours: Monday through Friday, 11 a.m. to 9 p.m. Saturday, 4 p.m. to 9 p.m. Closed Sunday
Price range: $2.35–5.65
Reservations: No
Specialty: Mandarin
Comments: Inexpensive, plain

Manuel's
Address: 2521-G Durant Avenue
Berkeley
Telephone: 849-1529

Hours: Happy Hour, Daily, 3 p.m. to 5:30 p.m. Daily 11 a.m. to 12 a.m. Sunday through Wednesday to 2 a.m.
Price range: $2.45–5.95
Reservations: No
Specialty: Mexican
Comments: Food to go is available

Margarita's Mexican Restaurant
Address: 1406 Solano Avenue
Albany
Telephone: 527-2025
Hours: Monday through Friday 10:30 a.m. to 10 p.m. Saturday 11 a.m. to 9:30 p.m.
Price range: $4–8.50
Reservations: Yes
Specialty: Mexican, and seafood
Comments: Banquets to 30 people

Mario's La Fiesta Mexican Restaurant
Address: 2444 Telegraph Avenue
Berkeley
Telephone: 540-9123
Hours: Daily 10:30 a.m. to 10:30 p.m.
Price range: $3.70–4.90
Reservations: Yes
Specialty: Mexican
Comments: Central location

Melting Pot
Address: 2519-G Hearst Street
Berkeley
Telephone: 843-4354
Hours: Tuesday through Friday, 11:30 a.m. to 2 p.m. for lunch. Daily for dinner, 5 p.m. to 9:30 p.m.
Price range: $7.95–9.95
Reservations: For six or more
Specialty: Fondue
Comments: European style

Metropol Restaurant

Address: 2271 Shattuck Avenue
Berkeley
Telephone: 848-3080
Hours: 11:30 a.m. to 10:30 p.m.
Price range:$6–15
Reservations: Yes
Specialty: "Cuisine Française"
Comments: Fine cooking in attractive surroundings

Ming's Kitchen
Address: 1761 Alcatraz Avenue
Berkeley
Telephone: 653-5866
Hours: Monday through Saturday, 11 a.m. to 9 p.m.
Price range: $2.59–3.39
Reservations: No
Specialty: Chinese
Comments: Plain, inexpensive

Narsai's Restaurant
Address: 385 Colusa Avenue
Kensington
Telephone: 527-7900
Hours: Sunday through Thursday, 5 p.m to 10 p.m. Friday and
   Saturday, 5 p.m to 11:30 p.m.
Price range: $22–35 (five-course dinner)
Reservations: Requested
Specialty: Gourmet French
Comments: Narsai's is one of the most elegant restaurants in North-
   ern California. Narsai David, the owner, is a wine connoiseur
   with one of the state's largest wine cellars.

Norman's
Address: College Avenue and Alcatraz Avenue
Berkeley
Telephone: 655-5291
Hours: Monday through Friday, 11:30 a.m.to 2 p.m. for lunch.
   Daily for dinner, Monday through Thursday, 5:30 p.m. to 10
   p.m. Friday and Saturday, 5:30 p.m. to 10:30 p.m. Sunday, 5
   p.m. to 9 p.m.

Price range: $4.95–14.95
Reservations: Yes
Specialty: Fresh seafood
Comments: Long established

North China Restaurant
Address: 1459 University Avenue
Berkeley
Telephone: 843-3966
Hours: Tuesday through Saturday, 11 a.m. to 9:30 p.m. Sunday 4
   p.m. to 9:30 p.m. Closed Monday.
Price range: $6–7
Reservations: Yes
Specialty: Mandarin
Comments: Food to go is available

Omnivore
Address: 3015 Shattuck Avenue
Berkeley
Telephone: 848-4346
Hours: Wednesday through Monday, 5:30 p.m. to 10 p.m. Closed
   Tuesday
Price range: $8.25–12.50
Reservations: Advised
Specialty: Fresh seafood, desserts
Comments: High quality, not inexpensive

Pasand Madras Cuisine
Address: 2276 Shattuck Avenue
Berkeley
Telephone: 549-2559
Emeryville Market
Emeryville
Telephone: 655-9020
Hours: Daily 11:30 a.m. to 10 p.m.
Price range: $3.45–6.95
Reservations: No
Specialty: South Indian
Comments: Indian music and entertainment is offered daily

Ravazza's
Address: 41st and San Pablo Avenue
Emeryville
Telephone: 654-2334
Hours: Daily 5 p.m. to 1 a.m.
Price range: $3.90–17.95
Reservations: Yes
Specialty: Home-made Italian
Comments: Ravazza's is a Bay Area landmark. Deliveries and take-out food available

Reza's Garden Restaurant
Address: 2426 Telegraph Avenue
Berkeley
Telephone: 848-2737
Hours: Monday through Saturday 11:30 a.m. to 9 p.m.
Price range: $4.25–9
Reservations: Yes
Specialty: Pizza
Comments: Reasonably priced Italian

Rod's Hickory Pit
Address: 11498 San Pablo Avenue
El Cerrito
Telephone: 234-3992
Hours: 24 hours daily
Price range: $4.25–9.75
Reservations: For groups over ten
Specialty: Barbequed ribs
Comments: For smoked meats

Salerno's
Address: 2468 Shattuck Avenue
Berkeley
Telephone: 549-2662
Hours: Monday through Friday, 11 a.m. to 12 a.m. Weekends, 5 p.m. to 12 a.m.
Price range: $5–7.50
Reservations: For six or more
Specialty: Pizza

Comments: Banquet facilities for groups up to 50

Santa Fe Bar and Grill
Address: 1310 University Avenue
Berkeley
Telephone: 841-4740
Hours: Monday through Thursday, 5 p.m to 10 p.m. Friday and
   Sunday, 5 p.m. to 11 p.m. Sunday 5 p.m. to 9:30 p.m. Lunch:
   Monday through Friday, 11:30 a.m. to 2 p.m.
Price range: $5.75–12.75
Reservations: Yes
Specialty: American char-broils, fish, poultry
Comments: This restaurant is housed in an old train depot which has
   been tastefully decorated. There is a cocktail lounge.

Siam Cuisine
Address: 1181 University Avenue
Berkeley
Telephone: 548-3278
Hours: Monday through Friday, 5:30 p.m. to 10 p.m. Friday and
   Saturday, 5:30 p.m. to 1 a.m.
Price range: $5.55–9.95
Reservations: Yes
Specialty: Thai
Comments: Banquet facilities to 30 people

Shattuck Avenue Spats
Address: 1974 Shattuck Avenue
Berkeley
Telephone: 841-7225
Hours: Monday through Friday, 11:30 a.m. to 2 a.m. Weekends, 4
   p.m. to 2 a.m. Food served until 11 p.m.
Price range: $4.15–14.45
Reservations: Yes
Specialty: Italian, seafood; exotic drinks
Comments: An eccentric decor and a cafe-bar in front which is a
   Berkeley hang-out. Banquet facilities to 90 people

Shin Shin
Address: 1715 Solano Avenue

Berkeley
Telephone: 526-4970
Hours: Monday through Friday, 11:30 a.m. to 3 p.m.; 5 p.m. to
  9:30 p.m.
Price range: $6.50–8
Reservations: For four or more
Specialty: Szechuan, Hunan, Mandarin
Comments: Middle level Chinese

Solomon Grundy's
Address: 100 Seawall Drive
Emeryville
Telephone: 548-1876
Hours: Sunday through Thursday, 10 a.m. to 10 p.m. Friday and
  Saturday, 10 a.m. to 11 p.m.
Price range: $5.95–22.95
Reservations: No
Specialty: Seafood
Comments:

Spenger's Fish Grotto
Address: 1919-4th Street
Berkeley
Telephone: 845-7771. Food to go: 548-0140. FishMarket: 548-2717
Hours: Daily 8 a.m. to 12 a.m. Fish Market: 9 a.m. to 10:30 p.m.
  daily
Price range: $3.85–11.50
Reservations: For groups of six or more
Specialty: Seafood, steaks, oyster bar
Comments: Spenger's has long been one of the most popular restau-
  rants in Northern California. Patrons should arrive early, as there
  can often be a long wait. The atmosphere is usually noisy. There
  are banquet accomodations for 25 to 350 guests.

Szechuan
Address: 1553 Solano Avenue
Berkeley
Telephone: 526-7234
Hours: Daily from 11 a.m. to 9:30 p.m. Closed Monday
Price range: $4.50–10.95

Reservations: Yes
Specialty: Szechuan
Comments: Inexpensive spicy Chinese

Szechuan House
Address: 2270 Shattuck Avenue
Berkeley
Telephone: 841-7303
Hours: 11:30 a.m. to 2:30 p.m.; 4:30 p.m. to 10 p.m.
Price range: $3.95–5.55
Reservations: No
Specialty: Szechuan
Comments: Inexpensive, plentiful servings

Taikoh
Address: 2519 Dwight Way
Berkeley
Telephone: 843-2017
Hours: Monday through Friday 11:30 a.m. to 2 p.m. for lunch.
Monday through Saturday, 5:30 p.m. to 9 p.m. for dinner.
Closed Sunday
Price range: $5.50–9.95
Reservations: Yes
Specialty: Tempura, sukyaki, teriyaki
Comments: Well-prepared Japanese cooking

Taiwan
Address: 2071 University Avenue
Berkeley
Telephone: 845-1456
Hours: Monday through Friday, 11:30 a.m. to 9:30 p.m. Weekends,
10:30 a.m. to 9:30 p.m.
Price range: $2.50–5.95
Reservations: For groups of five or more
Specialty: Taiwanese special, Beijing, Szechuan, Mandarin
Comments: Spicier Chinese

Three C's Cafe
Address: 2507 Hearst Avenue

Berkeley (Northgate Mall)
Telephone: 848-2856
Hours: Monday through Friday, 7 a.m. to 10 p.m. Weekends, 8
   a.m. to 11 p.m.
Price range: $5.50–7.75
Reservations: Yes
Specialty: Imported beers and wines, cappuccino, crepes, salads
Comments: Quick

Thu Song
Address: 1267 University Avenue
Berkeley
Telephone: 549-3168
Hours: Daily 11 a.m. to 9 p.m. Closed Monday
Price range: $3–4.50
Reservations: Yes
Specialty: Vietnamese-French
Comments: Unique in region

Tijuana Joe's
Address: 2556 Telegraph Avenue
Berkeley
Hours: Daily, 12 p.m. to 9 p.m.
Price range: $3–5.75
Reservations: No
Specialty: Nachos, chile rellenos, guacamole
Comments: A Berkeley landmark

Tora-Ya
Address: 1695 Solano Avenue
Berkeley
Telephone: 524-7000
Hours: Lunch: Tuesday through Sunday, 11:30 a.m. to 2:30 p.m.
   Closed Monday. Dinner: Monday through Friday, 5 p.m. to 9:30
   p.m. Weekends, 5 p.m. to 10 p.m.
Price range: $2.50–11.95
Reservations: Yes
Comments: Inexpensive Japanese

Toyo
Address: 2556 Telegraph Avenue
Berkeley
Telephone: 548-7420
Hours: Wedesday through Sunday, 11:45 a.m. to 2:30 p.m.; 5:30
    p.m. to 9:30 p.m.
Price range: $3.50–7.25
Reservations: Yes
Specialty: Tempura, teriyaki
Comments: More inexpensive Japanese

Trader Vic's
Address: 9 Anchor Drive
Emeryville
Telephone: 653-3400
Hours: Monday through Friday, 11:30 a.m. to 12 a.m. Saturday, 5
    p.m. to 1 a.m. Sunday, 4 p.m. to 11 p.m.
Price range: $10.75–19.25
Reservations: Yes
Specialty: International, Polynesian
Comments: One of the more expensive gourmet restaurants

Trevino's
Address: 1235 San Pablo Avenue
Berkeley
Telephone: 524-3167
Address: 11795 San Pablo Avenue
El Cerrito
Telephone: 234-7462
Hours: Daily, 11 a.m. to 2 a.m.
Price range: $3.75–6
Reservations: No
Specialty: Mexican
Comments: Long popular

Tsing Tao
Address: 1767 Solano Avenue
Berkeley
Telephone: 526-6223
Hours: Monday through Thursday, 11:30 a.m. to 9:30 p.m. Friday

and Saturday, 11:30 a.m. to 10 p.m. Sunday, 5 p.m. to 9:30 p.m.
Price range: $5.50–8.50
Reservations: Yes
Specialty: Mandarin, Szechuan and Hunan
Comments: Banquet facilties for groups of up to 80. Take-out orders
are available.

Tung Yuen Restaurant
Address: 2506 Telegraph Avenue
Berkeley
Telephone: 845-5864
Hours: Tuesday through Sunday, 11:30 a.m. to 8:30 p.m. Closed
Monday
Price range: $3.60–4.50
Reservations: No
Specialty: Northern Chinese and Cantonese
Comments: Good buy

Upstart Crow Company
Address: 2 Shattuck Square
Berkeley
Telephone: 845-5712
Hours: Sunday through Thursday, 9 a.m. to 10 p.m. (coffee and
cakes 'till 11 p.m.) Friday and Saturday, 9 a.m. to 12 a.m. (dinner
service ends at 11 p.m.)
Price range: $5.95–9.95
Reservations: No
Specialty: Salads, quiche, scallops in wine sauce, fine desserts
Vivoli's ice cream
Comments: Pleasant pub, bookstore attached

Vegi Food
Address: 2083 Vine Street
Berkeley
Telephone: 548-5244
Hours: Tuesday through Friday 11:30 a.m. to 3 p.m.; 5 p.m. to 9
p.m. Weekends 11:30 a.m. to 9 p.m. Closed Monday
Price range: $3.25–5.75
Reservations: Yes

Specialty: Vegetarian Chinese
Comments: Features unique vegetarian dishes

Vio Veneto
Address: 5356 College Avenue
Oakland
Telephone: 652-8540
Hours: Daily 5 p.m. to 10:30 p.m. Weekends, 5 p.m. to 11 p.m.
Price range: $3.95–11.45
Reservations: For five or more
Specialty: Home-made Italian
Comments: Banquet facilities; cocktail lounge

Walker's Pie Shop
Address: 1491 Solano Avenue
Albany
Telephone: 525-4647
Hours: Tuesday through Saturday, 5 p.m. to 8 p.m.
Price range: 7.50–8.50
Reservations: No
Specialty: Fresh pies
Comments: Pies to go are available

Warszawa Polish Cuisine Restaurant
Address: 1730 Shattuck Avenue
Berkeley
Telephone: 841-5539
Hours: Sunday through Thursday, 5:30 p.m. to 10 p.m. Friday and
Saturday, 5:30 p.m. to 11 p.m. Closed Tuesday
Price range: $7.70–11.50
Reservations: Yes
Specialty: Full-course Polish meals
Comments: A popular restaurant which features "Old World hospitality." Food to go is available

Yenching
Address: 2017 Shattuck Avenue
Berkeley
Telephone: 848-2200
Hours: 11:30 a.m. to 9:30 p.m.

Price range: $3.15–25
Reservations: Yes
Specialty: Mandarin, Hunan, Shanghai, Szechuan
Comments: Banquet facilties for groups of 20 to 60.

Yoshi's
Address: 6030 Claremont Boulevard
Oakland
Telephone: 652-9200
Hours: Monday through Friday, 11:30 a.m. to 2 p.m.; 5:30 p.m. to
9:30 p.m. Fish bar is open until 12 a.m.
Price range: $7–12
Reservations: Yes
Specialty: Japanese Tempuras, Teryaki, Sukyaki, fish bar
Comments: Jazz nightly

A GUIDE TO ORGANIZED TOURS

Many visitors to Berkeley enjoy one-day tours of San Francisco and other cities in the Bay Area. What follows is a list of tours to San Francisco, Oakland, Berkeley, the Peninsula, the South Bay, and the Golden Gate National Recreation Area. Some are free, others, where noted, charge a nominal fee.

San Francisco

African-American Historical and Cultural Society
Building C, Fort Mason Center (Marina District)
Tours for adults cost 50 cents. Children are admitted for 25 cents.

Architectual

California Historical Society
Telephone: 567-1848
Docent tours of the Whittier Mansion, 2090 Jackson Street; 1:30 p.m. and 3 p.m. Wednesdays, Saturdays and Sundays. Adults $2, students and seniors, $1.

The Foundation for San Francisco Architectural Heritage offers a house tour and a walk.
Telephone: 441-3004

Haas-Lilienthal House
45-minute tour given Wednesdays noon to 4 p.m. and Sundays 11

a.m. to 4:30 p.m. at the historic home, 2007 Franklin Street. No reservations required; adults $2, children and seniors $1.

Victorian and Edwardian Pacific Heights
12:30 p.m. Sundays; two-hour tour begins and ends at the Haas-Lilienthal House and makes 12 stops along the 1-mile route; $3, no reservations needed.

Asian Art Museum, Golden Gate Park
Telephone: 558-2993
Free docent tours are scheduled by subject matter.
China, 11 a.m. and 2 p.m. weekdays, noon and 3 p.m. weekends; Japan and Korea, noon weekdays, 1 p.m. weekends; India and Southeast Asia, 1 p.m. weekdays 2 p.m. weekends; Middle East, 11:30 a.m. on July 25 and August 5, 13, 21 and 29; special Japanese Netsuke exhibit, July 25 and August 5, 15, 19 and 25.

Cable Car Museum
Corner of Mason and Washington Streets
Telephone: 474-1887
A self-guided tour of the central control of the cable system; there is a miniature and pictorial history. No charge. Hours: 10 a.m. to 6 p.m. daily.

California Academy of Sciences
Golden Gate Park
Telephone: 221-4214
   Offers tours for groups of students to which individuals may join by pre-arrangement.

California Palace of the Legion of Honor
Lincoln Park
Regular docent tours are at 2 p.m. Wednesdays through Sundays; special tours of the current Phillips Collection exhibit at 11 a.m. *Telephone:* 752-5561

Chevron U.S.A., Inc.
555 Market Street

Telephone: 894-4895

"A World of Oil." Tours Monday through Friday, 9 a.m. to 4 p.m. Closed on major holidays

Chinatown walks
Telephone: 986-1822

Chinese Cultural Foundation of San Francisco offers two China-town Walks:

Culinary Walk—A look at the markets and food shops plus a Dim Sum luncheon; adults $9, children $5; reservations are required.

Heritage Walk—2 p.m. Saturdays; adults $5, children under 12 $1.75.

City Guides

These guides are volunteers who are sponsored by the Friends of the San Francisco Public Library. Reservations are not necessary. To join a tour, show up at the appointed place. Guides are identified by badges that say "City Guide."

The following tours are offered at no charge:

City Hall

Thursdays at noon; leaves from the San Francisco History Room on third floor of the Main Library, 200 Larkin Street.

Civic Center

Saturdays at 10 a.m., leaves from the San Francisco History Room on third floor of the Main Library, 200 Larkin Street.

Coit Tower

Saturdays at 11 a.m.; leaves from the reception desk of the tower on Telegraph Hill.

Fire Department Museum

Thursdays through Sundays from 1 p.m. to 4 p.m., 655 Presidio Avenue.

Neighborhood walks

In May and October, City guides conduct neighborhood walks. Walks will begin at 10 a.m. and 2 p.m. Saturdays, October 10, 17 and 24. Neighborhoods include: Noe Valley, Inner Mission, Nob Hill, Bernal Heights, Glen Park, Eureka Valley and Crocker-Amazon.

North Beach

Saturdays at 10 a.m., leaves from the steps of Sts. Peter and Paul Church, 666 Filbert Street.

Pacific Heights Victorians
Third Saturday of each month at 10 a.m. and 2 p.m.; leaves from
Mary Ellen Pleasant Park, 1801 Bush Street at Octavia Street.

Presidio Army Museum
Saturdays and Sundays at 1 p.m., Building 2 inside the Presidio at
the corner of Lincoln Way and Funston Avenue.

Forty-nine Mile Drive
The City of San Francisco has placed a well-marked self-guided tour
around the entire circumference of the city. By car, this is one of
the best ways to get to know San Francisco. For route descriptions
and maps, contact the San Francisco Visitor's Bureau in Hallidie
Plaza on Market Street, immediately adjacent to the Powell Golden
Gate Park Street BART station.

Golden Gate Park
Friends of Recreation and Parks have weekend walks through Octo-
ber in Golden Gate Park.
Telephone: 221-1310

East End—10 a.m. weekends, leaves McLaren Lodge at the corner of Fell and Stanyan Streets; concentrates on the park's role in
Victorian San Francisco.

Japanese Tea Garden—10 a.m. and 11 a.m. Saturdays, 2 p.m.
and 3 p.m. Sundays, meets inside main gate of the Tea Garden;
free, exept for 50-cent entrance fee to the Tea Garden.

Strawberry Hill—2 p.m. Saturdays, beginning at the north end
of the Rose Garden.

West End—2 p.m. Sundays, meets on the stairs of the Angler's
Lodge parking lot opposite Buffalo Meadow off Kennedy Drive;
includes windmills and neighborhoods on Saturdays during the
school year.

Grace Cathedral
1051 Taylor Street
Telephone: 776-6611
Tours between 1 p.m. and 3 p.m. weekdays; 11:30 a.m. and 1:30
p.m. Saturdays, and 12:30 p.m. and 2 p.m. Sundays.

Historical walks
Galileo Marina Community College Center offers historical and ar-

chitectural walks through Historic Market Street Museum 2 p.m., leaves from the De Anza equestrian statue at the foot of Market Street.
Telephone: 931-3595

Literary Walks

Don Herron offers three-hour literary walks that cost $3, $1.50 for seniors. Reservations are not required.
Telephone: 564-7021

There is a tour of the places where mystery novelist Dashiell Hammett lived and worked. The walk starts at noon on Sundays from the steps of the main library.

There are additional literary tours. One starts at Coit Tower at noon, and goes through Telegraph Hill, North Beach, the Financial District and the Union Square area; Saturdays, August 8 and 22, and September 5 and 19.

Another walk starts at the southwest corner of Sacramento and Mason Streets. It goes through Nob Hill, Russian Hill, and Pacific Heights. The tour starts at noon on Saturdays, August 15 and 29, and September 12 and 26.

Mexican Museum mural walk
1855 Folsom Street
Telephone: 621-1224

10 a.m. on second Saturday of each month. Tours begin at the museum. Adults, $3, students and seniors, $1.

M.H. de Young Memorial Museum
Golden Gate Park
Telephone: 387-5922

The de Young Museum offers free docent tours, scheduled by subject matter, Wednesdays through Sundays. The tours are organized by subject matter: Ancient and European, 1:30 p.m.; Africa, Oceania and the Americas, 2 p.m.; America, 2:30 p.m. children's tour, 1 p.m. Saturdays.

Old Mint
Fifth and Mission Streets
Telephone: 556-3630

Open 9 a.m. to 4 p.m. Tuesdays through Saturdays with free

tours on the hour beginning at 10 a.m.

San Francisco Zoological Society
The "Zebra Zephyr" train runs every half hour, starting at about 11 a.m. daily during the summer near Children's Zoo. The driver provides commentary during the 20-minute ride. Adults, $1; 50 cents for children and seniors.

Temple Emanu-el
Arguello and Lake Streets
Telephone: 751-2535
Free docent tours are offered of the Temple daily during the summer from 12:30 p.m. to 3:30 p.m. Reservations are not required.

Wine Museum
633 Beach Street
Telephone: 673-6990
Free docent tours are offered between 2 p.m. and 4 p.m. Tuesday through Sundays.

Peninsula

Ames Research Center
(NASA—National Aeronautics and Space Administration)
Moffett Field, Mountain View
Telephone: 965-6497
Free tours of the world's largest air hanger.

The Filoli Gardens
Telephone: 364-2880
The gardens and mansion in Woodside are one of the most popular guided tours in the Bay Area; reservations must be made well in advance; 10 a.m. and 1 p.m. Tuesday through Saturday from mid-February through mid-November; $5; no children under 12 allowed; 10 a.m. and 2 p.m.

Fitzgerald Marine Reserve
Coast Highway 1, Moss Beach
Telephone: 728-3584

Tours of the Tidal Pools at the Sanctuary led by a naturalist on weekends when the tide is cooperative.

Marine Ecological Institute
811 Harbor Boulevard, Redwood City.
Telephone: 364-2760
Half-day bay tours provide the chance to examine life aboard an 85-foot research vessel; primarily for groups, but sometimes space for individuals; make arrangments two weeks in advance; adults $12.50, students $10.

Stanford Linear Accelerator Center
2575 Sand Hill Road
Menlo Park
Telephone: 854-3300, ext. 2204
Free two-hour tours include audio-visual presentation and a bus ride around the facility; call ahead to arrange for a tour time.

Stanford University
Telephone: 497-2862
Tours are conducted by the student-staffed Guide and Visitors Service at 11 a.m., and at 2:15 p.m. Mondays through Saturdays and at 2:15 p.m. Sundays; free; starts at the end of Palm Drive at the entrance to the Main Quad.

South Bay

Frito Lay, Inc.
650 North King Road
San Jose
Groups (minimum of 15) may tour the facility to observe how potato chips are made. The tours are offered each Wednesday from 10 a.m. to 11:30 a.m. Book early, as the tours fill up quickly.

Rosicrucian Museum
Park and Naglee Avenues
San Jose
Telephone: (408) 287-9171
Tours of the tomb on the half hour; museum is open 9 a.m. to 4:45

p.m. Tuesday through Friday and noon to 4:45 p.m. Saturday through Monday; no charge.

San Jose Historical Museum
635 Phelan Avenue
San Jose
Telephone (408) 287-2290
Guided tours weekdays at 10:30 a.m., 1:30 p.m., and 3 p.m., weekends between noon and 4:30 p.m.; each building is staffed with a guide; adults, $1; children, 50 cents.

San Jose Museum of Art
110 South Market Street
San Jose
Telephone: (408) 294-2787
Docent tours at 10 a.m. and 3 p.m. Tuesday through Sunday; no charge.

Winchester Mystery House
525 Winchester Boulevard (at Highway 280)
San Jose
Telephone: (408) 247-2000
The widow of the rifle magnate had carpenters build 24 hours a day to ward off the ghosts of people killed by Winchester rifles. There are guided tours daily. Summer hours: 9 a.m. to 5 p.m. Charge: $5.95 for adults; $3.95 for children; those under 4 years old are admitted free.

Golden Gate National Recreation Area

Alcatraz Island
Telephone: 546-2805
Tours are conducted daily by park rangers. Ferries leave Pier 43 in San Francisco every 45 minutes between 8:15 a.m. and 4:30 p.m.; adults $3; ages 5 to 11, $1.50; ages under 5 years, free; make ferry reservations two weeks in advance.

Battery Chamberlain Tours
Telephone: 751-2519
Weekends at Baker Beach. Conducted by the National Park Service, the tour includes a look at a turn-of-the century 6-inch cannon, and other batteries left over from the Old Presidio. A walk to the Golden Gate Bridge, which is about 1 mile, is included.

Fort Point Historic Site
Telephone: 556-1693
Tours every 20 minutes on the weekends.

Marin Headlands
Guided tours begin at the Visitor Center. (follow Bunker Road to Rodeo Beach); reservations are needed.
Telephone 561-7612 for the following tours: "Headlands exploration," "Lunch with a ranger," "A walk in the dark," and "Getting out with children." Most of these tours occur only one day during the summer, and are conducted by the National Park Service.

East Bay

Alameda County Sheriff's Department
15001 Foothill Boulevard
San Leandro
Telephone: 557-1031
The Sheriff's Department offers a 30-minute tour of its facilities. All ages are welcome, but there should be at least one adult for every five children. Reserve one week in advance.

East Bay Municipal Utilities District (EBMUD)
Telephone: 835-3000
There is a 45-minute tour of filtration plants in Oakland, El Sobrante, and Kensington. The guides can accommodate groups from 15–35 persons; there should be one adult for each group of 10 children; third grade students and older are welcome. The tours are offered Monday through Friday, every hour on the half hour.

The East Bay Regional Park District (EBRPD)
Telephone: 525-2233

Offers a number of walks and tours both on a regular basis and on special occasions.

Bird Walks—Thursdays at 7 a.m. or 7:30 a.m. (depending on the season) at various sites in the park district.

Black Diamond Mine—Weekends at 9:30 a.m. to noon, 1 p.m. to 2:30 p.m. and 3 p.m. to 4:30 p.m.; at the foot of Somersville Road, Antioch; reservations are needed for all three Saturday tours and the one on Saturday morning; $1.50 for those 12 years and older, 50 cents for children aged 6 to 11;
Telephone: 757-2620

Horseback tours in the Black Diamond Mine Regional Preserve will be conducted 7 p.m. to 9 p.m. on August 2, 7, 16 and 28; $12; reservations are needed.
Telephone: 432-7881

Coyote Hills—2 p.m. Saturdays; a guided tour of an Indian shell mound with a park naturalist; 8000 Patterson Ranch Road, Fremont.
Telephone: 471-4967

Crab cove—Wednesdays through Sundays at Crown Beach in Alameda; tour of the cove with a naturalist; times vary.
Telephone: 521-6887

Tilden Botanic Garden—One-hour walks at 2:30 p.m. Saturdays and Sundays; garden specializes in California native plants; Berkeley.

Cameron-Stanford House
1418 Lakeside Drive
Oakland
Telephone: 836-1976
Tours between 11 a.m. and 4 p.m. Wednesdays and between 1 p.m. and 5 p.m. Sundays; 1418 Lakeside Drive, Oakland.

Dunsmuir House
2958 Peralta Oaks Court
Oakland
Telephone: 562-7588
Sundays at 1 p.m. 2 p.m. and 3:15 p.m.; charge: $1.50

General Motors Assembly Plant
Highway 17 (exit after Durnham Road)

Telephone: 498-5500
There is a one-hour tour of the plant by electric train. Children 6
and older are welcome. The tour is between 8:30 a.m. and noon, or
may be arranged at other times for groups.

Historical/Architectural tours of Oakland
Discovery Walks, coordinated by Volunteers of Oakland, has five
guided tours.
Telephone: 273-3234
    City-Center-Downtown Business Tour—1 p.m. on the second
Wednesday and Saturday of the month, leaves from the steps of
City Hall, 1421 Washington Street.
    Oakland Chinatown
The tour leaves at 1 p.m on the first Saturday of the month from
City Center Towers, 801 Franklin Street.
    Old Oakland—a visit to the business district of the 1870's. 1 p.m.
on the first and fourth Wednesdays and Saturdays of each month.
The tour leaves from Ratto's International Grocery, 821 Washing-
ton Street.

    Preservation Park—1 p.m., fifth Wednesday and Saturday of the
month, 2025 Broadway Avenue
    Uptown to the Lake—Includes a trip to the Kaiser Roof Garden,
1 p.m., third Wednesday and Saturday of the month, leaves from in
front of the Paramount Theatre of the Arts, 2025 Broadway.

Numano Sake
Addison Street
Berkeley
Telephone: 540-8250
Tours Monday through Friday, 2 p.m. to 4 p.m.; Weekends, noon
to 4 p.m. 25 cent charge for plastic shoes which are required for the
tour.

Integral Urban House (Farallones Institute)
1516-5th Street
Berkeley
Telephone: 525-1150
This is a model of what a self-sufficient house could look like. It has
a vegetable garden, beehives, crayfish, and chickens. There are

self-guided tours, Monday through Friday, from 10 a.m. to 4 p.m. There is a self-guided tour on Saturdays at 10:30 a.m. and 2:30 p.m. with a workshop at 1:30 p.m. Charge: $3 for adults, 50 cents for children.

Kilpatrick's Bread
955 Kennedy Street
Oakland
Telephone: 436-5350
Kilpatrick's offers a half-hour tour of its bread bakeries and a taste of its bread. The guides can accomodate groups from 10–30 persons. Reservations are required one month in advance of the tour.

Lake Merritt boat rides
Sailboat House 568 Bellevue Aveneue
Oakland
Telephone: 444-3807
Daily betweeen noon and 4:30 p.m.; 25-minute cruises with historical comments by the captain. Adults, 75 cents; those under 12 or over 55, 50 cents.

Mormon Temple
4770 Lincoln Avenue
Oakland
Telephone: 531-1475
Free tours of the Temple daily from 9 a.m. to 9 p.m.

Oakland Museum
1000 Oak Street
Oakland
Telephone: 273-3514
Offers bicycle and foot tours.

   Bicycle tours—based on historical or natural science themes—are conducted on selected Sundays during the summer; the 2 1/2 hour tour covers five to six miles; 10 a.m. at the museum; no charge; reservations are needed.

   Docent tours of each of the three permanent galleries—art, history and natural science; 2 p.m., Wednesdays through Saturdays; no charge; no reservations are required.

Oakland Society for the Prevention of Cruelty to Animals
8323 Baldwin Street
Oakland
Telephone: 521-8677
There is a one-hour tour of the animal shelter and dog obedience classes. The tour is designed for children of pre-school age through high school.

The Paramount Theatre of the Arts
2025 Broadway Avenue
Telephone: 893-2300
The Paramount is a classic example of the Art-Deco style of architecture. It is well worth a visit. The Theatre offers occasional Saturday tours. Tours begin at 10 a.m. in the summer; no reservations are needed; charge: $1.

Patti McClain's Museum of Vintage Fashion
2960 Peralta Oaks Court (adjacent to the Dunsmuir House)
Telephone: 638-1896
Sundays 1 to 4 p.m. Adults $3, children $1.50.

The Port of Oakland
Telephone: 444-3188
Offers free tours of the port facilities at 10 a.m. and noon on Thursdays, May through August; reservations are required. (the port begins taking reservations each April.)

Safeway Ice Cream Plant
2240 Filbert Street (near West Grand Avenue)
Oakland
Telephone: 891-3454
Safeway can accommodate groups of 10 to 30 persons, ages 6 and older. There is a 40-minute tour of the plant. Visitors may sample the ice cream. The best time to take the tour is during the summer when the plant operates at full capacity. Reservations are required one month in advance.

Shasta Beverages
26901 Industrial Boulevard

Hayward
Telephone: 783-3200, ext. 300
There is a 45-minute tour of this automated bottling plant. The best time to to the plant is during the summer, when it operates at full capacity. The tour is offered on Thursdays at 10 a.m. Reservations are required; book 6 months in advance.

Sierra Club *(San Francisco Bay Chapter)*
6014 College Avenue
Oakland
Telephone: 658-7470
The Sierra Club leads a wide variety of hikes, bicycle tours, and nature walks throughout the Bay Area. A schedule of events is sold for a nominal charge.

The University of California
Telephone: 642-5215
The University has free tours of the Berkeley campus at 1 p.m. daily. The tours begin in the main lobby of the Student Union Building, off Bancroft Way near Telegraph Avenue, Berkeley.

Visitors wishing to tour the Lawrence Berkeley Laboratory and the Linear accelerator should call the LBL Visitors Center directly. (See *University: Plan*)

Marin

Audubon Canyon Ranch
4900 Shoreline Street (Highway 1) north of Stinson Beach
Telephone: 383-1644
The Ranch is a 1,000-acre bird sanctuary. Primarily Egrets and Great Blue Herrons nest there. Hours: 10 a.m. to 4 p.m. weekends and holidays. Group tours are available by arrangment, Tuesdays through Friday. The Ranch is closed from July 5 to March 1.

Audubon Education Center
376 Greenwood Beach Road
Tiburon
Telephone: 388-2524
800 acres of bird sanctuaries on Richardson Bay. The Center holds

classes, conducts field trips, and offers guided nature walks in the marshlands and shoreline pools. These are held each Sunday at 1 p.m. Hours: 9 a.m. to 5 p.m., Wednesday through Saturday.

Farallone Islands Boat Trip

Natural Excursions, of the Point Reyes Bird Observatory, offers an all-day trip to observe one of the largest seabird rookeries on the Pacific Coast. Tufted Puffins and Rhinoceros Auklets make their nests on the Farallon Islands, just west of San Francisco. Cost is $35. For further information, contact Natural Excursions, Point Reyes Bird Observatory, 4900 Shoreline Highway, Stinson Beach, California 94970.
Telephone: 868-1221

Morgan Horse Farm
Bear Valley Trailhead
Point Reyes National Seashore
Point Reyes Station
Telephone: 663-1092

The horses are raised for use by the Park Rangers. There is a 40-minute tour of the ranch and blacksmith shop; and there is also a bridle and saddling demonstration. The Morgan horse is a unique American breed.

Point Reyes Lighthouse
Point Reyes (16 miles southwest of Inverness.)
Telephone: 669-1534

The lighthouse has been operating since 1870. Point Reyes is known as one of the foggiest points in the United States. The Lighthouse and Visitor's Center are open 10 a.m. to 5 p.m., Thursday through Monday, weather permitting.

San Francisco Bay and Delta Model
2100 Bridgeway
Sausalito
Telephone: 332-3871

There is a self-guided tour of the exhibits, and a slide-show. The Model is used by the U.S. Army Corps of Engineers to predict weather patterns, to plan shipping routes, and to plan for oil spills. A guided tour is available for groups of 10 or more. Hours: 9 a.m. to 4 p.m, Tuesday through Saturday. No charge.

A CALENDAR OF EVENTS

Actual dates of annual events vary from year to year. For specific dates, contact the San Francisco Convention and Visitors' Bureau, 1390 Market Street, San Francisco, California 94102, (415) 626-5500 for San Francisco events. For events in Oakland, contact the Oakland Convention and Visitors' Bureau, 1330 Broadway Avenue, Oakland, California 94612, (415) 839-9008.

January

Sports:

Horse racing, Golden Gate Fields, Albany (through May); sturgeon and striped bass fishing, San Pablo Bay; Shrine East-West Football Classic, Stanford Stadium, Palo Alto; San Francisco Giants Baseball, Candlestick Park, San Francisco, through October; San Francisco Pioneers. (Women's Professional Basketball) at Civic Auditorium, through March; Colllegiate Basketball; Wrestling at the Cow Palace, San Francisco, through April; Thoroughbred Racing, Bay Meadows, San Mateo, through May; San Francisco Fog, (Professional Soccer) at the Cow Palace, San Francisco, through March; San Francisco Soccer League (amateur soccer) plays each Sunday, weather permitting, at Balboa Stadium in San Francisco.

Exhibitions:

Annual Roadster Show, Oakland Coliseum. (four days in late January-early February.); Golden Gate Kennel Club All-Breed Dog Dog Show, at the Cow Palace in San Francisco. (30th to the 31st.);

Sports and Boat Show, Cow Palace, San Francisco; International Boat Show, George R. Moscone Convention Center; California International Antiquarian Book Fair, San Francisco.

Festivals and Fairs:
Chinese New Year Celebration. Parade in San Francisco's Chinatown. Festivities are continuous for the last week in January or the first week in February, with a parade in Chinatown on the final day.

Art and Music:
San Francisco Ballet Repertory Season, through May.

February

Sports:
Ice Follies, at the Cow Palace in San Francisco.

March

Festivals and Fairs:
St. Patrick's Day parade, downtown San Francisco. 12:30 p.m.; Annual St. Patrick's Day parade, Oakland. (mid-March)

Art and Music
Annual Gospel Academy Awards, Paramount Theatre of the Arts, Oakland. (mid-March)

Floral Exhibits and displays:
In the last week of March, the cherry trees bloom in the Japanese Tea Garden in Golden Gate Park. The blooming extends into the first week of April.

April

Sports:
Yachting Season opens on San Francisco Bay. (late April)

Festivals and Fairs:
Easter Sunrise Services, Mt. Davidson in San Francisco; Annual Easter Egg Roll, Children's Fairyland, Oakland (ages 4–10); Macy's Easter Flower Show, Macy's, Stockton and O'Farrell Streets, San Francisco (near Union Square.); Cherry Blossom Festival, Japantown, in San Francisco; and the Japan Center Parade on the last day of the Festival.

Art and Music:
Annual Duke Ellington Memorial Concert, Oakland Auditorium Theatre. (late in the month, 8 p.m.)

Exhibitions:
Grand National Junior Livestock Exposition and Horse Show at the Cow Palace in San Francisco. (coincides with Easter holidays); Annual Bay Area Science Fair (High School students), California Academy of Sciences, Golden Gate Park, San Francisco.

Floral Exhibits and Displays:
Apple blossom time in western Sonoma County, where there is a 44-mile marked tour of them; redbuds bloom in Lake County; fruit trees bloom on Mount St. Helena; peak blooming of the rhododendrons in Golden Gate Park, Union Square, and Civic Center. Blooming extends into May; California Spring Blosssom and Wildflower Show, Hall of Flowers, Golden Gate Park, San Francisco; California Spring Garden Show, Oakland. (late April, early May.)

May

Sports:
Sailboat racing on the Bay (each weekend through September); San Francisco 49'ers Football, Candlestick Park, San Francisco, through December; Thoroughbred horse racing, Golden Gate Fields, Albany, through June; Bay to Breakers Cross-City Foot Race, Mission and Spear Streets, San Francisco, 8 a.m.

Festivals and Fairs:
May Day Parades; Memorial Day observance, San Francisco Presidio; Festival Cinco de Mayo at The Cannery, San Francisco; San Francisco Rose Show (the largest show in the state devoted exclu-

sively to roses) Hall of Flowers, Golden Gate Park; Annual Book Sale (benefits the San Francisco Library); Latin American Fiesta Parade, 18th and Folsom Streets (reviewing stand at South Van Ness and 24th Street, San Francisco) 1 p.m.; Wild West Days on Treasure Island; Annual Asian/Pacific American Heritage Week Festival, Oakland Museum Gardens. This is an outdoor festival, with entertainment, ethnic food, and an arts and crafts sale. The event is free to the public; Greek Festival, Oakland Auditorium. (mid-May.); Annual Barbershop Harmony Show, Oakland Auditorium. (May 30, 31.) (Sponsored by the Society for the Preservation and Encouragement for Barbershop Quartet Singing in America.)

Art and Music:
San Francisco Symphony's Beethoven Festival; San Francisco Opera Summer Festival.

Floral Exhibits and Displays
Rhododendrons bloom at Lakeside Park, Oakland, Fort Bragg; roses in full bloom in municipal gardens of Berkeley, Oakland, and San Jose.

June

Sports:
Annual Coors International Water Ski Jumping Championships, Marine World/Africa USA, Redwood City.

Festivals and Fairs:
Union Street Spring Festival and Crafts Fair in San Francisco. (Franklin to Fillmore Streets); Upper Grant Avenue Street Fair in San Francisco. (from Vallejo to Filbert Streets) (Father's Day weekend.); San Francisco Birthday Celebration, Mission Dolores and Presidio of San Francisco. (June 29.); Polk Street Art Fair in San Francisco. (Polk Street from Post to Washington Streets.); Ringling, Barnum, and Bailey Circus, San Francisco; Annual San Francisco Fair and Exposition, George R. Moscone Convention Center, San Francisco; Gay Freedom Day Parade, Market Street in San Francisco.

Art and Music
Midsummer Music Festival, Stern Grove, San Francisco. (through August) Features, classical, jazz, pops, Country Western, and dance performances; (no charge) Folk Music Festival, Fort Mason, San Francisco.

July

Sports:
San Francisco Marathon, Golden Gate Park.

Festivals and Fairs:
Fourth of July Celebration. Fireworks celebrations sponsored by the City of San Francisco take place at Crissey Field on Marina Green, 8 p.m.; Fireworks display, Berkeley Marina 8 p.m.; Annual Independence Day Celebrations also take place in Jack London Square in Oakland. There is free entertainment sponsored by the Port of Oakland, narrated charter boat tours, the Oakland Symphony Pops Orchestra, the Oakland Ballet, mimes, jugglers, and puppeteers. Call 444-3188 for information.; Annual Fourth of July Picnic and Turk Murphy Jazz Concert, Fort Point, San Francisco; Japanese Cultural Festivals, Japan Center, San Francisco (Tanabata Festival and Bon Odori Street Dance); Alameda County Fair, Pleasanton; Marin Art and Garden Fair, Ross; Napa County Fair, Napa; Annual Irish Fair, Pier 2, San Francisco.

Art and Music
San Francisco Pops Concerts, Civic Auditorium; Band Concerts, Golden Gate Park Bandstand, 1 p.m.; Midsummer Mozart Festival, San Francisco; Mayor's Annual Folk and Square Dance Festival, Oakland Auditorium; Bach Festival, Carmel.

August

Sports:
San Francisco City Tennis Championships, Golden Gate Park courts (no charge); KNBR Bathtub Regatta. (mid August.)

Art and Music:

Pacific States Crafts Fair, Piers 2 and 3, San Francisco.

Floral Exhibits and Displays:
San Francisco County Fair Flower Show, Hall of Flowers, Golden
Gate Park.

September

Sports:
Collegiate Football; Thoroughbred horse racing, Bay Meadows,
San Mateo, through November.

Festivals and Fairs:
Japanese Fall Festival (Aki Matsuri), Japan Center, San Francisco;
(Friday through Sunday); Annual Preservation Fair, Oakland (late
September.); Renaissance Pleasure Faire, Blackpoint Forest,
Novato (Information, Telephone 434-4625); Annual Festival of the
Sea, Maritime Museum and Hyde Street Pier, San Francisco;
Sheriff's Posse Horse Show, Bercut Field, Golden Gate Park, San
Francisco.

Art and Music:
San Francisco Opera Season, through December; San Francisco
Symphony Season, Louise M. Davies Symphony Hall, through
May. Annual San Francisco Blues Festival, Kezar Pavilion.

Exhibits:
Annual Boat Show, Oakland Auditorium. (late September.)

October

Festivals and Fairs:
Blessing of the Fishing Fleet, Church of Sts. Peter and Paul, and
Fisherman's Wharf, San Francisco—in combination with Colum-
bus Day Celebration; Columbus Day Celebration and Parade,
North Beach and Aquatic Park, San Francisco (1 p.m.); Black Cow-
boy's Parade, Oakland (mid-October); Annual Great Milk Carton
Boat Race, Marine World/Africa USA, Redwood City; Chinese
Double Ten Celebration and Parade (Independence of the Repub-

lic of China), San Francisco; Annual Culinary Carnival, Trade Show Center, San Francisco.

Art and Music:
San Francisco International Film Festival, Palace of Fine Arts Theater and Castro Theater (10–12 days);

Exhibits
The Grand National Livestock Exposition, Rodeo and Horse Show, Cow Palace, San Francisco.

Floral Exhibits and Displays
Annual Fall Flower Show, Lakeside Park Garden Center, Oakland. (early October, 10 a.m.–5 p.m.)

November

Festivals and Fairs:
"Quartz Dynasty," the annual gem and mineral show of the Galileo Gem Guild, Hall of Flowers, Golden Gate Park, San Francisco; Veterans Day Parade, 1 p.m., Market Street, San Francisco.

Art and Music:
American Indian Film Festival, Palace of Fine Arts Theatre, San Francisco (tickets available from San Francisco Indian Center, 552-1070)

Exhibits:
San Francisco International Automobile Show, George R. Moscone Convention Center.

December

Sports:
Oakland Marathon. (late December)

Festivals and Fairs:
Annual Christmas Pageant, Oakland Auditorium (mid-December);

Annual Christmas Tree Lighting Ceremony, Jack London Square, Oakland (December 1); Christmas at Dunsmuir House, Oakland (late December); "An Elegant Celebration of Christmas," sponsored by the American Conservatory Theatre at the Trade Show Center, San Francisco; "The Nutcracker," a tradition of the San Francisco Ballet at the Opera House *(ticket information: 621-3838)*.

A GUIDE TO CONCERTS

Campanile *(Sather Tower, Berkeley Campus)*
During the academic year, the carillon is played weekdays at 7:50
a.m., noon, and 6 p.m. On Saturdays, it is played at noon and 7
p.m., and there are more extensive concerts on Sundays at 4 p.m.
For information on the programs, write to: Office of the Carillon-
neur, University of California, Berkeley, University Hall, Berkeley, California 94720.
Telephone: 642-1198

Carmel Bach Festival
Telephone: (408) 624-1521

Grace Cathedral
Nob Hill, San Francisco
Telephone: 776-6611
There are Sunday afternoon organ recitals twice monthly.

Hertz Hall *(University of California, Berkeley)*
Telephone: 642-2678
Wednesday noon classical music concerts are offered to the public
during the academic year.

Hyatt Regency Hotel, San Francisco
Big Band Jazz concerts are open to the public at no charge each
Friday at 6 p.m.

Inverness Music Festival
Box 2, Inverness, California 94937
Telephone: 457-3750

Monterey Jazz Festival
This festival is one of the most popular and important jazz events in
the United States. It occurs in mid-September each year in Monterey. For information, write: P.O. Box Jazz, Monterey, California
93940.
Telephone: (408) 373-3366

Music Concourse Band Concerts
Golden Gate Park, San Francisco
Classical and operatic concerts are offered at no charge each Sunday
during the summer and holidays. Concerts start at 1 p.m.

Oakland Lake Merritt Band Concerts
Near Fairyland and Lakeside Park
Telephone: 273-3091
On Sundays at 2:30 p.m. during the summer and holidays, concerts
are offered at no charge.

Paul Masson Winery
Box 97 Saratoga, California 95070
Telephone: (408) 257-7800
(Jazz concerts)

Robert Mondavi Winery
Box 106 Oakville, California 94562
Telephone: (707) 963-9611
(Jazz concerts. Festival begins June 28)

St. Mary's Cathedral
Geary and Gough Streets, San Francisco (known as "Cathedral
Hill")
Telephone: 567-2717
Periodic organ recitals. Call for concert schedules.

Sigmund Stern Grove, San Francisco

19th Street and Sloat Avenue
Summer Sunday afternoon classical concerts, no charge.

The Cannery
Leavenworth and Beach Streets, San Francisco.
Modern music. Concerts are offered daily, noon to 5 p.m. at no charge.

Woodminster Amphitheater, Oakland
Joaquin Miller Park
Telephone: 531-9597
Periodic musical productions.

A GUIDE TO NORTHERN CALIFORNIA WINERIES

Many visitors to the Bay Area enjoy taking tours of the wine country in Northern California. There are many wineries in the counties north of the Bay Area, but only selected ones with guided tours and tasting facilities will be listed in this guide. The counties which made California wines internationally famous are Napa and Sonoma. Selected wineries from these and other counties follow. Wineries with tasting facilities are marked with an asterisk (*); those with guided tours are marked with (#).

Sonoma

Buena Vista (The Haraszthy Cellars)
On Old Winery Road
Sonoma
Telephone: (707) 938-1266
Open daily 10 a.m. to 5 p.m. There are reservable picnic facilities.

* Sebastiani Vineyards
389 Fourth Street East
Sonoma
Telephone: (707) 938-5532
Open daily 10 a.m. to 5 p.m.

Russian River Valley

*Italian Swiss Colony
Asti
Telephone: (707) 894-2541
Mid-way between Geyserville and Cloverdale on U.S. 101. From U.S. 101, take the Asti exit, go east 1/4 mile.
Open daily from 9 a.m. to 6 p.m. during the summer, and from 9 a.m. to 5 p.m. during the winter months.

*Korbel
Guerneville
Telephone: (707) 887-2294
From U.S. 101 north, take the River Road exit. Go west 14 miles.
Open for guided tours from 9:45 a.m. to 3:45 p.m.

Napa

*Beringer/Los Hermanos
2000 Main Street
St. Helena
Telephone: (707) 963-7115

Open for tours daily from 9 a.m. to 4:45 p.m. (the last tour leaves at 3:45 p.m.) Groups may arrange tours by appointment.

*The Christian Brothers
Napa
Telephone: (707) 226-5566
Mont La Salle: From State Highway 29 at Napa, go west on Redwood Road for 7 miles.
Open daily from 10:30 a.m. to 4 p.m.

Greystone Cellar:
Telephone: (707) 963-2719
Just west of State Highway 29 near St. Helena.
Open daily 10:30 a.m. to 4 p.m.

*Inglenook
Rutherford
Telephone: (707) 963-7184
West of State Highway 29 on Rutherford, which is a private drive.

Open daily 10 a.m. to 5 p.m. Picnic areas are available for reservation.

*Hans Kornell
St. Helena
Telephone: (707) 963-2334
5.9 miles north of St. Helena. From State Highway 29, go east for 1/4 mile on Larkmead Lane. Open daily from 10 a.m. to 4 p.m.

*Charles Krug
St. Helena
Telephone: (707) 963-2761
On the east side of State Highway 29, on the northern edge of St. Helena.
Open daily from 10 a.m. to 4 p.m.

*Louis M. Martini
Telephone: (707) 963-2736
Just south of St. Helena east of State Highway 29.
Open daily from 10 a.m. to 4 p.m.

*Robert Mondavi
7801 St. Helena Highway
Oakville
Telephone: (707) 963-9611
Open daily from 10 a.m. to 4:30 p.m.

*Sutter Home
St. Helena
Telephone: (707) 963-3104
One half-mile south of St. Helena west of State Highway 29.
Open daily from 9:30 a.m. to 5 p.m.

Santa Clara Valley

#Almaden
1530 Blossom Hill Road
San Jose
Telephone: (408) 269-1312

From U.S. 101 or Interstate 280 southbound, exit at Santa Cruz-Los Gatos at State Highway 17. Exit at Camden Road. Go south east for 4 miles to Blossom Hill Road. Then go east for one half-mile.
Open Monday through Friday, 10 a.m. to 4 p.m.

* *Paul Masson*
13150 Saratoga Avenue
Saratoga
Telephone: (408) 257-7800
From U.S. 101 southbound, take the Lawrence Expressway exit. Go south for 7 miles to Saratoga Avenue. Then go west for 1 mile.
Open daily from 10 a.m. to 4 p.m.

Concerts at Wineries

Several wineries in Northern California offer popular summer jazz and classical music concerts. Since dates and prices vary from year to year, readers should contact the wineries listed here directly for exact information.

Geyser Peak Winery
Geyserville
Telephone: (707) 433-6585
On Canyon Road west of U.S. 101.
The annual performances of the Brown Bag Opera of the San Francisco Opera Company take place here. The concerts are held on Sunday afternoons in June. The concerts usually last one hour, and are featured by complimentary wine tasting in advance of the performances. Bring a picnic lunch.

Guild Wineries
Lodi
Telephone: (209) 368-5151
From State Highway 99, take the East exit. Go east for 3/4 mile to Myrtle Avenue. Then go north 1/4 mile to the winery drive. There are picnic facilities.
The Winemaster's Concert Series, which includes jazz and pops programs, takes place here each summer. During intermission, complimentary wine is served. The concerts are outdoors, and are usually in the evenings.

Johnson's Alexander Valley Winery
8333 State Highway 128
Healdsburg
Telephone: (707) 433-2319
East of Healdsburg. Two miles southeast of the intrsection of Alexander Valley Road and State Highway 128.
Pipe and organ concerts are held at the Alexander Valley Winery one weekend each month.

Charles Krug
(see above for address and telephone.)
The August Moon Concerts take place here. Call Charles Krug for ticket information.

Paul Masson Vineyards
(see above for address and telephone.)
Paul Masson's classical "Music in the Vineyards" series began in 1957. There is also a jazz and folk concerts series called "Vintage Sounds." Call Paul Masson for ticket information.

Robert Mondavi
(see above for address and telephone.)
There is a Jazz Festival on the last Sunday in June and every Sunday in July at 7 p.m. Picnics begin after 3:30 p.m. Wine and cheese are offered during intermission. There is also a Shakespeare Festival which takes place in August.

Sonoma Vineyards
Windsor
Telephone: (707) 433-6511
From U.S. 101, take the West Windsor exit. Go west to the Old Redwood Highway, then go north for 3 miles to the winerey.
At least one concert takes place each year. For ticket information, contact the winery directly.

Souverain
Geyserville
Telephone: (707) 433-6918
From U.S. 101, take the Independence Lane exit. The winery is just south of Geyserville, and 5 miles north of Healdsburg.
Contact Souverain to be placed on its mailing list for a series of concerts, theater, and opera performances.

Diablo Press seeks manuscripts. We are looking for scholarly works which appeal to a wide audience. We focus on history, political science, sociology, music, and the environment.

Diablo Press, Inc.
P.O. Box 7042
Berkeley, California 94707